SPUD JOHNSON &

Laughing Horse

SHARYN UDALL

Spud Johnson &

LAUGHING HORSE

UNIVERSITY OF NEW MEXICO PRESS
ALBUQUERQUE

Library of Congress Cataloging-in-Publication Data

Udall, Sharyn Rohlfsen.

Spud Johnson & Laughing Horse / Sharyn Udall.

p.   cm.

Includes bibliographical references (p.   ) and index.

ISBN 0-8263-1469-4

1. Johnson, Walter Willard, 1897–1968. 2. Periodicals, Publishing of—New Mexico—History—20th century. 3. Literature publishing—New Mexico—History—20th century. 4. Poets, American—20th century—Biography. 5. Journalists—New Mexico—Biography. 6. American Literature—20th century. 7. American literature—New Mexico. 8. Editors—New Mexico—Biography. 9. Laughing Horse.

I. Title. II. Title: Spud Johnson and Laughing Horse.

PS3519.028684Z93   1994

810.9'9789—dc20   93-42070

                                                                                                        CIP

Contents

v

The idea for this book developed very gradually, out of sporadic art historical research which led the author repeatedly to the pages of *Laughing Horse*. Over a period of years it became clear that this publication and its editor had collected a body of work, both visual and literary, that had seldom been seen since the 1930s. Much of it deserves to be seen again. Here were the expressions of artists and writers exploring the American, and later southwestern, experience in the 1920s and 1930s. The sustaining force behind the publication was Walter Willard "Spud" Johnson (1897 — 1968), a quirky, energetic man with a knack for eliciting material from a broad range of talented contributors.

Twenty-five years after Johnson's death seems an appropriate distance from which to view his life, his personal achievements, and whatever contribution he may have made to his era. In 1993 some of Spud's friends and associates still possess vivid memories of him. Their wide spectrum of opinions, generously given, has helped to provide a balanced view of the man.

On the other hand, most of these people knew Spud in Taos

or Santa Fe after 1940. Because he seldom talked of his upbring-
ing, most were unacquainted with the facts of his early life and
of his early literary exploits. Fortunately, Johnson was a saver: at
his death his voluminous correspondence, diaries, and other
writings were preserved in his little house at Taos. Friends, especially Milford Greer and Chilton and Judy Anderson, helped to
sort and arrange them, while Spud's niece, the late Sue Lovejoy,
arranged for their ultimate acquisition by the Harry Ransom
Humanities Research Center at the University of Texas in
Austin. There the Spud Johnson Collection of papers, including
some 950 photographs and hundreds of drawings, paintings,
and other artifacts, is preserved. It will continue to be of value to
researchers studying the milieu Johnson inhabited.

The author wishes to thank the following persons, who have
kindly provided information, advice and encouragement for this
book.

Jane Abrams; Chilton and Judy Anderson; James Colegrove;
Lou Criss; John E. Dixon; Georgette Ely; Elizabeth Glassman,
president, Georgia O'Keeffe Foundation; Char Graebner, Kit
Carson Foundation, Taos; Laura Holt, librarian, Laboratory of
Anthropology, Santa Fe; Tricia Hurst; Helen Kentnor; Dr. U. C.
Lovejoy and Michael Lovejoy, Barboursville, West Virginia; Ila
McAfee; Orlando Romero, History Library, Museum of New
Mexico, Santa Fe; Mrs. Albert Rosen; Verne Sackett; Henry
Sauerwein, Helene Wurlitzer Foundation, Taos; Harrison Smith;
Pam Smith, printer, Palace of the Governors, Santa Fe; Earl
Stroh; Mildred Tolbert; David Witt, Harwood Foundation, Taos.

The staffs of the following institutions have also provided
valuable help: the Harry Ransom Humanities Research Center,
University of Texas, Austin; New Mexico State Library, Santa Fe;
Center for Southwest Research, Zimmerman Library, University

of New Mexico; Beinecke Rare Book and Manuscript Library, Yale University; *Sunset* Magazine; Amon Carter Museum; Bancroft Library, University of California, Berkeley.

Excerpt by H. L. Mencken is published by permission of the Enoch Pratt Free Library in accordance with the terms of the will of H. L. Mencken. Laurence Pollinger Ltd. and the Estate of Frieda Lawrence Ravagli have granted permission for publication of D. H. Lawrence material. Excerpts from the writings of Witter Bynner have been reprinted with permission from the Witter Bynner Foundation for Poetry, Inc.

I also wish to thank the National Endowment for the Humanities for a Travel to Collections grant. And, as always, special thanks are due to my husband, Kimball Udall, for his unflagging support of my projects.

SHARYN UDALL
Santa Fe
January 1993

SPUD JOHNSON &

Laughing Horse

Spud Johnson:
Biographical Introduction

"If Spud Johnson had not come to Taos," wrote a longtime friend, "I suppose we should have had to think him up. Spud was the aesthetic and intellectual conscience of Taos."[1] Shy and self-effacing, Johnson would have put it less grandly; though aware of his influence, he preferred to think of himself as a gadfly—darting here, stinging there—but reluctant to take himself too seriously. To the end he remained improbable material for a legend. Asked in the 1930s for a poem about himself, he produced the following lines, at once amusing, vaguely wistful, and quintessentially Spud. He called it "Autobiography":

> One of my dreams is very old
> And never has been told—
> But three of them have long been sold,
> And ten have caught their death of cold.

Only once was he obliged to produce a serious autobiographical statement, and even then he made light of his literary abilities. In his application for a Guggenheim Fellowship in the late 1930s, Johnson described his first attempts at writing:

> I wrote an essay about a house-finch when I was in the seventh grade, which was so highly praised by my teacher that I at once decided to be a "writer," since that was the first indication I had been given that I excelled in anything![2]

That was in Greeley, Colorado, where the family resided during most of his youth. Christened Walter Willard Johnson, but known to everyone as Spud, he had been born in Illinois in 1897. From there, when Spud was about nine, the family moved to a comfortable house on Eighth Avenue in Greeley. There he grew up, with parents and siblings, in what sounds like a conventional, bustling, middle-class household. Describing it later, Spud constructed a childhood prototype of his adult self—curious, watching, taking it all in:

> I can see a stew pan on the stove in the corner, my mother going from the pantry to the stove and through the swinging door to the dining room. My father sitting in the old wicker chair at the side of the stove smoking his pipe. Gladys setting the table in the kitchen, or perhaps the one in the dining room, almost running into Mom as they try to go in through the swinging door at the same time. Van coming down the short staircase from the landing in the other room and saying "Gee that sassafras tea smells good!" Lila peering into the oven at some hot biscuits. And I? Probably getting in everyone's way trying to hover

near the stove and see everything without being actually useful. . . .[3]

Johnson's father was in the lumber business, but the world of commerce never interested young Willard. Spurred by that seventh-grade praise for his writing, he took on every journalistic job he could find. While at Greeley High School he started and edited the school newspaper, worked on its yearbook, and contributed pieces to a local newspaper. After graduation in 1916, he remained at home, enrolling at the school then known as Colorado State Teachers College.

There was never any doubt about a career choice: he knew he wanted to write, and he convinced college officials to let him take all the available English courses during his first year. At the same time he worked as a cub reporter for a Greeley newspaper and wrote humorous sketches for the school's monthly magazine. He began to use his nickname in print around this time; his columns, collectively, were known as "The Spud." Individual articles carried titles like "Rise and Fall of the Chewing Gum Dynasty," "The Hermit and His Treasure," and "The Beaux Boogie."

After two years at Greeley, Johnson transferred to the larger University of Colorado in Boulder, where he took advanced courses in literature and composition and again wrote for the student newspaper. But Johnson increasingly felt the constraints of small-town life. In 1920 Colorado was something of a cultural backwater—definitely not the kind of place for a young man with literary ambitions. That year Sinclair Lewis brought out his immensely influential *Main Street,* and *Babbitt* would appear two years later. These two books of searing satire vastly accelerated a nascent revolt of the American intelligentsia against what Frederick Lewis Allen described as "the ugliness of the American small town, the cultural poverty of its life, the tyranny of its mass prejudices. . . ." [4]

The seat of this postwar intellectual unrest was New York, but there were enclaves of such thinking based in other American cities. Mostly artists and writers, their numbers extended to include "the intellectually restless element in the college towns." [5] Spud Johnson, in the college town of Boulder, was part of that "restless element." Week by week he became increasingly disaffected with the provincialism of the place. He wanted a larger context and the varied life possible in a metropolitan area. Berkeley—not so distant as New York, but with the next-door sophistication of San Francisco—beckoned. He could finish his education, he reasoned, at the University of California, while associating with like-minded writers and thinkers, and escaping the environment of constraint he felt in Colorado.

Not long after his arrival in the Bay Area, Johnson met the man who would introduce him to the larger world of bohemianism, of avant-garde arts and letters. This was Witter Bynner—a poet sixteen years his senior, Harvard-educated, urbane, well-traveled, and blessed with more money than he needed. He taught poetry at the university and moved with ease among the literati of the Bay Area, socializing with prominent figures like Jack London, George Sterling, the printer John Henry Nash, and art patron Albert Bender. Bynner was a member of the Bohemian Club and was probably responsible for finding Johnson a job as librarian there.

He also made Spud think seriously for the first time about poetry. Bynner's poetry course, a favorite among students, was an unconventional class with no texts or tests. Poems were read and criticized, often out of doors, and Bynner's literary friends came as guests. Soon Johnson was turning out his own poetry, with the advice and criticism of Bynner. The older, established poet took a special interest in Johnson, and the two grew very close. According to Bynner's biographer, they eventually became "lovers, friends, father and son, teacher and student."[6]

But Bynner came and went from the university during those years, traveling, writing, and lecturing around the country and abroad. Spud was in and out as well, forced to juggle studies with the constant need to earn a living. At one point he headed back to Colorado for a whole year as full-time reporter on the *Pueblo Chieftain.*

Returning to Berkeley with some savings in his pocket, he again enrolled in classes and found a job reporting for the *Richmond Independent.* In later years he liked to tell the story, probably embellished, of his summary departure from that position:

It [Richmond] was a small town, and you had to milk it for news. Every day I'd get a release across my desk about Reverend Little. What he had done or said or thought. He was in everything, and, frankly, I began to get just a bit bored with the Rev. Little.

One morning I got a release about the Reverend's having addressed a large group of people who were becoming naturalized citizens. Just for the fun of it, I wrote the story and added that Rev. Little had said many trite things about patriotism and that all his bunk was received with much noise. I thought my editor would catch it, get a laugh and take it out, but he was so used to my stuff, he never read beyond the first paragraph.

The story, unedited, appeared on the next day's front page. An outraged citizenry, led by Rev. Little himself, trooped into the newspaper offices and made clear its indignation to the embarrassed editor. "Did you ever see an editor in tears?" chuckled Spud, recalling the event. "Naturally the only thing for my boss to do was to ask me to remove myself from the premises— as a matter of fact, I believe he said 'county.'"[7]

Johnson was discovering himself to be a devout iconoclast, distrustful of moral certitude, and especially disdainful of public piety. He had been amused by the incident at the *Independent*, but he had also been given a sharp taste of public pressure in journalism. On balance, he decided he would prefer the editor's chair to the reporter's beat. And in fact he was already laying plans for such a change.

With fifty dollars of his salary saved from the *Independent*, Johnson and two friends embarked on a publishing venture of their own—a small-format magazine to be known as *Laughing Horse*. It was undertaken, as Johnson later recalled, because the three were "exasperated with the existing conventional campus newspaper, literary journal and monthly comic book." Convinced they could do better, and linked only by a youthful spirit of rebellion against outworn tradition, they set out to "give a thorough and unrestrained horselaugh to the entire academic setup to which they felt so scornfully superior."[8] The two co-collaborators were James Van Rensselaer, Jr., and Roy Chanslor, whom Johnson had met in a literature class. Their adventures with *Laughing Horse* are detailed in Chapter Two.

The first two issues of *Laughing Horse* had already appeared in the spring of 1922 when Bynner reappeared in Berkeley and gave his immediate endorsement to the impudent new magazine. By that time Bynner was living mostly in Santa Fe. In

February of that year, during one of his lecture tours, he had fallen ill. Exhausted and unable to overcome a respiratory ailment, he accepted an invitation from an old friend to convalesce in New Mexico. The friend was Alice Corbin Henderson, poet and former editor of *Poetry* magazine. Bynner went to Santa Fe, gave a well-received lecture, collapsed, and entered the local sanitorium for a rest. By the time he was feeling better, he decided that Santa Fe seemed a congenial place for a writer, and he found himself a house.

Bynner invited Johnson, who was planning a summer visit to Colorado, to visit Santa Fe en route. When he arrived he was instantly infected, like Bynner, with the charm of the place and lingered long after the summer ended. Spud found he could contribute to *Laughing Horse* from New Mexico and began to solicit contributions from visiting and resident members of its literary and artistic community.

Besides, his academic future at Berkeley was in dispute: the university authorities insisted that he, like all male students, take military training during the afternoons. Spud objected, claiming that because of his morning job schedule he needed afternoons free for classes, not military drill. The feud developed into a stand-off: without military training, the university refused to admit that he was properly enrolled and gave him no credits for his classes. Spud refused to capitulate; he simply did not return to the university after the summer of 1922. Many years later he cast the whole incident in a bemused tone. Because he was not officially enrolled, he chuckled, the university was "cheated, later, of the opportunity to expel me from the university when *The Laughing Horse* became a serious menace to its dignity." Years later, in his Guggenheim application, he recalled a slightly less politicized version of the events:

Moving to Santa Fe, New Mexico, I became the secretary to the poet, Witter Bynner, who coached me in my initial efforts at writing verse. I therefore did not return to finish my course at the University of California, believing that the medieval idea of apprenticeship to an already accepted artist was more practical in learning my chosen craft of writing than continued academic studies. At any rate it was an opportunity not to be scoffed at, and I thought that more college studies could come later.

There is truth in both tellings. Johnson could be an extremely stubborn man, unwilling to bend to what he saw as unfair university rules. He did not shirk from controversy, but he would soon discover, to his simultaneous delight and chagrin, that being 1,500 miles away from Berkeley would not exempt him from the scandals provoked by *Laughing Horse.* By the fall of 1922 his equine offspring was launched on a trajectory that would bring Johnson more controversy than he could imagine.

But before that happened, he experienced the joys of being away from the hive of activity at Berkeley. Suddenly he had time to think and write without constant interruptions. He could test Max Eastman's famous dictum: that poetry was not just writing, but the "living of life."[9]

Symptomatic of a counter-trend opposing that heralded by Sinclair Lewis, New Mexico was welcoming refugees from the bohemian enclaves of Greenwich Village and Chicago. They came in search of a new world of experiences, based not on urban values and messianic technology, but on values derived from a rediscovery of America. John Dewey's article "Americanism and Localism" (*The Dial*, 1920) had begun to explore such ideas. William Carlos Williams was also urging America to return to its own roots and find authenticity in native subjects. A few years later Lewis Mumford would characterize this cultural diffusion as the infancy of regionalism, when nonurban areas would begin to discover their own cultural resources:

> Once we recognize that difference does not mean inferiority, once the other regions of the country become sure enough of their own bottom and reason for existence to stop aping New York, and once, partly as a result of this, the increasing dominance of New York and Chicago, through their control of finance and advertising, is undermined and lessened—regional cultures will perhaps grow more vigorously, since they will represent a conscious effort to make the most of their own resources.[10]

Fueled by such ideas, the Santa Fe literary scene was lively in the 1920s. At first it was nurtured mostly by Alice Corbin who, with her painter husband William Penhallow Henderson, invited many poets and writers to the town. Vachel Lindsay and Carl Sandburg, both friends of Bynner's, had lectured there shortly before he arrived.

Soon Spud also met Mabel Dodge, installed as self-appointed cultural doyenne at Taos. Five years after her own arrival in 1917, she was engrossed in efforts to build a utopian cultural community at Taos. She made certain her activities, her guests, and her writings were often talked about—both in Santa Fe and in New York, whose pool of writers, musicians, and painters she tapped for potential guests.

Her friend and sometime rival, Mary Austin, had already visited New Mexico and from 1924 on would reside in Santa Fe. And, within three months after Spud's arrival, D. H. and Frieda

Lawrence had answered Mabel's urgent summons to experience the cultural Eden she envisioned for New Mexico.

Internationalists like Lawrence visited in an effort to understand how America, which he believed to be psychologically and sexually repressed, operated outside its cities. Others were convinced, with Marsden Hartley, that America needed a major effort toward aesthetic education, and that its hope for finding a cultural identity lay somehow in an identification with native traditions and the land. Still another approach was taken by Bynner, who searched for correspondences between Chinese and Native American cultures; to him the diverse cultural patterns he encountered in New Mexico supported such cross-cultural research.[11] The house he had purchased and began to remodel would become an eccentric mix of Chinese, Indian, and Mexican influences. It was eclectic both in its furnishings and its guests: Bynner's rambling adobe became the site of legendary, stimulating, sometimes raucous parties.

JOHNSON'S POETRY: BEGINNINGS

To Johnson, it was exhilarating to be accepted into a community where the writer and artist mattered, where everyone seemed to be trying poetry or painting or playwriting. He divided his days between editorial chores for *Laughing Horse* and typing for Bynner (Fig. 1).

But he found time too for his own poetry. Encouraged by Bynner, he submitted his verses to national publications, and soon saw his work in print. One of his poems was anthologized in *The Best Poems of 1924,* and by 1926 his verses had appeared in *Poetry, Echo, Pan, Palms,* and the *New Republic.* He recalled later that "Movie Comedy," the poem for the latter publication, was written to pay a car repair bill.

Johnson's poems had been anthologized six times by the end of the twenties, but nowhere in better company than in Alice Corbin Henderson's *The Turquoise Trail,* a collection of New Mexico poetry published in 1928. Its distinguished list of poets was made up of thirty-seven residents or visitors to the state. Many of their names were familiar far outside the Southwest: Harriet Monroe, Carl Sandburg, Willa Cather, Paul Horgan, Lynn Riggs, D. H. Lawrence, and Vachel Lindsay were all contributors. Spud's two poems drew heavily on his personal experience of nature and humanity in the Southwest.

Desert Night

Walking
Under the moon,
Conscious of something deep
Beneath the calm—like life itself
Breathing in its sleep ...

The Living Root

I paused and stepped back, half entranced,
    Through the darkness of the alley-way,
As naked Indians gravely danced
    Into the plaza where the moonlight lay.

When they had passed, I waited there
    And listened to the drum and shout
Die slowly into shaken air;
    And then I sighed and turned about

FIGURE 1.
Spud Johnson typing,
probably at Witter
Bynner's home, Santa Fe,
1920s. Photography
Collection, Harry Ransom
Humanities Research
Center, University of
Texas at Austin.

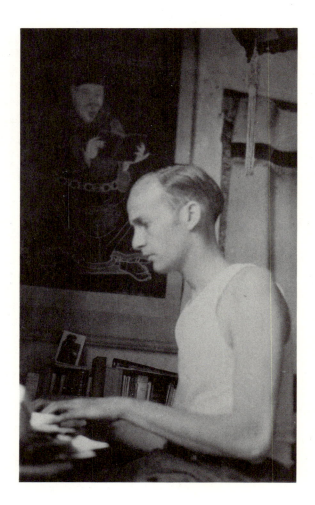

To find between me and the wall
    That held the alley's deepest shade
An Indian standing, still and tall,
    So near me that I felt afraid.

He was a part of silence and of night,
    And when I tried I could not see
His eyes flash any glint of light.
    ...I passed him as I would a tree.

In 1926 Johnson was asked to contribute an essay on south-western poetry to the *Anthology of Magazine Verse* and *Yearbook of American Poetry*. His efforts show a sensitivity to the multicultural literary sources of modern southwestern poetry, including Spanish and Mexican songs, cowboy ballads, and Indian poetry. He gives credit to the pervasive influence of Bynner and Austin, but recognizes the promise of emerging poets as well.

Poetry of the Southwest II

WILLARD JOHNSON

It is not easy to discuss the poetry of an entire region in a limited space, especially when its origins are prehistoric and when even its first published expression in a European language antedates the landing of the Pilgrim Fathers by a decade.

Personally, I believe that the most important poetry of the Southwest is that of the Indians and I am not sure but that the next in importance is the work of moderns who have been influenced by Indian art—although perhaps next in interest is the other folk poetry of that section, which includes the Spanish and Mexican as well as the cowboy songs. But since practically all of this wealth of material has been unearthed and made available to English readers through the work (not entirely of course) of contemporary poets, it can be appropriately mentioned in its entirety through a discussion of the modern group.

Captain Gaspar Perez de Villagra, was the poet to whom I referred as having preceded Plymouth Rock. He was one of the first of the Spanish adventurers and was with Onate in the settlement of Santa Fe, later publishing his rhymed narrative in thirty-two cantos entitled *Historia de Nueva Mexico* in the year 1610. However, I cannot vouch for the artistic merits of this work, although without being familiar with its text, I doubt its interest except as a his-

(continued on following pages)

toric fact. He does not tell, as Alice Corbin Henderson laments in her introduction to Mrs. Mary Van Stone's recent collection of Spanish ballads, "what love songs the soldiers sang in Coronado's camp at Bernalillo in the winter of 1541." So that the Spanish folk songs of New Mexico and Arizona that are known and sung, are in reality modern verses, some of them extremely recent—such as the ballad *La Realera*, which is that of a bootlegger whose life is declared to be "no better than if he were living underneath a train."

Besides these songs, new verses of which are constantly being written, the old custom of improvising "coplas" still prevails, but these are not yet available in English translation, although Mrs. Henderson and Maurice Lesemann have both collected them for some years and may eventually publish the best of them.

The cowboys ballads, on the other hand, have appeared frequently in collections. John A. Lomax' *Cowboy Songs and Ballads* and the anthology made by Jack Thorpe (himself a cowboy and the composer of some of the ballads) in collaboration with Mrs. Henderson, are representative. *The Old Chisholm Trail*, with its hundreds of verses, many of them obscene, is a typical example. Like so many of the cowboy songs, it contains a refrain of meaningless syllables which reminds one startlingly of the Indian songs:

"With my knees in the saddle and my seat in the sky,
I'll quit punchin' cows in the sweet by and by.
Coma ti yi youpa ya, youpa ya;
Coma ti yi youpa ya!"

Then there is *The Boozer* type:

"He's a killer and a hater,
He's the great annihilator,
He's a snorter and a snoozer,
He's the great trunk line abuser . . ."

And *Git Along Little Dogies* is one of the best of them, augmented by a haunting tune:

"Cloudy in the west and lookin' like rain,
Damned old slicker's in the wagon again.
Whoopee ti yi ho, git along little dogies,
For you know Wyoming will be your new home."

But as I mentioned before, next in importance to the Indians themselves, are those poets who have very definitely been influenced by the Indians and by the Southwest landscape and life as the Indians are. Alice Corbin, former editor of *Poetry*, is not only indefatigable in sponsoring all sorts of Indian causes and studies, and a collector of Spanish and cowboy verse, but is perhaps the most representative poet of the Southwest, and is probably more responsible than any other one person for Santa Fe's present reputation as one of America's literary capitals. She is the author of several books of which the most important is *Red Earth*—a slim volume but full of the charm and beauty and wisdom of the deserts and mountains. She has made few attempts to actually "translate" Indian verse, but on the other hand, I think that she has been as successful as

any in catching the spirit of it and presenting in English
form its rhythms and ideas. She sees, far into the past,

> "In the place where the fight was,
> Across the river:
> The women go wailing
> To gather the wounded,
> The women go wailing
> To pick up the dead . . ."

And hears,

> "The noise of passing feet
> On the prairie—
> Is it men or gods
> Who come out of the silence?"

And again:

> "Far in the east
> The gods retreat
> As the thunder drums
> Grow small and sweet.
>
> The dancers' feet
> Echo the sound
> As the drums grow faint
> And the rain comes down."

Finding at last,

"After the roar, after the fierce modern music
Of rivets and hammers and trams,
After the shout of the giant,
Youthful and brawling and strong
Building the cities of men,
Here is the desert of silence,
Blinking and blind in the sun—
An old, old woman who mumbles her beads
And crumbles to stone."

Mary Austin, who disclaims her reputation as "an authority on things Indian, which I am not; as a translator, which I never pretended to be; and as a poet, which I am only occasionally and by induction," has nevertheless contributed an important essay on the subject: *The American Rhythm*, which I think is based on sound theories. At the same time, I do not consider that her own "re-expressions" prove her point, even though many of them are very good poetry. But comparisons of the more stark translations of Natalie Curtis Burlin (in *The Indian's Book*) and of Washington Matthews with the original verse of distinctly American poets, prove the premise that there is some relation between the purely physical life-rhythms of a race and its poetic meters.

"Lo, the flint youth, he am I, the flint youth . . .
Clearest, purest flint the heart
Living strong within me—heart of flint:
Lo, the flint youth, he am I, the flint youth . . ."

And again:

"He, the blackbird, he am I,
Bird beloved of the wild deer.
Comes the deer to my singing."

The insistent reiteration of I; the identification of self
with animals and things, is reminiscent of Whitman—and
in the original is probably much more similar. The translations I offer are those of female anthropologists. The repe-
titions which are continually used in Indian songs, and
which of course are found in all poetry, nevertheless recall
similar recurrences in Lindsay and Sandburg—who, inci-
dentally, have both been influenced by the southwestern
country, visited it often and written about it, Sandburg in
Slabs of the Sunburnt West, and Lindsay in his humoresque,
The Santa Fe Trail in which he sings of "the cattle on the
thousand hills" and "in which many autos pass west-
ward"—

"While I sit by the milestone
And watch the sky,
The United States
Goes by."

And in which the trains,

"Screaming to the west coast, screaming to the east,
Carry off a harvest, bring back a feast. . . "

I like, too, to note these Indian lines:

"Newborn on the naked sand,
Nakedly lay it . . "

in comparison with Margaret Larkin's,

"I am a sun child.
When I first crept out of the darkness
They laid me in the sun . . ."

Very little of Miss Larkin's verse, however, deals with the Southwest, despite the fact the she is one of the few poets of that section who can be considered a native. Influenced more by the Spanish than by the Indian, she is one of the truest poets to come out of New Mexico, especially of the younger group, and sings her own songs along with the old Spanish and cowboy ballads to the accompaniment of her guitar in genuine troubadour fashion. But certainly she gets her love of snakes—about which she writes so frequently and so well—from the desert.

Eda Lou Walton is another native New Mexican, I believe, and her volume, *Dawn Boy* shows how intimately and thoroughly she has studied the Indian and his poetry. Perhaps they are not translations; like Mary Austin's they are probably "re-expressions," but they are lovely renderings of authentic Indian themes and an important contribution to our knowledge of aboriginal American verse. Her activities have by no means been limited to these translations, but they are her only poems which are available in book form. Here is one, however, which was not included in the book, unfortunately:

"Pity me and I will pity you.

Because of my sadness
This world is covered with feathers,
Because of my brother's death
The mountains are covered with soft feathers.
The sun comes over them
But it gives me no light,
Night comes over them
And has no darkness for my rest.

Pity me, pity me—
And I will pity you!

When I thought I was holding all sadness
There was yet a stronger sadness,
For my brother came and stood upon my breast,
His tears fell down on my body.
I tried to hug him,
And hugged only myself!

Pity me.

From the shadows of trees
I have learned it could be done:
Now I will gird on my bowels for belt,
Make sandals of my scalp,
I will fill my skull with blood
and talk like a drunkard.

Out of my own bones
I will make a great fire:

It shall light me to the Land of Death!"

Miss Nellie Barnes' recent *Indian Love Lyrics* covers the same ground less successfully and restates the American rhythm theory with still less actual proof, although it contains a few lovely lyrics and will doubtless prove one of the "documents" of American poetry along with George Cronyn's *Path on the Rainbow* and other anthologies of Indian verse.

Of the eastern poets who have been influenced by the southwestern country and whose work shows their adopted if not native allegiance to its hills, Witter Bynner is probably the best known. His *Dance for Rain at Cochiti* seems to me an admirable adaptation of the tom-tom dance rhythm to an English verse metre, and what is more important, it captures the religious magic of an Indian dance. Others of his western verses on Indian and Mexican subjects seem to bear out his theory that the similarity of southwest landscape to that in Chinese painting and of the Indians themselves to Orientals, creates a similarity of verse structure and treatment. Of course this may be due only to the influence of his Chinese translations which have occupied him for so many years.

But where does one draw the line? Mabel Dodge Luhan, more of a "native" than most of the colonists, has sporadically turned poet in a few surprising verses, which, however, have seldom reflected the influence of her adopted landscape and might have been written in Buffalo. Haniel Long, on the other hand, is only an infrequent visitor in that region, but has been profoundly influenced by the desert and by the Indians. The same can be said of Maurice Lesemann and Janet Lewis, of the younger group—and of Ivor Winters, perhaps the only "modern" southwesterner.

And where, too, is one to draw the geographical line? Is Lynn Riggs, the Oklahoma lyricist, a southwesterner by virtue of a New Mexican sojourn, or are he and Stanley Vestal from the South (West)?

There are two others of the younger group, however, not yet much known, who may be considered authentic natives: and they are Peggy Pond Church and Loren Mozley. Both of them have published poems of distinction and will undoubtedly make themselves more clearly heard within the next few years.

The list is not complete; my survey is scattered and my comments are slight. But I have tried to view a rather large and uneven field without being either exhaustive or exhausting. I have, with rare modesty, failed even to mention myself.

HORIZONTAL YELLOW

In the mid-1930s Johnson joined with other writers who had formed Writers' Editions, a cooperative publishing venture undertaken in the belief that "regional publishing would foster the growth of American literature."[12] Each author paid for the publication of his or her own volume, but was entitled to 90 percent of any profits. Other members would help with bookkeeping and mailing, for which Writers' Editions retained the other 10 percent of profits.

In 1935 Writers' Editions published 400 copies of Johnson's *Horizontal Yellow*, a collection of fifty-six poems—some new, some reprinted from regional and national publications. In previous appearances, one or two at a time, the poems had given only glimpses of the poet's vision of the world. Now, collected into a single volume, the range and conviction of Johnson's poetry are visible for the first time. The title demonstrates his ability to synthesize the visual and the verbal: "The Navajo calls the West/Land of Horizontal Yellow." Johnson arranged the verses thematically, with the first section, "The Living Root," devoted to poems of Indian life. Included were evocations of both Pueblo and Navajo culture:

Taos Dance

Hands outstretched, the girls danced slowly,
Long shawl-fringes swaying with the drums;
Danced around the old-men-chorus,
Sitting with thundersticks and drums.

Boys in blankets, side-stepped slowly
Around the girls and around the drums.

Making the third of the magic circles,
Repeating the circles of the drums.

Thunder sticks and eagle bones,
Voices, gestures, and the drums,
Merged into a single rhythm,
The living heart-beat of the drum.

Sixth Song of the Holy Young Men
(FROM THE NAVAJO)

On either side was a god,
But the Holy Young Man
Was the god on top of the mountain
Down which the rivers ran.

And this branch on the summit,
His talisman, his charm,
Was cut from the sacred pine-tree:
Fate could not do him harm.

The young girls who became bears
Said, "O Young Man, we know—
We know you are not divine,
There's no use saying so."

But on either side was a god,
And the Holy Young Man
Was the god on top of the mountain
Down which the rivers ran.

"Inland" was a more diverse selection of the poet's encounters
with the West. Its final poem is the moody "Winter," a fine

poetic counterpoint to Mabel Dodge Luhan's prose *Winter in Taos,* published the same year.

Winter

Winter will be a solace, I had said.
Winter will be pale with snow
And restful with the great black shadows
Of trees at night against a shrouded earth.
There will be grey-lace cottonwoods
Of filigree tangling the clouds
And branches cased with ice
As colorless as glass.
Winter is earth's failure in a fight for color,
I had said—and death is a drabness
Of protruding earth. . .

And then I remembered the dazzle
Of a snowdrift;
And then I remembered the sun-shadows
Painting the snow in subtle strips of lavender;
And then I remembered going a hundred miles
Over a prairie-land of dunes and clouds
Until a glacial peak had pierced
The uttermost part of the sky for me—
And there was the blue I had forgotten. . .

But there is always the drabness of earth:
(Rich, chocolate-colored, sometimes,
As though it were only waiting for a sunny day
To grow a thousand blades of green.)
There is always the drabness of earth

Among the hills—and I can numb my senses
By counting a century of fence-posts
Along a never-ending road of brown;
Or notice, here, the grama grass
Curling its tan seed-plumes above invisible stems
In frigid immobility.

Perhaps I'll sit a year or two
Believing in the drabness of the season
Where snow has sprouted into enormous tubes
Of birch and aspen stalagmites,
Or where bare columns of gigantic trees
Drill in the hills, precisely, as I pass:
The front row left, the back row right,
And all of those between walking sedately—
A forest wheeling in marshal time
Without the movement of a single twig. . .

And yet, who can point his finger and say,
This is winter, this is spring?
In my garden are all the seasons now.
There where the sheltering wall casts shadows,
The snow has drifted and has covered all
Save one bleak branch of hardy brown.
And there where the wind swoops down,
Dead leaves have gathered in an autumn pool.
And here in the sun by the southern window
Are green leaves still and one last apple clinging.
But not even I had known until today
That one brave, buried bulb had sprouted
Points of tender green in the farthest sunny corner,

And that a little lizard warmed himself
Beside it there at noon. . .

So never mind, I won't believe
That utter dullness ever was.
Death may be the drabness of earth,
But even the clods and pebbles glisten
With the color of a thousand lives;
And with what hidden fire
Must the very worms that plow the grave
Flash crimson, blood-shot eyes
And preen their jade-green claws
When we have closed our eyes to life
And colorlessly died. . .

"Yellow," which had been included in Henderson's *The Turquoise Trail*, is one of eight poems in the section Johnson called "Autumnal":

Yellow

We drove out miles this afternoon
To see the yellow in the woods:
Mountain-sides of aspen.

And when the eye is tuned
To yellow and when autumn
Warms the very air with gold,
Who can see crimson or distant blues?
Each moment that I watched
A flock of magpies

Making a design,
Or glanced aside to note
An old-rose window frame,
I saw, instead,
Chamisa, finger-tipped with saffron,
Or even sage, blooming to yellow,
Or dust, touched by the sun,
Or the road itself, unwinding itself;
And remembered that we had driven miles
To see the yellow in the woods.

Mountain-sides of aspen only?
There bloomed a daisy still
Against an adobe wall as yellow as the road;
Here a stubble-field where grain had ripened,
And under the shelter of a yellow hay-cock
A girl in a lemon-colored dress.

Wheat before and during and after threshing;
Corn, leaning in the wind as fodder,
Drying on a wall as food,
Scattered on the ground as shucks:
Yellow, everything.

This stone, this parched hill,
This halo around the holy head
Of Jesus in an ancient church,
And the nimbus, glowing in the sun,
Around the tow-head of a boy.
Even the yellow glint of iris
In the eye of an old woman.

Yellow, reminder of fruit
Piled beneath canopies
In Mexican markets;
Bananas, limes, pitayas;
Reminder of sunsets and of stars,
Of moons, suns, planets and every straw
That ever broke a yellow desert camel's back.
Yellow of sunrise
Of jewelry, of pirate gold;
Yellow background of a painting of Salome,
Yellow parchment of an ancient tome
And a story written by O. Henry
On cheap, yellow copy-paper.
Yellow Chinese silk and Chinamen themselves.
Sallow skin of scholars in dark libraries;
Sunlight on the ocean, golden dreams,
And saffron cake made by Cornishmen
In California mining towns.

Yellow, chrome, cadmium, canary—
Synonyms, suggestions. . .
A novel by Aldous Huxley,
And one by Oppenheim;
The Yellow Book and sunflowers,
Kansas and yellow journals,
Honey, butter and yellow-jackets,
Canary cottage, cages and circus-wagons;
Whole worlds of flaming yellow fire—
And oblivion, yellow with the dust of ages!

. . . We drove out miles this afternoon
To see the yellow in the woods:
Mountain-sides of aspen.

"Blue Day," from the section "Patio" is a color-saturated poem that captures the sensory crossovers, visual and verbal, of a brilliant summer day:

Blue Day

There have been blue skies all summer long,
But I had not realized until today
How intimately they had encompassed me.
And there have been blue-birds in the corn,
But now, suddenly, I see the blue of leaves as well:
Leaves of the corn and wild plum trees and alderbush,
Even the leaves of cottonwood and oak.
How had I failed to see this blue before?

The unbelievable color of hills,
The incredible distance. . .
Blue from a knife-edge grey of dawn
Until a vivid noon;
An azure day that bends to turquoise,
Then the saturated heaviness of evening.

Where has there been a blue like this before?
Pale asters, corn-flowers, delphinium
Are domesticated colors.
Who wants to lock himself in a garden
When he can thrust himself, on a mountain,
Into the cerulian of the day;
Or when he can swim, submerged,
In the copper colors of a mountain lake:
Green-blue—
Reflecting the deepest of the sky,
Dyed with subtle minerals:

Cobalt, molybdenum and malachite. . .

I do not dare
Even to think of the indigo hull
And the mauve sails of a sunset cloud—
Even to remember the tourmaline translucence
Of a desert hill at dusk. . .
Bring me blue glasses to see, darkly,
A purple eclipse of the sun;
Bring me violets for the grave
Of my lost youth in which I knew
Only a jazz-band, deep second-street blue. . .

But who said summer sky?
Who mentioned lapis lazuli?
Who hinted that the bird-bath in the garden
Reflects the universe?
Mercifully it is hidden.
A jay flies, screaming, through a blue fir tree,
Heralding the storm—
And now the lavender serpentine
Of summer carnival
Has hidden the hyacinthine hills.

That daytime brilliance is contrasted with the night silence of
Johnson's own garden pool, beside which he writes:

Song For Saying Good-Bye

Quietly, all night long,
The frail fish in the garden pool
Flash in the moon-flecked water.

The cool night wind,
Lifting a scented bough,
Sends one slow petal falling

And fragile leaves,
Trembling on the trees,
Whisper to themselves

As the slow breeze,
An old calligrapher,
Writes with the shadows.

The soft sigh of pen-strokes
On the low table,
Is only another branch

Weaving, like the wind,
Its slow words to tell
Things that cannot be said.

The final section of *Horizontal Yellow* is "Adobe House," a collection of sixteen varied works. A persistent theme throughout *Horizontal Yellow*, but especially in the final section, is a wistfulness, and a recognition that Johnson's life was changing. His propensity for forming impossible attachments to younger men, often through fleeting encounters, had often left him (as it did Marsden Hartley, for example) disappointed, unfulfilled, and lonely. Despite his many friends, he could sometimes foresee an isolated existence stretching before him. We begin to meet the mature Johnson in these poems, which are among his most personal.

Faun

I thought last night that hoof-steps on my bed
Had wakened and carried me into a myth,
And that a whispering faun had laid its head
Upon the pillow by my own, and with
A voice that sounded like a wind in trees
Had muttered from the void (where beauty lies
All night beyond eternal sleepy seas)
A thousand things that would have made me wise.
I might have learned the mystery of death
And all of life without the hell of fear,
If I had listened to the gentle breath
Which trembled in the dark against my ear. . .
But now I have forgotten what it said;
The faun has vanished, and the dream is dead.

Whisper

My candle flickers
And I put it out.

A whisper breathes
over the edge of silence. . .

When I Am Left

When I am left standing in an empty house,
All the forgotten days of my life
That have been stark with loneliness
Come and pass over me.
When I am left without a word or touch,
There is no time, and I hear again

The wheels of a horse-drawn hearse
Creak in the winter snow
And feel the strange, cold
Shiver of a child;

I stand upon a windy hill
Leaning against a tree
And feel again the rough bark
Against a boy's wet cheek;

I clutch a pillow in a dismal room
And know the ache will never go away
From my heart;

I feel a smile
Lost on my face
As unsuspecting words
Thrust their sharp certainties
Into a beauty
That will not live again.

When I am left standing in an empty house,
When I am left without a word or touch,
All the forgotten days of my life
That have been stark with loneliness
Come and pass over me.

PROSE WORKS

Aside from the pieces Johnson contributed to *Laughing Horse*, discussed in Chapter Two, he edited or wrote for a variety of publications after college. At first he consulted closely with Bynner, but a contest of wills developed. As early as 1923

Johnson had begun to chafe under his perennial role as student. Bynner's biographer explains Spud's incipient resistance to authority: "Spud refused to commit himself to anyone, which . . . slightly disturbed both his teachers [Bynner and Lawrence]—it was an affront to their doctrines."[13]

By 1924 a partial rupture of Johnson's personal and professional relationship with Bynner took place. Though they would continue to be friends, the apprenticeship was over. Johnson had benefited enormously from the older poet's mentoring, from watching a creative mind at work, from communing with an intellect of wide grasp and sympathies. Bynner had also given Johnson entrée to the world of American art and letters through his extensive acquaintance with its leading figures. The younger man had learned much in the years they spent together, but it was time for a change.

The reasons for the Bynner-Johnson break are more complex than have been reported. True, Mabel was jealous of Bynner's and Johnson's invitation to travel to Mexico with the Lawrences. True, she did make efforts after the 1923 trip to lure Spud to Taos, perhaps in retribution against Bynner's "capture" of the Lawrences. But the separation was a gradual one, over several years. Though he spent much time in Taos beginning in 1924, it was not until 1927 that Johnson was actually installed as Mabel's secretary at Los Gallos.

Before that time, during their long stays at Taos during 1924 and 1925, the Lawrences had developed a special fondness for young Spud. "I often did secretarial work for D. H. Lawrence and was given the benefit of his criticism of my verse during many sojourns at his ranch," recalled Johnson.[14]

In addition to his own writing, his frequent work for Mabel, and *Laughing Horse*, for which he had now assumed primary responsibility, Johnson began to undertake other publishing jobs as well (Fig.2). He had purchased a printing press at Taos, on which he produced many small pamphlets and broadsides. One project was a 1,500-line poem by Arthur Davison ficke,

PRINTING - BOOKLETS A SPECIALTY

Willard Johnson
PAMPHLETEER

Laughing Horse Press -- Taos, N. M.

FIGURE 2. Advertisement for Spud Johnson's printing business, from *Laughing Horse*, no. 14 (1927).

which Spud compiled into a small booklet for private distribution. In 1930 his Laughing Horse Press published *Adobe Notes*, a booklet written by Kate Chapman and Dorothy N. Stewart about building with adobe. Illustrated with thirteen woodblock prints (by the authors and the printer), it outlined the history, the virtues, and rewards of the old ways of building, espousing traditional materials and time-honored methods.[15]

When not at his press, Johnson began to seek other venues for his own writing. In 1924 he contributed amusing bits about New Mexico for the "Americana" section of George Jean Nathan and H. L. Mencken's influential periodical *The American Mercury*.

But he wanted to write more than snippets of local color. Following tearful farewells to the Lawrences, who left Taos in September 1925 for what would be the last time, Spud arranged his own departure, to explore the larger world of New York publishing. The visit turned into a whole winter, during which he assembled contributions for a D. H. Lawrence number of *Laughing Horse*. That issue was published in the spring of 1926 at Ossining, New York, not far from Mabel Dodge's Finney Farm at Croton-on-Hudson, where Spud was spending time. During these months he also began to write articles for a recently established popular magazine, the *New Yorker*. After a summer in New Mexico, he was invited back to the city in the fall of 1926 as a regular staff contributor.

Johnson's *New Yorker* sketches are breezy, irreverent, and youthful—writing aimed at a socially ambitious, jazz-age readership. He tossed in casual remarks about the "good old days" in New York and made knowing references to *au courant* places and events. Years later he liked to joke about his affectation of big-city *savoir faire*. Called into the office of legendary *New Yorker* editor Harold Ross, Johnson was praised for his pieces—just the kind of bright, urbane writing the magazine wanted. "Thanks," said Spud, "but I've only been in town for a couple of winters. I'm from the West." Gulping and sputtering, Ross replied, "Don't ever tell anyone that!"[16]

Flippant and whimsical, Johnson's pieces for the *New Yorker* poked gentle fun at society horse shows, love-struck stenographers, and skyscraper architecture. One example recasts Shakespeare as a modern New Yorker whose plays face the modern censor's axe. It was a subject close to Johnson's heart.

Another English Author Comes to New York [17]

SPUD JOHNSON

William Shakespeare threw his copy of the *World* onto the breakfast table in front of Anne Hathaway with an exclamation and took a long drink of coffee before he said anything. In fact, Anne was the first to speak.

"But, William, there's nothing here about you."

"Not until next week!" he said bitterly, taking a piece of toast, and then exclaiming, "It's burned."

"I don't know what you're talking about," she said.

"The toast, of course, dummy—and don't you realize that my play opens next week and that if *these* plays are suppressed and the actors and producers arrested, the same thing will happen to me? And that if the play doesn't go on we shan't be able to pay the rent?"

"Oh, William," she moaned, "and I was counting on a new fur coat! They wouldn't stop your play, would they? It's so poetical. Not nearly so bad as some of your others. The way Hamlet talks to his mother, for instance, is shameful."

"Well, Sidney Howard got away with that sort of stuff, debunking sweet motherhood, so I guess I can. 'Hamlet's' a better play than 'The Silver Cord,' too, even if I do say it myself."

"And the way *Lady Macbeth* talks about dashing her

(continued on following pages)

baby's brains out and all. Why, all your plays are just full of murders and everything."

"Murders! Neither the moralists or the police—nor yet the Great American Public bothers about murders. Murderers always repent, anyway, or are killed in the end, themselves. What they object to is sex."

"But how can they object to that? We all have it, haven't we? Even if some of us haven't got the appeal," she whimpered wistfully.

"Well they do object, anyway. And I suppose I've got to rewrite 'Midsummer Night's Dream.' I shouldn't have been surprised if it had been 'Merry Wives of Windsor' or 'Henry IV'— Falstaff is pretty rowdy for a nation that has Prohibition. But this sweet comedy will simply have to be wrecked."

"You mean because *Hermia* and *Lysander* wander in the woods all night together? I thought *Hermia* was very firm and sweet about it," said Anne.

"There were at least *six* lovers in the woods all night," replied Shakespeare with the righteous annoyance of an author whose play has been forgotten. "And must I remind you that the whole plot turns on the quarrel between the King and Queen of the fairies and remind you *what* the quarrel was about? Have you forgotten that *Titania* makes violent love to an ass? 'Sleep thou,' she says to *Bottom,* 'and I will wind thee in my arms'; and then, 'entwisted like woodbine and honeysuckle vines,' they fall asleep? How can I get away with that?"

"Well, I suppose you'll want to lock yourself up in your

study all day, now, with a bottle of gin and a carton of Camels, and will get mad if I call you to lunch!"

"I suppose I will," he replied, pacing the floor distractedly. "And I suppose I'll have to do something about that new edition of my sonnets Knopf is bringing out in the spring. I guess I'd better change the dedication, at least."

"Well, it serves you right," said Anne, having the last word, as usual, "for writing all those sonnets to that young man. At least, the critics give me credit for being the dark lady of the later sonnets, anyway."

Shakespeare went out and slammed the door behind him.

Following his second winter in New York, Johnson returned to Taos, where he produced issue fourteen of *Laughing Horse* and then went to San Francisco for the winter of 1928–29. For an organization called Californians, Inc., he wrote profiles of westerners, several of which were published in *Sunset*—then a more literary, public affairs kind of publication than now. One of these sketches was about Bynner, whom Johnson styled "A Poet in a Raccoon Coat." Using the pen name Walter Mallon, Johnson sketched a vivid picture of the gregarious Bynner:

He literally doubled up with laughter at his own splendid story, clapping himself in the stomach with one hand and with the other grabbing the arm of his nearest neighbor for support in his uncontrollable paroxysm of mirth which made him look rather like a great frog about to explode.[18]

While in California Johnson spent time with Lincoln Steffens, the socialist writer and journalist, helping him edit his autobiography.[19] He also persuaded Steffens to contribute a political humor piece on Al Smith, printed by *Laughing Horse* in 1928 (see Chapter Two).

TAOS: PUTTING DOWN ROOTS

Back in Taos, Johnson settled into the little adobe house he would occupy for most of the next four decades (Fig. 3). As in many Taos homes, its rooms served multiple purposes. Once the day began, his bathroom became a "morning room," where he spent much of his time; a board and Indian blanket spread across the tub transformed it into a couch. Another room was added on, built around an old covered well which Spud adorned with plants and flowers and used as a coffee table. Spud's press occupied a corner, and his books, magazines, and paintings were everywhere, as described in Luhan's *Winter in Taos.*[20]

As the famous passed through Taos, Johnson came to know many of them. In the summers of 1929 and 1930 John Marin, already a highly successful watercolorist, visited Taos at the invitation of Mabel Dodge Luhan.[21] Since Spud was working for Mabel during those years and was often on hand at her compound, he and Marin undoubtedly met. Probably they also spent time together, since Johnson's collection contained drawings and a watercolor sketch by Marin; on the reverse of the watercolor was attached a typed notation that the painting was "collected by Mr. Johnson from Marin. Painted in the vicinity of Taos, N.M." (Fig. 4). Spud also collected six drawings of Indian dancers, presumably studies for Marin's paintings of the Santo Domingo corn dance; they remain in his papers (Fig. 5).

FIGURE 3.
Spud Johnson at his
home in Taos, 1931.
Photograph courtesy
Dr. U. C. Lovejoy and
Michael Lovejoy.

FIGURE 4. John Marin, New Mexico landscape sketch, watercolor and pencil. Collected by Spud Johnson, 1929 or 1930. Photograph courtesy Dr. U. C. Lovejoy and Michael Lovejoy.

FIGURE 5. *(opposite)* John Marin, charcoal and watercolor study of Pueblo Indian dancer, obtained by Spud Johnson from Marin in 1929. This is one of six Marin figure studies owned by Johnson. Probably they were made in preparation for Marin's monumental watercolor *Dance of the San Domingo Indians* [sic], 1929, now in the collection of the Metropolitan Museum of Art. The sketches are now in the Art Collection, Harry Ransom Humanities Research Center, University of Texas at Austin.

Throughout the 1930s Leopold Stokowski made repeated visits to Taos in search of Indian music. He wanted to record ceremonial chants and brought along specially designed sound recording machines. Tony Luhan and Spud, each driving a car, took on the task of driving the legendary conductor to villages in New Mexico and Arizona, where he painstakingly tried to capture the sound and rhythms in permanent form. Ultimately the venture proved a failure, for the equipment produced poor recordings and the music resisted attempts at conventional written notation.[22]

Celebrated playwright and novelist Thornton Wilder was another Taos visitor starting in the 1930s. When buffeted by the changing winds of critical opinion, Wilder found visits with Mabel and conversations with Spud both restorative and bracing.[23] Slight, like Johnson, and refined, Wilder represented the literary success coveted by an aspiring writer like Johnson (Fig.6).

During the summer of 1929, her first in New Mexico, Georgia O'Keeffe and Spud began a friendship that would last for decades. He was working for Mabel that year, but she was away in the East having surgery and recuperating for most of the summer. In her absence the visitors to her home created their own diversions. As a newcomer O'Keeffe was given a great deal of attention, and expeditions were arranged in her honor. Toward the end of the summer she and four other intrepid travelers— Spud, Charles Collier, Marie Garland and filmmaker Henwar Rodakiewicz—set out on a spontaneous trip through some of the West's most spectacular country. In a letter to her friend Rebecca Strand, O'Keeffe recounted the highlights of the adventure:

FIGURE 6. Spud Johnson and Thornton Wilder at the Taos Inn.
Photograph by Regina Cooke, courtesy the Harwood Foundation, Taos.

Henwar and Spud had supper with us at the Hotel and
Marie decided we must take a real trip—go to the Grand
Canyon and Navajo Country—Well—a day later we started—in the Rolls Royce and Packard—Marie—Henwar—
Charles—Spud and I—I wont go into it now—We went
to both rims of the Canyon—crossed the new Lees Ferry
bridge—through as much Navajo country as heavy rains
would permit—up to Bryce Canyon—almost to Salt Lake

City—across the Great Mesa—or maybe it is called Grand
Mesa—I dont remember—over Independence Pass to
Colorado Springs and down to Taos by Raton—We were
ten days—terrible roads—heat that made you feel your
eyes were frying—We crossed Painted Desert too—incredible color—and what shapes! even had such a bad hail
storm that the ground was almost white—There seemed
little left to do when it was all over—all sorts of hotels and
sandwiches—We drove with tops of the cars down most of
the time—greased faces and peeling noses and everybody
loved it—[24]

In the years to come Johnson and O'Keeffe would share other
adventures on the road. In October of 1934 O'Keeffe, following
her first summer visit to New Mexico in three years, prepared to
return east. She asked Spud to drive her across the country in her
Ford. Since she was willing to pay all expenses, Spud accepted at
once, glad for a chance to visit old friends in New York. With
Spud at the wheel they set out, filling the long miles with generally pleasant conversation. During the trip they shared many
confidences, including the details of one of O'Keeffe's long visits
to Bermuda earlier that year.[25]

Nobody loved gossip more than Johnson, but with close
friends he was a discreet and sympathetic listener—qualities
which help to account for his long friendship with O'Keeffe. But
during the 1934 cross-country trip, with only each other's companionship, the miles began to wear on both. At one point, after
O'Keeffe complained about accommodations and breakfast,
Johnson confided to his journal that he found her "more per-
snickety and old-maidish than usual."[26] En route to the city they
breakfasted with Arthur Dove, and in New York Johnson

FIGURE 7.
Left to right:
Georgia O'Keeffe,
Tinka Fechin, Dorothy
Brett on the occasion
of Brett's seventy-ninth
birthday, Taos, 1962.
Photograph by Regina
Cooke, courtesy the
Harwood Foundation,
Taos.

renewed acquaintance with friends from his mid-twenties stays in the city: Countee Cullen, Philip Wylie, the Stettheimer sisters, Henry McBride, and the Jean Toomers.

When O'Keeffe resumed annual visits to the Southwest, she and Spud saw each other frequently, either in Taos or at Ghost Ranch. Following her permanent move to the state in 1949 she often invited him to her home in Abiquiu for holiday visits, usually in the company of Dorothy Brett. Especially memorable was the Christmas of 1950, which he recounted in a letter to his friend Gina Knee:

> Brett and I went to Abiquiu Christmas eve and spent a very pleasant two days with Georgia O'Keeffe. To be more exact, I commuted between Taos and Abiquiu over the holiday. After dinner on the 24th we lit Christmas trees (one inside, one out in the patio) built the traditional 9 bonfires on the cliff-edge outside, drank mulled wine, and gossiped cozily before the fire, went to midnight mass in the nearby church. On the 25th we drove to Taos to see the Deer Dance, returning to Abiquiu for turkey dinner that night. And on the 26th Brett and I returned home.[27]

Despite his occasional waspishness and her frequent need to control those around her, O'Keeffe and Johnson adjusted to each other's eccentricities. More, they forged a durable friendship. Early in 1951, a few months after that memorable Christmas at Abiquiu, they again traveled together, motoring to Mexico in the company of Eliot and Aline Porter. Johnson had spent long periods in Mexico—first with the Lawrences, later with the Luhans, and he knew it well. O'Keeffe had never been south of the border, but she was entranced by its history, architecture, color, and art.

To O'Keeffe and to many other women Johnson was a non-threatening friend, in part because of his homosexuality. Besides, they liked him for his vital interest in life and literature, and for his astute, often wry, observations on human nature. Over the years he developed close friendships with many women, including Mabel Luhan, Mary Austin, O'Keeffe, Brett, Frieda Lawrence, Ida Rauh, Rebecca James and painter Gina Knee (Fig. 7). Austin and Luhan, respectively twenty-nine and eighteen years older than Johnson, exercised their maternalism on him. So did Frieda Lawrence, who affectionately called him "the Spoodle." But sometimes his natural reserve prevented real closeness with these older women; Frieda, for example, once remarked, "I've known Spud and loved him for thirty years, and I still don't know whether he even likes me."[28] With those closer to his own age Spud's reticence broke down, allowing closer friendships. To him they spoke freely of their loves and their lives. O'Keeffe, for example, wrote him intimately, searching in words—as she was in her art—for meaning and identity:

FIGURE 8.
First page of a hand-
written note from
Georgia O'Keeffe to
Spud Johnson,
undated. Harry
Ransom Humanities
Research Center,
University of Texas at
Austin. See note 29,
Chapter 1.[29]

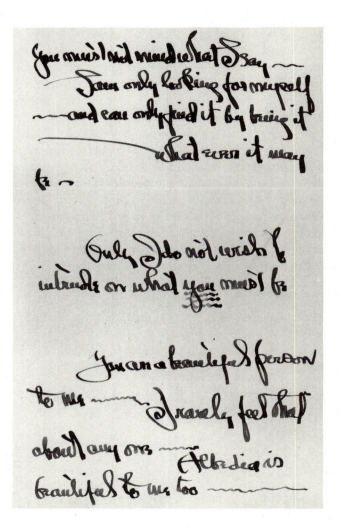

Sojourns in Santa Fe

Johnson called both Taos and Santa Fe home, so comfortable was he in each town. He willingly left the little Taos adobe for sojourns in the capital from time to time. One such opportunity arose when the editor of the *Santa Fe New Mexican* joined a delegation to Mexico early in 1930. In his absence, Spud was invited to take over some of the editorial chores and provide local stories during the month of February. He wrote a number of feature articles, some "silly" (as he termed them), but others serious in intent. He conducted an informal survey (probably through his friends in the local bookstore) of what Santa Feans were reading in 1930. Not surprisingly, books of regional interest headed the list.

During his brief stint at the newspaper he also wrote a daily column of local gossip, "The Perambulator," which included such items as the imminent visit of the poet and mythologist Robert Graves, and a report on the recent visit of Dr. Albert Barnes. Barnes, the wealthy Philadelphia inventor (whose art collection became the Barnes Foundation in Merion, Pennsylvania), had been in town buying, as Spud reported, "carloads" of santos, Navajo blankets, and silver.[30] "The Perambulator" proved so popular that when Johnson's month-long job ended, a group of locals presented a petition asking that Spud and his column be retained. They addressed the petition to Senator Bronson Cutting, owner of the *New Mexican*. Its list of signatories is a Who's Who of local writers, artists, and dignitaries.

Despite his excellent connections, no extended position was available, so Spud returned once more to Taos, where he began work on a novel set in Mexico. Neither that manuscript nor another, begun later in the 1930s, was ever completed, though excerpts were published as sketches and stories over the years.

Johnson's newspaper career resumed when he was offered the editorship of the *Taos Valley News* in 1933. Among the features he initiated on its pages was a series he called "Kindly Karicatures," sketches of local citizens he found colorful. Mabel was one of them, as was Dr. T. P. (Doc) Martin, whom Johnson remembered as the first man he had met upon arriving in Taos many years earlier. Johnson stayed at the *Taos Valley News* until 1935, when he was again offered a position in Santa Fe. This time it was a job managing the Villagra Bookshop, haunt of all the local writers. It was a bibliophile's dream: customers dropped in to sit by the fire, browse through new editions and exchange views on every conceivable subject. With access to all the latest releases, Spud wrote a book review column for the newspaper, in which he included news of local and visiting writers.

Spud was also active during his stays in Santa Fe in all kinds of community affairs. As part of the hilarity one year during the Santa Fe Fiesta a mock bullfight was announced, to be staged in front of the Palace of the Governors. Featured were "Tres Toros Terribles" and three equally formidable "Matadores," one of whom was Spud, nicknamed "La Papa" (Fig. 9).

FIGURE 9.
Santa Fe Fiesta poster
announcing a mock bull-
fight with Spud Johnson
("La Papa") as one of the
matadors. Woodblock
print by Gustave
Baumann. Poster
courtesy of History
Library, Palace of the
Governors, Museum of
New Mexico.

Thorough Survey of Reading Habits of Local Book-Worms

SPUD JOHNSON

A comprehensive survey of just what Santa Feans read has been occupying our statistical department for some time along with the vital question: "What is behind the cathedral?" (a question which arose recently when it was suggested that a local duel be fought there).

Apparently local book-worms follow the remainder of the country's readers with certain of the best-sellers, but are not at all influenced by the mob and the book-reviewers with regard to others. With the war books, yes. "All Quiet on the Western Front" has led the national (as well as international list of best-sellers) and it has led in Santa Fe. So has "A Farewell to Arms". But with the exception of "Scarlet Sister Mary" and "The Bishop Murder Case", the other leaders have not been much read.

Biography Goes Strong

Among the non-fiction best sellers, the biographies "Elizabeth and Essex" and "Henry the Eighth" have been Santa Fe's choice—with the addition of one other—and here we blush—Chic Sale's "The Specialist!"

But the most interesting revelation that came as a result of this investigation, is that Santa Fe readers are loyal to local talent. Frank Applegate is a best seller in the ancient city. People read "Stories From the Pueblos" in preference to war and murder stories. And Willa Cather's "Death Comes for the Archbishop" has been a more or less continuous best-seller here ever since its publication. Witter Bynner's books come perhaps third in the list, and Mary Austin, Oliver La Farge's "Laughing Boy" and D. H. Lawrence's "Mornings in Mexico" are all hard to keep in stock.

Books on Mexico are also big sellers here, especially during the past few months when the Mexican exodus set in. Anita Brenner's "Idols Behind Altars", "The Frescoes of Diego Rivera, "Viva Mexico," by Flandreau, "Mornings in Mexico" by Lawrence, and even "Indian Earth" by Bynner, although this last is not strictly a book about Mexico.

It is a little early to state now what the fate of Harvey Ferguson's "Footloose MacGarnegal" will be from the hands of local book buyers, but it will doubtless have a good sale and in any event will exceed the murder stories so popular elsewhere.*

---

*This piece originally appeared in the *Santa Fe New Mexican,* February 8, 1930.

MARCH 5, 1930
SANTA FE, NEW MEXICO.

Senator Bronson Cutting,
Senate Office Building,
Washington, D. C.

Our Dear Senator:

We protest. For years we have faithfully subscribed to the Santa Fe New Mexican through the trials and tribulations of the many political campaigns, seiges of state educational boards, highways, labor commissioners, odd tales, springeritis and trips to Mexico. At last we found a haven in the "Perambulator".

We are now informed that the Perambulator has been sidetracked. We learn that no longer shall we be able to hear of the peculiarities of one Jasper. We are told that never again shall we be able to read of what really happens in the innermost chambers of the La Fonda, let alone Taos. We fear that our dinner conversation will degenerate to pre-Perambulator dullness.

Never before has the New Mexican been so freely quoted, so spiritedly discussed, as since the Perambulator started ambling through its pages.

We will continue to read your publication under any circumstances—even if the pains in the solar plexus should ease. In fact, we might buckle up the old belt and stand the gaff even if famous people should stop coming and

(continued on following pages)

going through Lamy. But please we hope, wish, beg, implore, plead and pray—keep the Perambulator rolling.

(Signed)

Major and Mrs. Holmes
John J. Zook
Mr. and Mrs. James
    MacMillan
Mr. and Mrs. Raymond
    Jonson
Mr. and Mrs.
    [unreadable name]
Dr. H.P. Mera
Mr. and Mrs. H.H. Dorman
Martin Gardesky
Mr. and Mrs. Haniel Long
Sheldon Parsons
Mr. and Mrs. W.M. Field
Mrs. L.A. Hughes
Datus E. Meyers
Mrs. G.H. Van Stone
Alice C. Meyers

Roberta Robey
Mr. and Mrs. Ashley Pond
Mr. & Mrs. Philip Stevenson
Joe Bakos
Will and Helen Shuster

Marjorie Breese
James L. Breese

Mabel K. O'Brien

Francis Linden Otis

Roscoe Matthews
Mr.andMrs. Hubert Galt
Betty Galt
Dorothy Ellis
Andrew Dasburg
Alice Corbin Henderson
Richard and Norma Day
Margaret Lemis
Mr. and Mrs. Carlos Vierra
Mrs. Sam Hamilton
Mr. and Mrs. Frank
    Applegate
Willard and Edith Nash
Mrs. William H. Nash
Teresa Bakos

Levi Hughes
Kenneth M. Chapman

Marian F. Winnek
Florence O. Harrington
Louise Pugh

Mr. and Mrs. Raymond Otis
Margaret McKittrick
Mrs. Byron Harvey
Dr. E.W. Fiske

Richie S. March

Liane Hall Adams
Ben Jaffa
E.P. Moore
Mr. and Mrs. O. A. Larrazola, Jr.
J.B.M. McGovern
Margaret Naumberg
Margaret Larkin
Cyril and Phillis Kay Scott
Dr. Robert O. Brown
Juan A. A. Sedillo
Howard and Elizabeth Patterson[31]

Arthur Seligman
William J. Barker
Mr. and Mrs. David
        McComb

Osborne Wood
Daggett Harvey
Mrs. Francis Harvey

NEW PUBLISHING VENTURES

Late in 1937 Johnson returned once more to Taos, where his hand-press awaited. It was never idle for long. *Laughing Horse* had not appeared for some seven years, but now Johnson began to assemble materials for number twenty, which he published in June 1938. As soon as that issue was out, Johnson turned his attention to a new publishing project, an experiment he had been planning for some time. It was a miniature one-sheet weekly newspaper called *The Horse Fly*, billed as the "Smallest and Most Inadequate Newspaper Ever Published." Filled with items of local news, it chronicled the comings and goings of residents, promoted arts events, and proclaimed causes dear to its editor's heart. To Johnson it was a labor of love—a one-person operation whose success rode entirely on his own efforts. Spud gathered the news, wrote copy, sold advertising, set type, and distributed by himself (Fig. 10). After a year he was exhausted by the effort; in July 1939, exactly one year and fifty-two issues after its first appearance, he declared *The Horse Fly* dead. More precisely, it ceased independent operation, except for some scattered reappearances in its original format during 1940 and 1941. Eventually it was absorbed into the county newspaper *El Crepusculo* (affectionately known as "The Creep" to many locals). That change of status greatly lessened Johnson's responsibilities; thereafter he merely gathered news and wrote opinions, with others handling the printing and distribution. Still later *The Horse Fly* became a highlight of the *Taos News*, where it continued into the 1960s (Fig. 11).

Even while editing his own publications, Johnson was always a free-lance writer as well. Besides submitting poetry and sketches to national publications, he wrote columns and notes

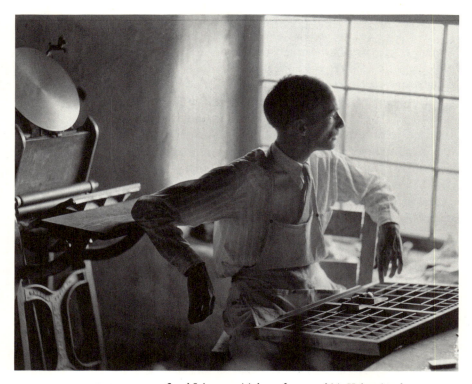

FIGURE 10. Spud Johnson with box of type and his Kelsey hand press, Taos, 1930s. Photography collection, Harry Ransom Humanities Research Center, University of Texas at Austin.

FIGURE 11. *(opposite)* First anniversary issue of Spud Johnson's *Horse Fly*, announcing the demise of the miniature newspaper, July 1939.

THE HORSE FLY

Smallest and Most Inadequate Newspaper Ever Published

Vol. I, No. 52. Five Cents a Copy.   *Taos, New Mexico, July 8, 1939*

"HORSE FLY" DIES IN CANDLE FLAME OF BIRTHDAY CAKE

At the very peak of his brilliant career and in the midst of a gay & ribald party celebrating his first birthday, *Horse Fly, No. 1* was fatally singed in the flame of his birthday cake candle and died miserably at an early hour this morning.

Rallying bravely, shortly before the end, friends who gathered 'round report that his last gallant words were: "Well, anyhow, I'm not the first host to pass out cold at his own party!"

He is survived by only one legitimate son, the well known *Vol. 2*, who told reporters today, that although he is completely crushed by his pappy's death, he hopes to appear soon again in public, & to carry on the noble work of his revered parent, at least spasmodically & at intervals; although he cannot attempt & will not promise to produce offspring with the unfailing regularity which characterized the virile efforts of his dear daparted dad.

Grandfather *Laughing Horse*, who was interviewed later in the day at his country

Horse Fly Succumbs On Unique Deathbed Of Angelfood Cake   *— by Ila McAfee*

estate, was violent in his denunciation of 'the deplorable weakness of the younger generation,' & announced his intentions of stepping into the breach himself, and assuming all obligations. "I will see to it that every one of my grandson's creditors is paid in full!" he said manfully.

Memorial services will be conducted in many a home throughout the week & genuine hand-printed replicas of the deceased will be on sale at all newsstands.

FIGURE 12. Spud Johnson in priest's costume, riding a burro in Taos Fiesta parade. Shaffer Studio photograph. Photography collection, Harry Ransom Humanities Research Center, University of Texas at Austin.

for the *New Mexico Sentinel* in the late 1930s. Often he took part in little theater productions and parades at Taos, where he took special delight in donning improbable or outrageous costumes (Fig. 12). A lifelong bibliophile, he supplemented his own collection (and his meager income) by buying and selling books. Sometimes from a pushcart, sometimes from his house, he ran a small lending library (Fig. 13). And during World War II he operated a bookstall next to the Heptagon Gallery in the Scheurich patio near the Taos plaza.[32]

FIGURE 13.
Spud Johnson with
his portable bookseller's
cart, Taos, c. 1930s.
Photography Collection,
Harry Ransom
Humanities Center,
University of Texas
at Austin.

FIGURE 14. Spud Johnson on the Plaza, Taos, 1939. Photography Collection, Harry Ransom Humanities Research Center, University of Texas at Austin.

Spud became an authority to be consulted on all things relating to Taos. When H. L. Mencken was revising his book *The American Language* he wrote Spud asking, "May I bother you to tell me what the correct local designation is for a citizen of Taos? Is he a Taosian, a Taosite, or what? . . . .Taos is pronounced, I believe, to rhyme with *house.* Isn't that correct? If you care to give me any help I'll be very grateful."[33] (Fig. 14).

Until shortly before his death in 1968 Johnson contributed Sunday columns called "The Santa Fe Gadfly" (some 300 in all) to that town's newspaper. In these columns he explored things that interested him: people, books, the arts. But he also began to

FIGURE 15.
Spud Johnson cartoon: "Taos: We have lots of room for improvement." Art Collection, Harry Ransom Humanities Research Center, University of Texas at Austin.

write increasingly about issues of ecology and civic beau-
tification. Having seen many changes in his forty years of residence, Johnson lamented unrestricted growth and irresponsible
development in Taos. As neon signs proliferated, he spoke out
against the over-commercialization of its historic streets and
reportedly stole through the night streets on occasion, chopping
down offensive signs (Fig. 15). Once he received (presumably
from those who disagreed with such activity) a broken windshield on his car. He crusaded for protection of the environs of
historic Ranchos de Taos church from a proposed road reloca-
tion. And, in a public-spirited "Horse Fly" column he chided
businessmen for chopping down trees and called for a bypass
(sadly lacking even now) that would divert heavy traffic from
narrow, already crowded streets.

El Crepusculo

THE TAOS NEWS
MARCH 22, 1966
SPUD JOHNSON

During many past years I have made it my business to record
and lament the sad death-rate of TREES in our valley. . . .

I protested the destruction of the entire row of cottonwoods on Pueblo Road when the Mariposa Market was
built, urged that the building could be erected only a few
feet further back, saving the trees and making a shaded
parking space in front, besides preserving the handsome
avenue that so beautifully framed the view of Taos
Mountain.

(continued on following pages)

Similarly, I protested the chopping down of the row of box-elders when the new Enco station was built at the corner of Pueblo and Armory Place. This station could have been entered through a judiciously clipped garden strip with very little sacrifice of the actual "service" area, and certainly no interference with their tall, identifying sign. . .

I remember, too, that I applauded when Spivey built his restaurant and surprisingly preserved one lone tree directly in front. It's still there, a happy survivor, and I can't see that it in the least interferes with necessary parking beside it.

Every year the carnage continues and I have, each year, written obituaries, while urging preservation of the old timers that are still with us.

I was reminded of all this just the other day when driving into town after being away for a mere week or two. On both sides of town lay newly-felled corpses! Two handsome trees—or was it three?—opposite Chet Mitchell's house, on Highway 3, just north of Placita Road, had apparently only a moment before been chopped down and had not yet been dismembered or removed.

And between the Sierra Sporting Goods building and the neighboring Texaco station on Santa Fe Road, it looked as though an entire forest had been levelled, for the pile of trunks and branches made a veritable mountain. Obviously a new building is to rise soon, the cinder blocks already there to replace inutile vegetation.

Painful News

The subject has been so personally painful during the writing of the last few paragraphs, that I could scarcely mind what I was saying and perhaps didn't make much sense for the simple reason that I was interrupted by a telephone call from a friend who had recently attended some kind of highway meeting, where it was announced that State Highway No. 3, north from Taos, is scheduled, as immediately as next fall, to be considerably widened, which will necessitate the destruction of ALL the trees on BOTH sides of the present road.

Since the construction of the long bridge at Placita some years ago, and the straightening of what once was a "winding road," took a large slice from my own property, and since I have spent the intervening 30 years nurturing and defending a new line of defense in a solid row of trees, many of which are now considerable giants, you can imagine how this news came as practically a knock-out blow.

And such a project will not only completely destroy the semi-rural aspect of this entire northern approach to Taos, but will inevitably slice spang into the middle of garages, kitchens, bed-rooms and living rooms of some of us already too near a country lane turned highway.

Can you blame me, then, for groaning aloud in public? For praying fervently for that often-discussed and controversial by-pass which will not only partially solve our local traffic problems, but divert at least a part of the heavier trucking? And, hopefully, save a lot of our cherished trees!

Perhaps it is time for a public announcement of the Highway Department's complete intentions and plans, and for a full-scale re-discussion the whole by-pass subject.

Save the trees! Save Taos!

Spud was a keen observer of people, both individually and in groups. Over many years in Taos he saw conflicts come and go, often with publicly mouthed platitudes masking the deeply divided nature of the place. Alarmed about ethnic strife among the Indian, Hispanic, and "Anglo" communities in Taos, Spud aired his impatience at old stereotypes and misbegotten efforts to homogenize the populations of northern New Mexico. It is a lament that might have been written, in nearly the same form, twenty-five years later.

The Santa Fe Gadfly

SPUD JOHNSON

Split Personality

Do you suppose Taos, as a community, is schizophrenic? I'm well aware that I shouldn't bandy about technical terms I don't understand, but my point is that Taos always seems to be over-violently SPLIT on almost every issue that confronts it, and perhaps the case should be studied as a psychological problem, if not as a psychopathic case.

Last week, for instance—if one can trust the local newspaper as an accurate reflection of public opinion—you would have thought another 1847 Revolution was in the works. Petitions, editorials, front-page stories, and countless separately-headlined letters from individuals crowded the pages, all protesting (again) the renewed Indian claim to Blue Lake and surrounding Wilderness Area acres.

(continued on following pages)

As usual, the Indians' quiet legal battle was attacked as a "land grab," which has always seemed odd to me, since almost all our land, from Cape Cod to the Golden Gate, has been a grab by Spanish, Mexicans, and so-called Anglos from the indigenous Indian population, so that it has always struck me that modern day protestors might at least acknowledge this situation by calling it a "counter grab," instead of labeling it an outrageous, unfounded, almost insane bid for power and property—property which, again and again the letters of protest, were designated as "belonging to all of us" and as "the birthright of the American people" to which a single, dwindling, unimportant ethnic group had no right, justification or claim. . .

Ancient Conflict

It was especially interesting to note that all but about half a dozen of the appended names to these petitions and letters were from our Spanish-American neighbors, so that it gave the impression of being a purely racial issue. In other words, it was a renewal and repetition of the ancient conflict between the descendants of the "Conquistadors" and the original Indian inhabitants with, this time, the "Anglos" (except for a few Forest Service personnel and a few businessmen mindful of their status, as a minority group) siding with the Indians!

All of this is a slight switch from the aforementioned "Revolution of 1847," when the Spanish and the Indians combined to combat the "American Occupation;" but the point is that, whatever the alignment, there always was in

the past, and there still is in spite of apparent friendly relations on the surface, a strong racial antagonism that crops
up in one way or another whenever a controversy erupts,
no matter how unrelated such an argument may be from
what fundamentally benefits or disserves all three races
alike.

Take as an example a fairly recent "fight:" a highway
by-pass was being considered. Inevitably, the "rich Anglos" were accused of trying to preserve the area as a kind
of primitive Shangri-La at the expense of the "poor
Spanish-Americans" who can barely make a living here and
often have to migrate to industrial areas or to richer agri-
cultural zones—this in spite of the protesting group's con-
victions and repeatedly stressed arguments that tourism is
one of the main industries of the area, and that all races
will benefit from keeping it an unsullied island in the
midst of an America that is becoming distressingly and
increasingly uniform.

I was thinking of all this the other day when I read Mr.
Colgrove's article in last Sunday's New Mexican about how
successful New Mexico had been in the matter of "desegre-
gation"—referring, of course, to the Negro problem. The
fact of the matter is that New Mexico, in spite of its lati-
tude, has never been what could be called a "southern
state," and has never had a Negro problem. Its racial problem is triple, relatively "uncolored," curiously complicat-
ed—and still unsolved.

In the end, races do mix, and prejudice disappears, but
it's a long bitter struggle that is perhaps never completely
settled without rancor.

Mud or Cement?

The latest Taos controversy is over the question of whether St. Francis Mission at Ranchos de Taos shall be hard-plastered. Will this also become a racial issue?

A number of disinterested, public-spirited well-wishers, who would like to preserve this fine and unusual example of primitive New Mexican architecture without a practical but ugly coating of modern cement, are contributing money and agitating to collect more funds in order to pay for its continued, but increasingly expensive mud-coating. But many of these contributors are Anglos.

Will the Spanish-Americans protest that this is THEIR church, that the "rich Anglos" had better mind their own business and leave the decision to the Mission's legitimate heirs?

Or will they, for once, recognize the gesture as a generous and genuine interest in the preservation of a heritage that belongs to all of us, irrespective of who our grandfathers were?

It remains to be seen.

TRAVELS: EXPANDED HORIZONS

In 1954 Johnson traveled to Europe in the company of Taos painter Earl Stroh. He had never been abroad and at fifty-seven was uncomfortable with the prospect of trying to communicate in foreign languages. Stroh, who knew some French, was sailing to France for an extended period of painting, so Spud booked passage on the same ship. Stroh recalls two events from the trip with particular clarity; the first was their experience of having tea in Paris with Alice B. Toklas. In New York before their departure for France, Spud had contacted some of his literary friends from years past and had been offered an introduction to the legendary companion of Gertrude Stein. Once in Paris, they sent along the letter of introduction and were promptly invited to tea. Though Stein had died eight years earlier, Toklas welcomed them to a light repast in her art-filled apartment and talked vividly of the lives and times of the Stein circle.

Another highlight of the trip was Spud's first visit to Sainte Chapelle, the jewel-like thirteenth-century chapel of Louis IX in Paris. After entering the dark, low-ceilinged lower church, they climbed a narrow corner staircase to the upper part of the structure. There Spud became temporarily separated from Stroh and another companion. When they located him a few minutes later he was seated on the socle bench along one side of the brilliant light-filled nave. There he sat, tears silently streaming down his face, utterly overcome by the unexpected splendor of the *rayonnant* windows.

With Stroh, Johnson also visited the south of France during that trip, then went by himself to Italy and England before returning to the United States.[34] It would be his only trip abroad. Mostly, he was content to visit old friends and relatives in California.

In 1960, before the construction of Glen Canyon dam flooded
many miles of Colorado River canyons, Spud helped organize a
week-long raft trip on the scenic river. In the company of pho-
tographer Eliot Porter and longtime friends Genevieve Janssen,
Claire Morrill, and Chilton and Judy Anderson, the group, with
two river guides, braved 120 miles of rafting on the Colorado.
At stops during the day Johnson scribbled notes in a black note-
book or made drawings of the scenery. Porter's big camera came
out during lunch stops along the riverbank. At the end, Johnson
and Morrill each wrote versions of the trip, which they published in a small volume illustrated with Porter's canyon photographs and Spud's drawings. A few excerpts from Johnson's
narrative suggest his response to the natural beauty, as well as
the joys and discomforts of travel on the river:

Six Taosenos Who Braved the Colorado River

TWO ACCOUNTS OF A TRIP THROUGH GLEN CANYON IN UTAH

SPUD JOHNSON & CLAIRE MORRILL
1960

Dream of Delight

. . . the first few days were a dream of delight, floating down the broad stream in warm sunlight, not too hot, between vermillion walls of constant variation as to height, shape and color: round-topped, monolithic waves of stone, looking like herds of mastodons, sheer drops which Powell, the first explorer of the river had called "Mural Cliffs" (even though he had doubtless never heard of abstract expressionism, which is surely the only way to describe the "style" of these "murals"), and great sculptural masses of rock tumbling in confusion above the cliffs, into the river, or retreating up a thousand estuaries and side-canyons—or merely framing the countless green tamarisk-, willow- and oak-festooned glens which give the canyon its name.

Noons and nights we stopped on narrow muddy shores which quickly rose to delightful sandy beaches backed by the green shrubbery and behind that the red cliffs again. Each night both boats had to be completely emptied of all gear, drawn up safely into the sand and turned over—after

(continued on following pages)

which the passengers scurried for driftwood and then were free to select their favorite sleeping spot, blow up their mattresses, unfurl their sleeping bags, delve for soap and towel in their duffle—and then go swimming (or at least get a bath on a flat rock that jutted comfortably out over the mud that almost always separated the fine sandy beach from the grey-green turgid river.)

Three Miracles

Leather jackets, ponchos, raincoats—and the ever-present bulbous life-preservers which we were required to wear at all times while aboard the boats—served as adequate insulation against cold, wind and rain next morning; but toward noon we suffered what threatened to be a major catastrophe.

Suddenly, the propeller-blade on one of our outboard motors JUST WASN'T THERE—and it seemed futile to attempt a search for it in the foot-deep silt, even though it might have sunk in the exact spot where we first discovered its loss.

At this vital juncture occurred the first of what I personally regarded as miracles. Miracle Number One: there was one extra propeller aboard (but nothing to attach or hold it to the drive-shaft). Miracle Number Two: Gene, Ken and Chilt somehow managed to secure the propeller blade in place with (1) a piece of an old coat-hanger, (2) a length of baling-wire, and (3) a rusty nail. Miracle Number Three: (most important and most miraculous)—

FIGURE 16. Eliot Porter, "Cliffs and River, Glen Canyon, Utah, 1960."
Copyright Amon Carter Museum, Fort Worth, Eliot Porter Collection.

the damned thing held until we landed at our destination at four o'clock that afternoon.

The harrowing point was that none of us thought it COULD survive those last fifteen painful miles. And this worry scarcely made the final hours any more comfortable as the weather worsened, the wind rose higher, the rain fell harder, and the waves broke over us with increasing violence.

Two of us lost our hats, and all of us were drenched from head to foot, all of us sitting in cold pools of water, all of us shivering and miserable, with feet caked solid in clammy mud.

Rescue

Those last twenty miles overland were as beautiful and spectacular as the landscape between Blanding and Hite the week before, and seemed even more glamorous because of the contrast to the last two days on the river and our dreary landing in the rain the night before.

Need I add that beds, baths, razors and restaurants seemed heaven sent? And that the great dam abuilding at Page seemed an exciting marvel of technology, in spite of the realization that someday soon it will cause the engulfment in three hundred feet of water, of all the beauties we had enjoyed with such awe during the previous week?

Glen Canyon will soon be the bottom of a lake fringed with "Recreational Area" for pampered tourists. But we were happy to be among a favored few who got ONE LAST LONG LOOK THE HARD WAY!

The Printer as Artist

Johnson's sketching during the river trip demonstrates his growing interest in making art. Long a friend to artists and a publisher of their work, his own artistic efforts had been confined to
casual sketches of places he visited or to carving simple wood
blocks (of his own or others' designs) for *Laughing Horse*. But in
the last fifteen years of his life Johnson turned more seriously to
forms of visual expression.

He enrolled in Taos Art Association classes in 1953 and
joined a drawing group called the Inner Sanctum. Working seriously on his drawing, Johnson sought advice from professionals
in Taos. In particular, artist William Rowe taught Johnson to
strengthen his line and to reduce the amount of detail in his
drawings. Usually he worked with pen and ink, setting out to
draw landscapes or the old houses and churches in the Taos area.
Once he took a trip to Nebraska and came back with drawings
of dinosaur bones. With time, his technique loosened and his
confidence grew, allowing him to make sensitive records of the
people and places he loved (Figs. 17 and 18).

As Johnson's health began to fail in the late 1960s, he traveled less and thought of putting his affairs in order. To the
Harwood Foundation he gave a portrait of himself by Taos
painter Louis Ribak (Fig. 19). Ribak had painted him in a characteristic pose—seated, pipe stuck in the corner of his mouth,
eyes narrowed like an Eastern sage. Spud was even more austere-
ly portrayed in a drawing by Emil Bisttram (Fig. 20). Both were
apt characterizations, for Johnson had indeed grown more ascetic
with the passing years. His friend Claire Morrill described his
social habits:

FIGURE 17.
Spud Johnson, "Man with
Guitar," ink drawing.
Art Collection, Harry
Ransom Humanities
Research Center,
University of Texas
at Austin.

. . . he was the only gregarious hermit I knew, and the only man who, in a room full of people, could sit silently in a corner all evening, smoking his Sherlock Holmes pipe, and still manage to give the impression of having taken a pleasant and active part in the proceedings.[35]

Listening had always been a special talent of Spud's; now it became one of his chief pleasures—to listen and reflect on the passing scene. If he was unobtrusive at public gatherings, he was never unaware of the impression he made on people. Photographs reveal that Johnson was always something of a dandy, fussy about his clothes, handsome in a delicate way, and vain. In later years he experimented with an all-too-obvious toupee to disguise his thinning hair (Fig. 21).

Always a lightning rod for controversy, in earlier years Spud had loved to stir things up, sometimes merely for the sake of doing it. Nowadays the mordantly witty tongue spoke in a milder tone, except when it came to needling readers on issues he cared deeply about. Ever a positive force for artistic integrity, he remained an advocate of excellence in all kinds of artistic pursuits.

But Taos was changing. By the mid-1960s many of his former targets, as well as some of the central characters in the New Mexico legends he had helped create, were gone: Mabel and Tony Luhan and the Lawrences all preceded him in death. Witter Bynner died just a few months before Spud, in the summer of 1968.

Late that year Johnson's always-thin frame grew even more fragile and spidery; in the last photographs papery skin barely conceals his fine bones.

With his cooperation friends organized a show of nearly 150

FIGURE 18.
Spud Johnson, ink
drawing of three
musicians: Joe
Baum, Chilton
Anderson, Milford
Greer. Art
Collection, Harry
Ransom Humanities
Research Center,
University of Texas
at Austin.

FIGURE 19.
(*opposite*)
Spud Johnson with
his portrait, painted
by Louis Ribak, now
in the collection of
the Harwood
Foundation, Taos.
Photograph by
Regina Cooke.
Photography
Collection, Harry
Ransom Humanities
Research Center,
University of Texas
at Austin.

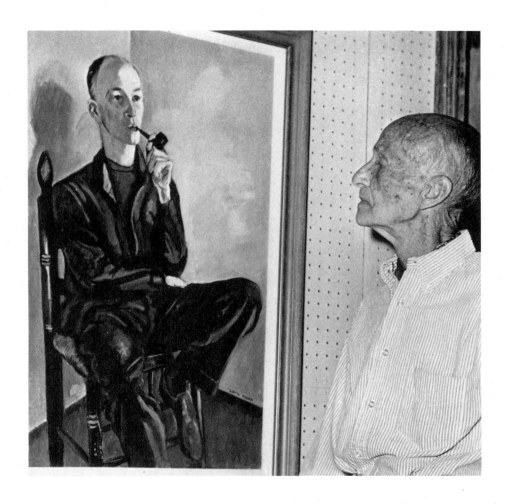

FIGURE 20.
Emil Bisttram,
drawing of Spud
Johnson.
Photography
Collection, Harry
Ransom Humanities
Research Center,
University of Texas
at Austin.

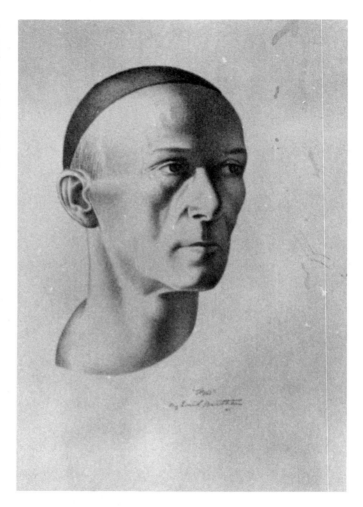

FIGURE 21.
Spud Johnson in
Taos. Photograph by
Mildred Tolbert,
courtesy the Harwood
Foundation,
Taos.

of Johnson's skilled, moody drawings. Included with them were portraits of Spud by some of the painters and photographers he had known: Emil Bisttram, Helen Blumenschein, Will Connell, Ernest Knee, Dorothea Lange, and Eliot Porter. But as plans for the show moved forward, Johnson grew steadily weaker. Friends drove him twice to the hospital in Santa Fe, where he died in November 1968. Instead of a living artist's retrospective, the planned exhibition became a memorial show and sale. Spud's sensitive drawings were the big attraction, with most selling for a mere five dollars or so.

His little Kelsey foot-powered press, sold and resold to several buyers, was given in 1976 to the Museum of New Mexico, where it is exhibited along with other historic presses in the print shop at the Palace of the Governors. Spud's little Taos house at the curve of the road became a bed and breakfast establishment called, appropriately, Laughing Horse Inn.

Johnson was a man whose life and art were never separated. He seemed to know everyone in Taos, but he was a public figure with a private nature. To friends he revealed himself, slowly and selectively, but he disclosed more of his inner being in poetry than in conversation.

In the guise of a rollicking horse Johnson had run roughshod over absurdities of all kinds; as a gadfly and a horsefly he had stung those who took themselves too seriously. With his seasoned intellect and sure instinct for the theatrical, Spud had learned how to isolate, frame and carpenter issues into a space where readers encountered every kind of unsettling idea. Quirky, urgent, and modestly heroic, he was a maker of New Mexico legends. In helping to shape a rich, vibrant era in southwestern cultural history he saw its uniqueness as a cultural moment. And in helping to preserve it—as poet, editor, and activist—he made himself a legend as well.

FIGURE 22. Spud Johnson, 1932. Photograph by Will Connell, courtesy the Harwood Foundation, Taos.

THE BALLAD OF
SANTA FEE SAL

Illustrated With Engravings on Wood

Being a Sad Song Without Any
Music, But With Much Rhyme, Reason
AND TRUTH; also A MORAL

Written, Illustrated & Printed
at Taos, New Mexico, in the Studio of

THE LAUGHING HORSE

Which is situated near one of the Curves of the
Acequia Madre about a Mile from the Village itself

by SPUD JOHNSON, a

PAMPHLETEER

of no Mean experience and Originality, believe
it or not. AND NOW OFFERED to the PUBLIC

at TEN CENTS per copy

oh, boy! only 10 cents!

Santa Fee Sal

A BALLAD

I always said, "it's a quaint little town."
And I always thought it was;
But listen, my boy, while I write down
My story and its cause.

It's a long time now since I left the city,
Though it's longer than its seems:
The reason is—oh, what a pity!—
That I've lost all my dreams.

I came to the town called Santa Fee
With all my youth and beauty;
I came with equanimity
And bringing all my booty.

I came to forget the smoke and grime
And all my misdeeds, too;
I came to forget the city's crime
And start my life anew.

A little house on the brow of a hill,
A quaint little house of mud—
(The dear old place is standing still
With a sign on it: "Help Wanted.")

That quaint little house with a door of blue,
A serape on the bed,

(continued on following pages)

Some ears of corn of colored hue
And chile scarlet red—

Oh, dear little house of my abode:
No basement and no attic:
You stood aloof from the dusty road
—So simple, yet erratic.

'Twas there I lived for a span of years—
(What happiness that covers!)
I lived with no regrets or tears,
Without bathrooms or lovers.

But listen, my boy, and I will show
How everything that mattered
Was taken from me, leaving woe,
And all my life was shattered.

They took the earth beneath my feet,
My dusty, winding trail
And made of it a hard paved street,
Despite my anguished wail.

They brought electric lights to take
The place of my sweet oil,
And telephones which simply make
My very blood to boil.

They brought out artists—oh, my soul!
And writers from the East.
My cup ran over-AND my bowl:
God, what a bitter feast!

They made a beastly city-thing;
A city council taxed us:
And now the city people fling
A golf-club in the cactus.

Contract bridge is now the rage;
Simplicity is dampened;
Orchids grow instead of sage—
Society is rampant!

And so, my boy, I came to live
Up in this big hotel,
And I've nothing now that I can give,
Except the key to hell!

Try to forget your Santa Fee Sal,
Go back to old New York
And find yourself a rural gal
In the wilds of Central Park.

CHAPTER TWO

Laughing Horse 1922-1939: Its Founding, History, and Influence

On April 10, 1922, the first number of *Laughing Horse* trotted off the press at Berkeley, the brainchild of four young University of California students. Their "Apologia" drew the battle lines with convention, stuffiness, and all things they deemed ridiculous:

 ## *Apologia*

Herewith is presented "The Laughing Horse," a magazine of polemics, phillippics, satire, burlesque and all around destructive criticism, edited, written and financed by four more or less like-minded young persons, who find education as it is perpetrated in America, and especially at California, a somewhat gaudy farce with lachrymose overtones but withal a spectacle par excellence.

We propose to take nothing too seriously, to hold nothing sacred, to subject anything or everything which seems to us to affect too pontifical an air, too solemn an attitude,

97

to ribald ridicule. Our aim is frankly destructive, regardless of the attitude of the English Club on that kind of criticism. We are not reformers; we are not architects. We are the wrecking gang, hurlers of brickbats, shooters of barbs, tossers of custard pie. We are not bitter; we are not ill-natured; we are not soreheads. We are simply tired of the incessant bleating of professorial poloniuses and their spineless imitators, the blather of campus politicians, the palpable tosh of Cal. and Pelly and Occident editorials, the silly chatter of our half-baked Hobsons, Bryans and Orison Swett Mardens. We seek not simply to shock by our derisive irreverence of sacred things which are largely ridiculous in their very nature, but merely to come out with a merry horse-laugh.

This magazine is deigned as a healthful reaction to the whole timid, vacillating conservative spirit which now prevails over this land. We Americans accept everything that is told us. We are the most credulous people in Christendom. What we, the editors, are seeking is a robust skepticism. It is possible that in our zeal we shall tend to swing the platitudinous pendulum too far. If we do, it will swing back, never fear. Meanwhile, we shall have our fun and our chuckles and we hope that you will, too.

Laughing Horse's four pseudonymous editors were listed in the first issue as "Jane Cavendish," "Noel Jason," "Bill Murphy," and a person known only as "L 13," the latter described in part as "a man with a middle-west background, a large stomach, and a voracious appetite for literature and beer." Knowing that anonymity bestowed freedom to wage their verbal attacks with impunity, the editors took care at first to protect their real identities.

Financed mostly with Johnson's fifty-dollar loan, they peddled 500 copies of the first run—printed, they bragged, "on Genuine Wrapping Paper." The look of the new periodical was, in fact, a poor-man's imitation of an admired Bay Area prototype. Johnson later recalled:

> I had picked up in old bookshops several copies of a charming little magazine called *The Lark*, which a group of gay San Francisco Bohemians had published at the turn of the century and printed on Japanese paper—and the size, the general appearance, and the spirit of this predecessor was our inspiration.[1]

The question was, at twenty-five cents each, would sales of the upstart, downscale *Laughing Horse* provide enough return to pay for the next month's issue? The gamble-on-a-shoestring paid off. The second number, out in May, proclaimed a small publishing triumph:

Victory

Well, we have done it. We have published a magazine, financed it ourselves and sold enough copies to pay the printer. We have been written up in The Berkeley Gazette, The Tribune and Post-Enquirer of Oakland, and the San Francisco Chronicle and Examiner. We have even achieved a notice in The Daily Californian.

Some cunning fellow, possessed of an uncanny power of penetration, has opined "that we strain for the brilliancy of the Smart Set's anti-social diatribes and achieve nothing but Mencken's coarseness without his wit." Excellent! A well-turned phrase, by the gods, and in the Daily Californian! This piece, the sole notice which we received in that gazette, is an excellent piece of prose. Any one of us would be proud to claim it. If its author will meet one of us under Sather Tower, hard by the alleged head of Lincoln, at midnight of the tenth of May, we will present him with an autographed copy of "The Laughing Horse" and a half-pint flask of Haig and Haig.

In this, our second issue, we are presenting a wider variety of material and a larger number of contributors. We hope in our next effort to still further broaden our publication and to present the work of more contributors. The next number will be a special Summer Session edition and will be on the stands the last few days of June—providing, of course, that we sell enough of this one to pay the printer.

In the first two issues Johnson invented reactions to *Laughing Horse* from the literary world, past and present:

A laughing horse and a silver spur soon outstrip the wind.
—GOETHE

"I hear the Laughing Horses, their gleaming flanks
a-shake,
(They'll surely tell their secret joy before the glad
daybreak!)
Their hoofs are clattering merrily, their teeth are
glimmering white,
Their laughs unroll and ring again far into the
purple night. . .
—CHARLES ALGERNON SWINBURNE

I would be willing to wager my best set of Conrad against
a single volume of Marie Corelli, that The Laughing Horse
will kick over the traces of college cant and run riot in the
green pastures of Higher Journalism before three more
issues have gone to press.
—H.L. MENCKEN in *The Smart Set*

With great delight Johnson later wrote to a subscriber who
thought the contemporary blurbs were legitimate:

. . .the blurbs were a huge joke, manufactured by me, in
which I attempted to burlesque the style of each of the
more prominent critics and amusingly forecast what we
thought ought to be said by them about us later. I am
sorry if they misled you—except that it is of course very
gratifying to think that you thought them genuine.[2]

The *Laughing Horse* editors were self-appointed satirists of almost everything, but especially of literature. In a piece called "Better Books Committee," they rummaged through the literary canon, sparing neither the classics nor the contemporary from their acid barbs. With tongues firmly in cheek, they moved beyond mere literary criticism to social criticism, mocking the perceived 1920s domination of American culture by the middle class.

☞ *Better Books Committee*

A. P. (CHAIRMAN.)

In connection with the general movement throughout the country for an improvement in Art, we have formed a "Better Books Committee" to report on various works of literature with the purpose of raising our standards of literature and bettering the public's taste. This department is conducted in the same spirit as the "Berkeley Better Films Committee," whose work in improving our motion pictures has met with such great success.

Report

HAMLET, by William Shakespeare. Cheap melodrama. Unsuitable for Juniors. A play in which a crazed young prince plans revenge on his mother and uncle for the murder of his father. An affront to the sanctity of the home, and a disgrace to the greatest love on earth—a mother's

(continued on following pages)

love. The scene between Hamlet and his demented fiancee is especially lewd, vulgar and suggestive, misrepresenting the pure clean love of a young girl. This form of drama should not be tolerated, as it has corrupting influence, especially dangerous to the impressionable minds of children. It is gratifying to note that very few people read the works of this lascivious author. Steps should be taken to purge our libraries and schools of all works of this nature.

THE RAVEN, by Edgar Allen Poe. Poor. Improbable. A description, in verse, of a meaningless conversation between a talkative crow and a man evidently under the influence of alcohol. The rhythm is enchanting but it is obtained by inserting such senseless words as Leanore, nevermore and evermore at random.

UNCLE TOM'S CABIN, by Harriet Beecher Stowe. Very good. A gripping tale of the wickedness and misery of slave owning. Especially suitable for Juniors. The entire book is filled with interesting scenes of life on the southern plantations before the Civil War. The description of the whipping of old Uncle Tom by two brutes is a good lesson to children, teaching them to be kind to their little black brothers.

THE APPRENTICESHIP OF WILHELM MEISTER, by Johan Wolfgang von Goethe. Waste of time. Poor plot. Moral obscure. A lengthy description of a young man's purposeless wanderings through Germany, filled with long discussions, often bordering on obscenity, which have no connection with the plot of the novel. The hero's shady dealings with an actress, although partially atoned for by his later good intentions, do not add to the general tone of the book. It is a shame that we should import books such as these from foreign countries, (especially from our late enemy) when our own authors are producing vastly superior works.

WHEN A MAN'S A MAN, by Harold Bell Wright. Very good. Suitable for adults and juniors alike. A story of the great West, but not of the ordinary melodramatic kind. It has a big vital message and the strong moral that justice and right always conquer in the end.

(For further reviews on books by this author see Daily Californian.)

THE REVOLT OF THE ANGELS, by Anatole France. Very poor. Evidently an atheist's attempt to ridicule the sacred teachings of the Bible. The actions are improbable, and show the wanderings of a demented mind. Aside from being vulgar and sacrilegious, it is a disgrace to the public taste, to expect to interest adult persons in the crude fantastic iconoclasisms [sic] of the author. The description of the faithless wife's immoral connections with various men is especially disgusting. Such things may be tolerated in a country like France, but our moral code is much cleaner.

THE CRIME OF SYLVESTER BONNARD, by Anatole France. Very good. A clean, wholesome novel, teaching the lesson that a kind act never goes unrewarded. The title is misleading. This is not a Sherlock Holmes story. The hero is a lovable old scholar, who, on a cold day sends food and fuel to a poor woman. This woman, upon becoming rich, presents the old man with a book which is worth much money. The old man also befriends an orphan girl, and later she becomes his chief solace and comfort. Upon reading this book it seems incredible that Anatole France is also author of the immoral "Revolt of the Angels."

THE LAUGHING HORSE. (Anonymous). A cheap, lewd, boorish, sensational publication, edited by smart-alecks evidently under the influence of communistic propaganda. Their conduct in reproving their elders and insulting our institutions savors of poor breeding. Evidently these misguided youths have failed to catch the fraternal constructive spirit of the university. They are only wasting their time and the state's money. These are the type of men who, in later life, become economic burdens upon our communities or clutter our state penitentiaries.

Beneath the verbal horseplay, however, there were serious efforts to upset the literary status quo, and to replace it with fresher voices. Along with other little magazines like the *Dial* and *Poetry*, they launched a lively assault on the leftover standards of the Victorians, especially in literature:

Suggestion

Why not a New American Academy of Art and Letters, to be called "The Young American Academy of Arts and Letters"? I hereby nominate, Waldo Frank, Scott Fitzgerald, The Benet brothers, Ring Lardner, John Farrar, John V. A. Weaver, Harold Stearns, Harvey Fergusson, Al Jolson, John Dos Passos, Gilbert Seldes, Francis Hackett, Lee Simonson, Eugene O'Neil, Thomas Wilfred, Donald Ogden Stewart, Susan Glaspell, Carl Sandburg, Hugh Wiley, Mencken and Nathan, Irving Berlin, John Peale Bishop, Ben Hecht, Floyd Dell, Zoe Akins, Robert Edmond Jones, Thomas Beer, John Murray Anderson, Fred Stone, Clare Kummer, Norman Bel-Geddes, Kenneth MacGowan, Don Marquis, Donna Schuster.

THE HORSE AND SOCIAL CRITICISM

Laughing Horse cheerfully adopted the mantle of social criticism at a time when intellectual bohemianism and radical politics were closely allied in the United States. In their general rebellion against the past, the editors related experimental literature with new attitudes in politics and society. But, unlike such publications as *Blast* or the *Little Review, Laughing Horse* was not a platform for manifestoes. Its editors preferred to take on, often in humorous guise, the preoccupations of a fragmented and disillusioned postwar generation—ideas that included socialism, anarchism, science, Freudianism, and feminism.

The latter idea, which encouraged women to expand their personal and professional horizons, had to compete with longstanding gender biases in most aspects of American life. One of them was the identification of intellectuality with effeminacy—a notion that grew out of American women's nearly exclusive support and cultivation of the arts in frontier times. Theodore Roosevelt, himself a man of letters, deplored men's alienation from cultural pursuits. "The scholarly career," he wrote in 1905, "the career of the man of letters, the man of arts, the man of science, must be made such as to attract those strong and virile youths who now feel that they can only turn to business, law, or politics."[3]

That this perceived estrangement of men from the arts still lingered in 1922 is clear from a piece in *Laughing Horse* which mocks the old attitudes, even as it professes outrage at women's excessive influence as teachers, artists, and students.

 ## The Feminine Menace in Education

MONTGOMERY CRAIG

All of the arts, without exception, are essentially masculine. In all history there is not recorded one single first-rate artist who was a female. And yet what a pass has literature and art come to in this day.

In the University of California, the gals outnumber the boys at least five to one in all courses in art, literature and education. Literature is looked upon as a plaything for women and half-baked "queer-ducks," who sleep in baby-

(continued on following page)

blue silk pajamas. Real men as a rule take courses in book-keeping or plumbing or the selling of malthoid roofing and leave literature to the women and the men who should have been women. They seem to take pride in their absolute lack of intellect and gaze with the bilious eye upon those who are alleged to be of their sex who go in for such silly stuff. Now it happens that this judgment often has some justification. Show me a man who is forever prattling about art and the little theatre and the poetic drama, and seven times out of ten I will behold an ardent admirer of root beer and a frequenter of maiden ladies' teas.

Now, why is it that our men take so little interest in art and literature? I grant you to start with that men are mainly concerned with the problem of getting on in the world or at least of making a living, while women expect either to get married or teach school. In the struggle to meet the competition of other men, men have less time to spend on such things than women. But even taking this undoubted fact into consideration, it does seem that men might at least spend a little of their time on such things and, if nothing else, learn to respect them. The trouble, I believe, lies in our educational system. Young boys are taught by women, first the mother in the home and then the woman teacher in the lower grades. These women teachers, in the case of literature at least, attempt to teach the subject to these vigorous, healthy and happily vulgar young males, in the manner of the Sunday School with overtones of the Ladies' Aid. They accomplish their purpose in some cases and we observe the feminized "literary" man, but in the long run they succeed in effectually scaring off ninety-percent of their charges. They have impressed the boys, not that literature is essentially the virile and vigorous expression of men, but that it is a weak and anaemic and puny thing, a thing for the Epworth League and the nursery, a thing for old maids and spindle-legged girls and sissified boys. Boys should be taught literature by a man who can lick anybody of his size in the neighborhood.

In 1913 Walter Lippmann, then a prominent radical in Greenwich Village, had argued that Freud's psychoanalytic research promised "the greatest advance ever made toward the understanding and control of human character."[4] Soon words like *neurosis, libido,* and the *subconscious*—new and faintly wicked-sounding—were on everyone's lips. In scholarly studies certain psychological disorders, construed as inherently a part of American culture, were blamed for the country's perceived literary and cultural failures. The whole discussion of art and literature was broadened to include critical awareness of the social and subconscious backgrounds of art. All that was serious business, but the *Laughing Horse* editors were determined to find the humor in Freud's exposé of modern society:

The Chocolate Complex

A psycho-analytical friend of mine has been working for years, on the sexual anomalies of Oakland lawyers; and a certain professor at the University worries along manfully semester by semester in the intricacies of the Oedipus Complex and a multitudinous welter of inhibitions—but it remains for The Laughing Horse to do some really practical research work along this line.

We have chosen for our first investigation, the Chocolate Complex; which is almost epidemic in campus circles this fall. The mania has seized even the most conservative, and is making ravages in the most exclusive sororities. Only three days ago a carton of chocolate doughnuts was seen by our agents as it hung in mid-air between the tradesman's entrance and a boudoir window, in the act of being hoisted up to the hungry stomachs of the chocolate complexioned coeds in a house on Channing Way. It is painful to cogitate on what the consequences would be should Dean Stebbins hear of this.

Even the most casual observer must have been staggered by the alarming number of chocolate products flooding the market, which this strange demand has created. There are chocolate bon-bons, chocolate shops, hot chocolate, razorettes, chocolate dough-nuts, chocolate sundaes, chocolate malted milks, chocolate ice-cream, chocolate cake, chocolate sodas, chocolate fudge, esquimaux pie, chocolate drops, chocolate-coated lollipops, chocolate mints, chocolate milk wafers, chocolate nut bars; and even chocolate

(continued on following pages)

cigarettes and chocolate cigars, to say nothing of chocolate pies and just plain chocolate and cocoa.

Manifestly something must be done about it. The failure of prohibition methods makes it clear that raids on malted milk dives would be ineffectual—in fact, even a stimulant to the trade. What then, is to be done? Shall the campaign issue at the next presidential election turn on a Nineteenth "Amendment? An Anti-Chocolate, sugar-coated, Peppermint-flavor Instead Act?

No. The logical and modern method is psycho-analysis.

The Laughing Horse has begun this investigation by collecting the data, and hereby announces that it will put this information into the hands of any serious analyst who will agree to make a profound and learned study of the whole situation; and will likewise award a chocolate-coated castor-oil bean or capsul (choice) to the one giving the best explanation and solution of the Complex.

We have on hand the following cases, which may be ordered by number from the editors:

1. Girl, 19, who dreamed she was chased to the fourth floor of Wheeler Hall by a chocolate malted milk; dream ending as the malted milk spilled on her new yellow organdie frock.

2. Boy, 39, whose parents could not break him of the habit of using chocolate cigarettes. He surreptitiously purchased on an average of nine boxes a day, and ruined his lungs inhaling the marshmallow fillings.

3. Case of college professor, age 21, who suffered from chocolate fits and required an esquimaux pie every hour during the period while he was obsessed.

4. Sophomore, age unknown, sex indeterminable, who dreamed a series of three dreams on six consecutive nights, the series repeating itself on the fourth, fifth and sixth nights. The dream-content was not always the same, but always culminated with the horrible certainty that the dreamer was about to fall into the hole of a chocolate doughnut. This dream was each time remembered by the dreamer on waking and resulted in a distinct aversion for bakeries and restaurants where this particular bete noir was sold. The sight of them became nauseating to him, and resulted once in a horrible scene in the Coop Cafeteria.

5. Coed, 22, who dreamed of chocolate all-day-suckers, and became a nervous wreck as a result of her suppressed desire to have a chocolate-colored negro chauffeur.

These cases are but representative of hundreds more, and should arouse a University-wide campaign in search of the solution. Jung has of course already advanced the theory of neuro-cocoaitis, and Freud's book on "Biliousness as a Result of Chocolate Drinking," is well known; but despite this, there is yet a broad and open field for the serious investigator, especially in a locality where the epidemic is so pronounced.

For who does not know of the whispered scandal that Dr. Colonel Barrow, Esquire's resignation was due indirectly to the fact that he was a chocolate snow-bird? A fiendish addict of the cocoa bean? A hot-chocolate swiller? (He required two cups of cocoa every morning at breakfast to keep him from going entirely to pieces under the stress of the day's work!) Although, of course, his sensational announcement of resignation in the spring was directly

traceable to the accusations and criticisms published in
The Laughing Horse.

Prohibition, alluded to in "The Chocolate Complex," was a
fact of American life by 1922. Enacted by the Eighteenth
Amendment in 1920, it polarized American views on public
morality and transformed campus life everywhere. Poet and critic Haniel Long, a friend of Bynner's, contributed an essay
humorously advocating socially acceptable alternatives to the
intoxicating effects of alcohol.[5]

The Moral Equivalent of Booze

HANIEL LONG

When some years ago it became known that I was engaged
upon an extensive inquiry into the moral equivalent of
Booze, I received letters from persons in every part of the
country, letters which moved me, from persons who
regarded prohibition (then imminent) as the approach of
something worse than death. Man being human must get
drunk, sighed Byron. He was right; and we who were
about to lose the bottle would need, I reflected, something
very unusual to distract us.

(continued on following pages)

I answered these letters at once. I advised my correspondents that the refuge of intoxication might still be theirs, inasmuch as history shows time and again that divine vertigo exists apart from certain distillations commonly employed to bring it about. And I instanced as typical causes of it,

LOVE,
RELIGION,
MOTION,
ART.

Most of my correspondents thought I was hoaxing them, and wrote me no more. But a few explained that it was impossible or inconvenient for them to fall in love. Others objected to religion because they were doing well in business. Still others wrote that in their cities it was impossible to resort to motion, and they preferred a substitute of a different sort, about which they remained vague. And some, who had never heard of art, inquired what brand of it I recommended, what form it came in, and where it could be obtained.

My magnum opus will not be accessible to the general public for some years, and I feel that I should make a brief statement of my conclusions for the benefit of those who may be concerned.

Anyone who has ever loved will agree that Love is an inebriation like no other. Its phraseology has been stolen, even. Wine is said to blush; a philosopher of the old school referred to his bottle as his Spouse. "Getting" religion also transforms the world, and suggests secrets of destiny which blind the wondering neophyte. Yet, if one is prudent, so deep a potation need bring in its train no dark mornings after. Even before 1920 the religious were never boozers. Why? They said they had something better. So with lovers; no lover was a hard drinker, so long as love ran smoothly. "Leave but a kiss within the cup," sang one popular poet to his lady. But if your beloved jilted you, it went without saying that you got drunk. People expected it. The pleasure of motion, whether skating or swimming or looping the loop, is a foundation of friendship and a persuasion that life is good. If there is no rapture in flying a kite, where are we to find it? Horsemen like so many centaurs on a polo field, ball players who leap as though at the press of a single button: those who live in cities where they never see such sights have only to organize themselves and wreck a sufficient number of buildings, clear the debris away, and lay out gymnasia, stadia, natatoria, and what not. In the very course of the adventure, which may amount locally to a kind of civil war with incidental bloodshed, they will find exercise and excitement.

There is today, I feel, a fair amount of falling in love; many persons go to gesture in the open, especially children and young men; and the number of religious persons, though unsatisfactory to a statistician, is far from small. But there are so few who find their happiness in art that it is to me a genuine pleasure to call this form of ecstacy to the attention of the great American public.

An artist may perhaps be defined as a man who has feelings about nature or human nature, anything or anybody, and who wishes to relieve these feelings of the ignominy of perishing by giving them, in his medium, a kind of deathlessness. He communicates his spirit to others as he can, it may be in irritating ways, by means of poetry, by means of the pipe-organ. At first, such a person may not seem armed with much power. But a feeling surpasses an idea in a dozen ways; it travels faster, it penetrates more mysteriously.

Let us imagine a man who feels the presence of a Future Thing, or descries a Tremendous Meaning behind the events of every day. A white flame plays upon the surface of his painting or above the periods of his prose, and passes into the being of all who touch his work. Imagine that among those so affected are persons who believe that life is a matter-of-fact affair and should be lived in a matter-of-fact way. That is, without any insane desire to make the present so delightful arrangements of society appear unsatisfactory or nugatory. What results from the encounter? A ruction terrible to the sobriety of the person concerned. Something has attacked him which he cannot combat. Can you argue with a white flame? Can you open the door and put it out? It is neither here nor there, it is everywhere: dissolved in one's veins, trembling in the air like music. The matter is exasperating, for it undermines the idea of matter-of-factness of life.

Without art, each successive generation might fall into the error of believing that things are what they appear to be, that human beings are merely bipeds capable of working at so much an hour to fatten their employer, of going to war and getting gassed or killed to protect him. Those who are ignorant of art or indifferent to it are apt to hold such views about other people, though even the toughest of them keep for themselves a romantic regard, unjustifiable of course, but in essence artistic.

Art at its highest is complete intoxication; at its lowest it is still the foe of sobriety. In the world of art there have been, one should admit, the occasional topers as well as the great habitual drunkards. It follows that men intent upon seeking inebriation through literature or the arts, should entrust themselves to the greatest and most divine Drunkard they can find, take hold of his hand, and let him lead them to the Vine where hand clusters of golden never-fading delight.

If Americans cannot learn to do this, is it pessimistic to feel that the worst is still to come?

With each issue of *Laughing Horse* its editors strained against convention. They wrote more and more boldly, seizing the reins of the *Horse* and charging directly at the complacency of their academic environment. It was all held within the bounds of respectability until their fourth issue: ". . .with *Laughing Horse* No. 4," recalled Johnson, "we really went to town."[6]

Taking courage from their survival and their success in attracting new contributors, the editors dropped their anonymity. They revealed themselves as three, not four: Johnson, Roy Chanslor, and James Van Rensselaer, Jr.

EQUINE OBSCENITY

Johnson, still in New Mexico, had taken the lead in recruiting pieces for issue four. He asked D. H. Lawrence to write something for *Laughing Horse* and received, in response, an outrageous book review from Taos. In the form of a letter addressed to the youth of America as "Chere Jeunesse," Lawrence lashed out at Ben Hecht and his book *Fantazius Mallare*. Lawrence railed against Hecht's sordid character: "Poor Fantazius is sensually, if not technically, impotent . . . .a poor, impoverished, self-conscious specimen." Long dashes substituted for the shocking words in Lawrence's vitriolic review, which was prefaced by the *Laughing Horse* editors with this note: "We were advised at the last moment to leave out words in this letter which might be considered objectionable. We hope that this censorship will in no way destroy the sense of the text."[7] On that account, the editors needn't have worried; the text was all too clear. So clear, in fact, that university officials found it impossible to ignore. What was worse, they surmised (wrongly) that Lawrence was Witter Bynner, their former faculty member, in disguise.

As if that weren't enough, *Laughing Horse 4* also contained excerpts (also solicited by Johnson) from an incendiary new book by Upton Sinclair. Sinclair, whose writings epitomize the early twentieth-century alliance between protest literature and revolutionary journalism, had long spoken out against corruption and perceived oppression wherever he found it.[8] Now, he said, he had found it at the University of California, and devoted five chapters of his new book *The Goose Step: A Study of American Education* to an exposé of university politics. These were the five chapters from which *Laughing Horse* published excerpts—chapters whose titles suggest Sinclair's views: "The University of the Black

Hand," "The Fortress of Medievalism," "The Dean of Imperialism," "The Mob of Little Haters," and "The Drill Sergeant on the Campus."

University officials were enraged. They immediately took steps to suppress *Laughing Horse* and punish those responsible. But instead of taking on Sinclair's myriad allegations against the university, they chose instead a simpler route: to charge *Laughing Horse* with printing obscene matter in the Lawrence letter. Trouble was, who exactly should be charged? At the center of the campus storm should have been Spud Johnson, responsible for soliciting both objectionable contributions. But Johnson was in fact far away, isolated in the midst of another storm—a snowstorm at Zuni Pueblo, where he had gone to attend the Shalako ceremonial. Johnson recalled frantic efforts to reach him: "telegrams from Van Rensselaer began to arrive, informing me of the Berkeley storm. Chanslor, the only one of the three editors still on the rolls of the university, had not only been expelled, but was actually being sought by the police on a charge of printing obscene matter."[9]

A warrant for Chanslor's arrest was issued, and he was eventually brought to trial on the obscenity charge. Almost immediately the judge dismissed the case, but the reputation, or at least the notoriety, of *Laughing Horse* was vastly enhanced by the whole incident. "It became a *cause célèbre* throughout the academic world," recalled Johnson.[10] And its editors lost no time in capitalizing on the free publicity by soliciting paid subscriptions and making repeated references in the next three issues to their successful assault on the establishment. In number five, for example, a full-page ad appeared for Sinclair's book *The Goose Step*, available by mail from *Laughing Horse*. Also included was an essay by Arthur Davison Ficke, "The Problem of Censorship."

Finally, as if to rub more salt in the wound, the editors published a scathing letter from Sinclair to David P. Barrows, president of the university, prefaced by their editorial note:

> With the publication of this able and convincing letter from Mr. Upton Sinclair to Mr. David P. Barrows, *Laughing Horse* drops the matter of its attempted suppression. The editors wish to do publicly that which they have already done privately—to thank Mr. Sinclair for his courageous stand for us, or, more properly, for the principles of justice and honesty.

Sinclair wrote:

> I have just learned that you have expelled Roy Chanslor, editor of the *Laughing Horse,* upon the charge of having published in his little paper a letter from D. H. Lawrence, the English novelist, whom you described to Chanslor as "decadent, obscene and degenerate." I have many reasons for believing that the reason you have assigned for the expulsion of Chanslor is a pretext, and that the real reason for your action is his reprinting of extracts from chapters of my forthcoming book, *The Goose Step,* dealing with your administration of the University of California. Your action in this matter starts a public fight, which is going to last for a considerable time. . . ."[11]

Though exonerated in the obscenity matter, Chanslor, Van Rensselaer, and Johnson had cut their political eyeteeth and had discovered the power of well-placed publicity. They lost no time in wading deeper into political waters, where the *Laughing Horse* would often venture in future years. Many of these future concerns would issue from the Southwest, where Johnson, closing in on a year's residency, had acquired a fast education on the state's political issues.

Of pressing concern to his activist friends in the New Mexico literary community in 1922 and 1923 was proposed legislation in Congress known as the Bursum bill. This bill, drawn up by New Mexico politicos and passed quickly by the United States Senate, was designed to settle a longstanding controversy between Pueblo Indians and non-Indians regarding title to lands adjoining the Indian villages. In effect, it would grant titles to most of the non-Indian "squatters"—title to land and water formerly owned by the Indians who, lacking the vote, seemed powerless to oppose it. But before the bill could pass the House, the artists, writers, and anthropologists of New Mexico, led by activist John Collier, rose up to oppose it. These people, whose support for Native people ranged from the scientific to the most maudlin "primitivism," mustered enough support across the country to thwart what most later analysts characterize as a grossly unjust piece of legislation.

Laughing Horse carried the story, supplied by Spud Johnson, of the opposition and defeat of the Bursum bill, and accorded to the Indians the last laugh in the whole affair. It was the first of many sympathetic articles on the culture and politics of Native peoples.

Poets and Indians in Politics

One of the most typical and Ballengerian, the most stupid and revealing fiascos of modern American politics, has just occurred in Washington. Secretary Fall, Senator Bursum, and many others seem to have been implicated in a gigantic and clever scheme to obtain valuable lands from the Pueblo Indians of New Mexico. The bill was miraculously recalled from the House owing to a widespread protest resulting from investigations made by the general Federation of Women's Clubs, and a better bill seems now about to pass the sleeping Houses.

Sixty-one artists and writers, including D. H. Lawrence, Stephen Graham, Zane Grey, Emerson Hugh, Vachel Lindsay, Witter Bynner, Mary Austin, Maxfield Parrish, Edgar Lee Masters, Stewart Edward White, William Allen White, Charles Erskine Scott Wood, Fremont Older, Carl Sandburg and countless other notorious scribblers and painters, wrote and signed a protest which got them into every newspaper and magazine in the country, and the atrocity was stopped. Even Warren Gamaliel woke up and Secretary of the Ulterior Fall was asked to resign. "The pen is mightier" . . . et cetera. Fall said there would be armed resistance if the Bursum Indian Bill failed to pass!

But the manifesto of all these noted writers is not half so good or convincing, either as a piece of prose or as a protest, as the succinct and naive letter written by the Acoma Indians on the same subject! Compare the following document with the famous letter of the writers which appeared in the "New Republic," November 18, 1922:

"The Acomas held here, this 13th of November, at Acomita, in the year 1922, a meeting; there met the Chief of Acoma and all of his principal men and his officers. Willingly we will stand to fight against the Bursum bill, which by this time we have discovered and understood.

"Our white brothers and sisters: This bill is against us, to break our customs, which we have enjoyed, living on in our happy life.

"It is very much sad, indeed, to bear, and to know, and to lose our every custom of the Indians in this world of men.

"Therefore we are willing fully to join to the others our Pueblo, where we may beat out the Bursum bill for the benefit of our children and of our old people and of all our future.

"We have held a meeting, assembling yesterday in the school house all day long. the meeting was very good. Every person was sworn and each did say that he is willing to help right along from now on.

"Yes, sir, we are all glad to do so to help through the name of our great God and to help those who are trying to stand for us, our American honorable people.

"This is all very much appreciated, and thanks for the help, and signed with all our names: we the chiefs of said Acomas."

The Last Laughers

Perhaps no group of people, either foreigners or our own crop of young complainers, extracts so much enjoyment out of the ludicrous spectacle of American civilization as the American Indians.

How quietly and hugely they are amused by our silly clothes, our ridiculous manners, our unbelievable conceit.

Nothing could be funnier than the sight of a wealthy prude of a woman in the midst of (say) a Hopi village in Arizona—and the natives laugh the loudest! They guffaw openly at her mincing ways and her hideous skirts—or trousers, whichever she happens to wear; and laugh almost as loud at her husband, though he wear a sombrero and puttees, overalls, or a tweed suit. It is yet to be recorded whether an Indian (untainted by contact with Americans would burst or simply have spasms in the presence of evening clothes. Even a derby hat might prove disastrous.

If a reversion to primitive beauty and simplicity in manners and clothes can only come about as a reaction to extremism, let us all become Ezra pounds and Whistlers wearing jade ear-rings and cerise velvet trousers to hasten the revolution!

Why not adopt the real American dress—that is, the Amerindian—at once, and have done?

With Johnson in New Mexico, *Laughing Horse* was increasingly flavored by the piquancy of the Southwest. Numbers six and seven featured the first visual art from that region: wood blocks by painters Vernon Hunter, Willard Nash, Jozef Bakos, and B. J. O. Nordfeldt.

laughing horse

FIGURE 23. Cover design for *Laughing Horse*, no. 6 (1923) by Vernon
Hunter. Hunter (1900–1955) would later become a prominent muralist and
Federal Arts Projects administrator in New Mexico.

FIGURE 24. "The Penitentes," woodblock print by Willard Nash from
Laughing Horse, no. 6 (1923). Nash (1898–1943), an old friend of Bynner's,
arrived in Santa Fe from Detroit in 1920. With four young colleagues he soon
formed "Los Cinco Pintores," whose paintings and prints span a broad range of
subjects and styles in the 1920s art of New Mexico.

laughing horse

FIGURE 25. Cover design for *Laughing Horse*, no. 7 (1923) by Jozef Bakos (1891–1977), who came to New Mexico from Buffalo and was active in Los Cinco Pintores and New Mexico Painters groups. He is best known for his vigorous, yet lyrical landscape and still life subjects.

FIGURE 26. Untitled linoleum-cut, frontispiece for *Laughing Horse*, no. 7 (1923) by B. J. O. Nordfeldt (1878–1955). During some twenty years in Santa Fe, Swedish-born Nordfeldt made paintings, etchings, and lithographs using formal innovation to analyze the rugged southwestern landscape or to make richly tonal prints portraying his Hispanic neighbors. Here, somewhat in the manner of Matisse, he demonstrates his skill with the human figure.

THE PORTABLE *Horse*

As the scope and ambition of *Laughing Horse* grew, so did its debts. Even with the publicity windfall from the Lawrence-Lewis affair, revenues failed to keep pace with rising production costs. Late in 1923 the three young editors began to feel the heavy burden of financial responsibility. Chanslor announced he was leaving for New York to pursue other literary opportunities. Van Rensselaer had left school and married; with Johnson he continued to publish the magazine for a time but was increasingly preoccupied with other matters. Unless rescued, it looked as if *Laughing Horse* might meet with a premature death.

Fortunately, Johnson was still vitally interested in the *Horse's* welfare and began to think of pasturing it in the Southwest. He had already sampled an abundance of material and contributors there; and he could imagine *Laughing Horse* filling a real need for New Mexico writers, most of whom had to publish outside the region to be published at all.

While traveling with Bynner and the Lawrences in 1923, Johnson had the leisure to put together a Mexico issue of the *Horse*—its first with a special theme—and to explore possibilities for the future of the periodical. Living in Guadalajara was Idella Purnell Stone, another of Bynner's former students, who was launching her own literary magazine, *Palms,* during that year.[12] As a friend of Spud's, she was helpful in finding a Guadalajara printer for *Laughing Horse,* no. 8. She also contributed a poem for the Mexico number:

The Serenade

IDELLA PURNELL

Jasmine-scent through the window,
   My darkened room,
On the high balcony, roses,
   A riot of bloom.
The garden below in flower-drowned
   Fragrance lay,
Holding its breath to hear him,
   'Tonio, play.
Soft through the star-hushed darkness
   Came the tune,
Singing a song of pleasure,
   Love, and the moon.
"Querida," the last words reached me,
   Plaintive, low.
"Querida, thou wouldst love me
   Didst thou know
How I have pined in silence,
   Pined for thee.
Give me a word of hope
   For charity."
Softly I went in the dark, then,
   One white rose
Plucked from the mass of blossom
   (No one knows
I dropped a kiss in its flushed heart),

(continued on following pages)

And the stars
Laughed as I flung the flower
 Through the bars.
Sprang he then from the others
 (Paused the tune),
Holding the rose in triumph
 Toward the moon.
"Hear compañeros," I heard him.
 "While I sing
My song of joy that shall rise
 Till the glad skies ring!"

—Si, Pablo, I am coming. . . . . .
 (Long ago,
When I was young I loved him—
 Antonio.)

Included as well in the Guadalajara number was
"Fanaticisms," an essay by Alvaro Obregon, president of Mexico.
It was probably obtained for *Laughing Horse* by the well-connect-
ed Idella Purnell. Obregon wrote of the powerful antipathy
between church and state in postrevolutionary Mexico. Johnson
added the following Editor's Note:

On January 10, 1923, President Obregon by authority
vested in him under article 33 of the Constitution signed
an order for the summary expulsion from the Republic as
an undesirable foreigner of Monsignor Ernesto Filippi,
Bishop of Sardica and Papal Delegate in Mexico. The [fol-
lowing]. . . article explains his views in the matter.

Fanaticisms

ALVARO OBREGON
President of Mexico

The fundamental program of the Catholic Church as it is theoretically presented to us by those in charge of its destinies, consists principally in guiding all souls along the path of Virtue, Morality and Brotherhood—in the broadest sense of the terms—aiming by means of these noble postulates to assure infinite happiness for all in the life eternal.

The fundamental postulates of the present government, which believes it is faithfully interpreting popular desire, may be summed up thus: to guide all the sons of Mexico along the path of Morality, Virtue and Brotherhood—in the broadest sense of the terms—aiming by means of these postulates to find a greater well-being for the earthly life. If these two programs could be realized, there would result the greatest possible gain of well-being for all of us who inhabit the earth because the happiness and well-being sought for would have been gained for all of us both in this life and in the life to come.

The Catholic religion requires of its ministers that they should nourish and direct the souls of its adherents. The Revolution which has just ended requires that the Government born of it should nourish the stomach, the brain and the spirit of each and every Mexican. In this basic view of the two programs there is nothing mutually exclusive, there is, on the contrary, indisputable harmony. I regret very sin-

(continued on following pages)

cerely that certain high members of the Catholic clergy have not sensed the transformation which has occurred in the minds of the people toward a modern outlook, in the course of which ineffective and abstract doctrines have day by day lost their force, while effective social programs have gained strength. To this vigorous evolution the high Catholic clergy have denied their share of cooperation. Many of them have opposed its fullest development with systematic obstruction although its postulates are essentially Christian in spirit and in form and their execution in no way conflicts with the doctrines which members of the Church theoretically support. If there has been any lack of harmony, it is rooted chiefly in the methodical difference between the clergy's theory and their practice.

It is certainly regrettable that lack of sincerity among high members of the Catholic clergy should foment a struggle between two that might well co-operate. If instead of continuing to fight and thereby inevitably to lose ground, they would only work with us, for no other object than the welfare of the people! For surely it is no longer a question of the single metaphysical fanaticism which for two thousand years has monopolized the spirit of the masses. Instead, we have two rival fanaticisms disputing that spirit, the one ineffective and abstract, the other material and effective. The first nourishes the spirit and prepares it for sacrifice; the second nourishes the stomach, the brain and the very soul to avoid such sacrifice. And in this struggle, very few would accept the first alternative if its protagonists espoused it to the exclusion of the other; if they asserted that it was not possible to be Catholic and to

FIGURE 27.
Spud's first visual arts
contribution to *Laughing
Horse* appeared in issue
eight, 1923. "La Canoa"
is a print based on a Lake
Chapala scene from his
1923 Mexican sojourn.
Compare with Figure 70.

serve God while seeking at the same time a minimum of well-being and equity and conscience in this life; especially since the foundations of true socialism have been inspired by the doctrines of Jesus Christ, who, with all justice, may be considered the greatest socialist humanity has yet known.

I therefore say to Catholic officials with the sincerity which characterizes men of the Revolution; I exhort you for the good of our people that you neither calumniate nor injure the progress of that essentially Christian and humanitarian program which the Government seeks to develop in our country. Its oppressed classes have for many long and bitter years experienced every injustice and have missed the spirit of brotherhood and equity which should have prevailed in the directing upper classes, who have neglected the noble part of man's mission on earth and instead have exerted all their efforts to piling up material fortunes. I assure you with all sincerity that you will encounter no obstacle in carrying out the tenets of your religion in this country. On the contrary, you will have the support and sympathy of each and every Mexican. We ask only that no systematic and unjustified obstruction be raised against a popular desire which has acquired such strength in the minds of the people that none but the most ignorant would deny its existence or oppose its definite realization.

The other visual arts contributions to *Laughing Horse*, no. 8 were all by New Mexico artists: a cover by Olive Rush and more woodblock prints by Vernon Hunter and Willard Nash.

Johnson let his readers know that the *Laughing Horse* would soon follow him back to Santa Fe:

Los Caballeros

WILLARD JOHNSON &
JAMES T. VAN RENSSELAER, JR.

Present "The Laughing Horse in Mexico" as a guaranteed thoroughbred, hundred percent Mexican caballo.

It has been pastured at Chapala, Jalisco, Mexico, under the care of Willard Johnson, saddled and bridled at Guadalajara, Mexico, by Gallardo y Alvarez del Castillo, and will be stabled in Santa Fe, New Mexico, U. S. A., until further notice. It is licensed in the United States by James Van Rensselaer, Willard Johnson, and Roy Chanslor, and is entered for registry as second-class matter (which refers in this case to first-class livestock) in the post office at Guadalajara.

Communications praising the animal, orders for a year's lease at $2.50 (5 pesos), or for single rides at twenty-five cents (cincuenta centavos), cheques for the support of starving young grooms, and also bundles of especially prepared fodder, should be addressed care of Managing Veterinarian Johnson, Box 1061, Santa Fe New Mexico.

All statements and bills, as well as pleas from the printer, should be mailed directly to the Dead Letter Office, Washington, D.C

PLANNING FOR SURVIVAL

Back in New Mexico, Johnson realized that *Laughing Horse* would have to change if it was to survive. Originally planned as a monthly magazine, the *Horse* had in fact appeared nine times during its first twenty months of life. As sole editor, Spud knew he could not publish that often. With issue nine he announced its official change from monthly to quarterly publication.

Though he, Chanslor, and Van Rensselaer were still listed as owners on the masthead, Johnson was certain that his would be the chief responsibility. He would have to look for new ways of financing the journal; hence, the beginning of advertising in *Laughing Horse*. For most of its New Mexico run, Johnson sold the ads himself, at twenty dollars a page. He also wrote most of the ad copy. Over the years the *Horse* contained dozens of advertisements—some straightforward, often extolling the virtues of tourist-related businesses or services in the Southwest—others humorous.

FIGURE 28.
Advertisement for the
Indian Detour, a joint
tourist venture of the Fred
Harvey Company and the
Santa Fe Railway.
From *Laughing Horse*,
no. 14 (1927).

Newest way to see oldest America on your Santa Fe - Fred Harvey way to and from California

The
Indian Detour

Three days personally conducted motor tour in luxurious Harvey cars through a region rich in history and mystery --- the Enchanted Empire. Only $50 extra with everything provided: meals, hotel accommodations and motor transportation. Westbound passengers leave train at Las Vegas, N. M., and join them again at Albuquerque, N.M., three days later. Eastbound is just the reverse. This unusual tour comprises visits to old Santa Fe, also the inhabited Indian Pueblos of Tesuque, Santa Clara, Isleta and other places in the Upper Rio Grande Valley, as well as the huge ruin of Puye, a cliff pueblo twenty centuries old.

There are optional side trips and "motor cruises" in charge of specially trained couriers for those who wish to extend their trip off-the-beaten-path.

Special motor land cruises may be made to Mesa Verde National Park (Sierra Verde Cruise) and Carlsbad Cave National Monument, starting from either Santa Fe or Albuquerque.

For further
details address: W.J. Black, Pass. Traf. Mgr.
Santa Fe Ry.
Railway Exchange, Chicago, Ill.

FIGURE 29.
Advertisement from *Laughing Horse*, no. 14 (1927). The Spanish and Indian Trading Company was founded in 1926 by five New Mexico artists and writers: Andrew Dasburg, Witter Bynner, B. J. O. Nordfeldt, Walter Mruk, and John Evans.

"Now I can Sleep at Night!"

Says Mrs. Horace Alwett of Punca City, Oklahoma

"Since patronizing

THE TAOS DRUG CO.

my blood-pressure has gone up, my bronchial tubes have expanded, my liver is functioning properly; and I read THE LAUGHING HORSE almost every year without having a sinking spell, indeed, very nearly enjoying it."

Do YOU Belong to the DISEASE OF THE MONTH CLUB?

It's cheaper to get your aspirin and castor-oil, phonograph records, coca-colas; and even your LAUGHING HORSES
at

THE TAOS DRUG CO.

Stanley L. Mollands, Proprietor

Ask "Moon" Mollands!

He Knows What's Good

For Everything

Where the Best Duck Shooting and Fishing is to be Found; What to do with a Recalcitrant Mother-in-law; and How to Cure:

Intestinal Fatigue
Athletes' Foot
PINK TOOTHBRUSH
Depilatory Disappointments
Housemaids' Knee
Halitosis
Green Nail-file
SUMMER COMPLAINT
Deodorizing Depressions
Small-pox

The Taos Drug Company

The Centre of Town

FIGURE 31.
Advertisement for the Taos Drug Company from *Laughing Horse*, no. 18 (1930).

DO YOU FEEL KNOCKED OUT?

**Never Mind, You Haven't Got a Disease,
It' Just New Mexican Receding Fever.**

EVERYBODY HAS IT!

Go To:

THE TAOS DRUG CO.

And Ask MOLLANDS To Prescribe

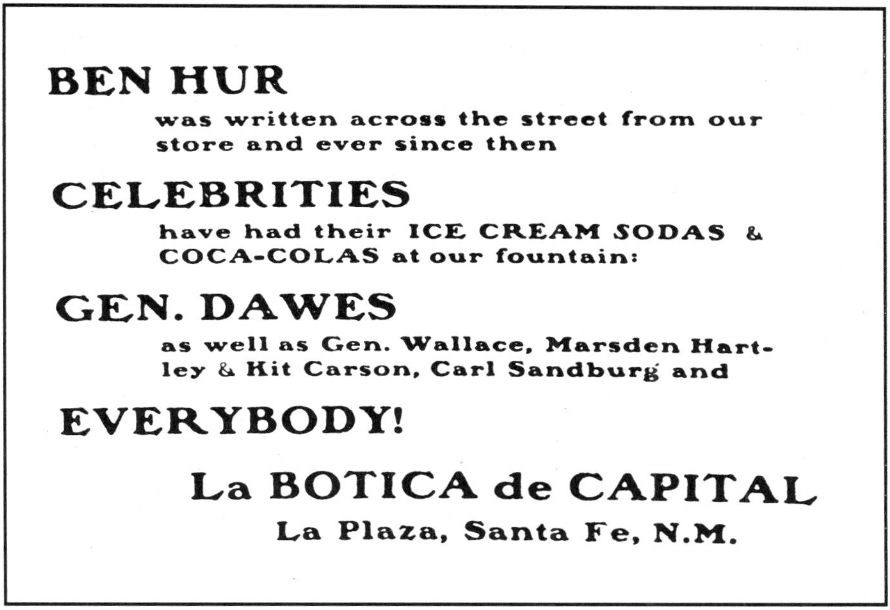

BEN HUR
was written across the street from our store and ever since then

CELEBRITIES
have had their ICE CREAM SODAS & COCA-COLAS at our fountain:

GEN. DAWES
as well as Gen. Wallace, Marsden Hartley & Kit Carson, Carl Sandburg and

EVERYBODY!

La BOTICA de CAPITAL
La Plaza, Santa Fe, N.M.

FIGURE 33. Advertisement for La Botica de Capital, Santa Fe, from *Laughing Horse*, no. 14 (1927).

When Spud entered the real estate business for a time, his ads for property appeared in *Laughing Horse*:

ROMANTIC

to own a tiny haci-
enda and Rancho in
New Spain.

FASHIONABLE

to spend a part of
the year in New
Mexico, summer or
winter.

EXCLUSIVE
JUST
IMAGINE!

owning an all modern house, an orchard, alfalfa fields, gardens
—in the hills near old Santa Fe for $15,000.

WRITE TO

Laughing Horse
Santa Fe,
N. M.

or

Willard Johnson
Finney Farm
Croton-on-Hudson,
N. Y.

FIGURE 34. Advertisement for Spud Johnson's real estate enterprise, from *Laughing Horse*, no. 13 (1926).

Besides advertising, support for *Laughing Horse* continued via the subscriber list, which Johnson tended carefully. An expired subscription might elicit a personal note from the editor, or a hand-printed reminder to renew.

It is our Painful

DUTY

to break the DREADFUL NEWS that your Subscription

to the

laughing horse

Taos, New Mexico

has

EXPIRED !

BUT THE LAUGHING HORSE

goes on FOREVER.

Send us $1.00 & See

what happens . . .

FIGURE 35.
Subscription expiration
notice, *Laughing Horse.*

A SHORT HISTORY OF
LAUGHING HORSES
. . . . *And* a Suggestion
For Developing Thoroughbreds

A Pamphlet With a Purpose . . . . . . *by Spud Johnson*

Once Spud ventured into the realm of creative financing, con-
cocting a scheme to provide capital for *Laughing Horse*. In
exchange for a one-time contribution of $100, patrons could
take advantage of a variety of services provided by the publisher
of the *Horse*.

A Short History of Laughing Horses

. . . . AND A SUGGESTION
FOR DEVELOPING THOROUGHBREDS

A Pamphlet With a Purpose

SPUD JOHNSON

NOT FOUR-SCORE, but seven years ago, three college boys brought forth on this continent a new magazine, conceived in liberty and dedicated to the proposition that all men are created to be laughed at. . . ′

They did this on an original capital of approximately fifty dollars, which amount they subsequently lost, and they did it under the name of *Laughing Horse*, the original meaning of which was lost as it became a magazine of the Southwest. But the name has been retained as a reference to a legendary Indian horse that had a joyous neigh, and the periodical has continued, irregularly enough, until the present time. It is still kicking and very much alive.

This brief historical preface is meant to direct your attention to the fact that the *Laughing Horse* has survived on its own merits. It has not been a charity child. No endowment has enabled it to weather the first hard years. It did not even ask for subscribers until after the fourth issue, and it did not begin to solicit advertising until after that, or to pay for itself through advertising until the ninth number was printed, several years later.

(continued on following pages)

Where, we ask you, is there a periodical with such a record?

Laughing Horse now has its own plant, and is edited, printed, bound, mailed from a country hut in the curve of the Rio del Pueblo, a mile outside the town of Taos, New Mexico, a village which is itself twenty-five miles from any railroad.

When, we ask you, has there existed a periodical of such distinction?

At the present time, *Laughing Horse*, (still issued in a limited edition) has a subscription list that increases every month of the year, and is sent to subscribers in Spain, Switzerland, Italy, England and Mexico, as well as all over the United States. It is sold in bookstores in Copenhagen, Guadalajara, Chicago, San Francisco, New York, Hollywood, Kansas City, Dallas, Boston and Alamogordo, to mention but a few of the cities where it is popular. It is even sold in museums and curio-shops.

Mr. Edward J. O'Brien has given it a one-hundred percent rating in his *Best Short Stories of 1928,* by listing all of the stories printed in the *Laughing Horse* during that year on his Honor Roll.

The editor of one of the most prominent of New York monthly magazines has said: "I read every issue of the *Laughing Horse* more carefully than any other magazine—French, English or American." The present editor and publisher of the *Laughing Horse* was, himself, one of the editors of a popular New York weekly for a time, and he also considers the *Laughing Horse* a superior publication. Such writers as Mary Austin, Carleton Beals, Witter

Bynner, Alice Corbin, Arthur Davison Ficke, Robert
Herrick, D. H. Lawrence, Upton Sinclair and Charles
Vildrac have contributed to it because they thought it
worth while. (And as a result, several anthologies, and at
least five recently published books have acknowledged
their indebtedness to *Laughing Horse* for privileges to
reprint.) Besides its distinguished contributors, *Laughing
Horse* has printed the work of utterly unknown artists, such
a drawings by Indian schoolchildren and Mexican cowboys.

But to go back, and to repeat: during all these seven
years of accomplishment, *Laughing Horse* has never asked
for money, did not ask for subscriptions or advertising
until it was well established; and is not now asking for
charity.

It has occurred to us, however, that with more money,
we could accomplish still more interesting things, and so
this is a suggestion, not a plea for help: a suggestion that
an investment in the *Laughing Horse Press* will bring you
yearly dividends of interest.

Not in cash, because all profits will automatically go
back into business until it is more firmly established. But
by a contribution you become a life member of the organization and receive all the publications of the press, including first editions of any books published, all the pamphlets
issued, the magazine itself regularly: and you will know
that you are a charter member of a unique publishing club
and are furthering an interesting and unprecedented experiment.

Let us outline our plan. Suppose you invest $100 in the

business. You will at once receive a Membership Book in the form of one hundred dollars worth of coupons. An issue of the *Horse* is published in November or December, let us say. You receive your copy and cancel one of your coupons. Then you decide to send copies to certain friends as a Christmas remembrance and so you clip ten twenty-five-cent coupons and mail them to us, receiving ten copies of the *Horse* in return—or you clip twenty-five coupons and we mail you twenty-five copies, etc. We publish a book. You receive your copy and cancel two dollars worth of coupons, but want more copies to use as gifts: so you clip more coupons, mail them to us with your order, receive a shipment of books corresponding in value to the number of coupons you have clipped.

Let us go still further. You decide to sell your house; you want to secure a private secretary; you are in business and undertake an advertising campaign. How simple. You clip coupons for a page of advertising space in the next issue of the *Horse*! Or perhaps you need some stationery; you want amusing invitations or programs printed for a party you are planning; you want your Christmas card printed, a Valentine, tickets for a club function; you are always needing printing of one kind or another. A cash outlay? Not at all. Clip coupons! And it is obvious that if you invest $500, instead of $100, the possibilities are multiplied by five. In any case, you will soon have got all your money back in merchandise received—meantime having the satisfaction of being a Patron of the Arts!

Could anything be more frank or straightforward? Have you ever had a stranger or more interesting business propo-

sition made to you? Have you your cheque-book handy?
SPUD JOHNSON
Pamphleteer

*Published with the permission and under the supervision of
Willard Johnson, editor of the* Laughing Horse *and owner of
the Laughing Horse Press, at Taos, New Mexico, U.S.A.*

Response to Johnson's capitalization venture must have been less than vigorous, for there is no record of any coupon-clipping in exchange for his services.

"A MAGAZINE OF THE SOUTHWEST"

With these 1920s changes in format and emphasis, *Laughing Horse* became a real Southwest publication. Years later Johnson looked back at one of the critical turning points for *Laughing Horse*:

It was then [1923] that I "inherited" the magazine and converted it into a journal of, by and for New Mexicans. Unearthing a Navajo legend about the sun-god riding a turquoise horse with "a joyous neigh," it seemed a natural transition to keep the title (which had proved wonderfully rememberable) but to change its nature to suit the new environment.[13]

FIGURE 36. Vernon Hunter, "The Turquoise Horse," from *Laughing Horse*, no. 8 (1923).

Johnson was willing to appropriate any suitable legend, whether from Mexico, California, or Navajo lore, to underpin the lineage of the *Laughing Horse*. He had already published Vernon Hunter's woodblock "The Turquoise Horse," crediting a "famous Mexican Legend."

Now, in issue nine, he hybridized the legends into a rambunctious new beast, who gathered strength from the sun and released it as "sun-noise," which might be interpreted either as a "joyous neigh" or a downright horselaugh, as the reader chose.

The Sun-Noise

There is a legend in California to the effect that the fabulous animal, the laughing horse, is a brute which expends all of its energy emitting ribald horse-laughs at any and everything which it sees or hears about. And there is a legend among the Navajo tribes of Arizona and New Mexico about a turquoise horse on which the Sun-God travels across the sky on clear, happy days, making the journey from the turquoise house in the east where his wife lives, to the newer turquoise house in the west, where his mistress, She-Who-Changeth, lives. He travels, the Indians say, "making the sun-noise", which is a joyous neigh. For this beast, also, is a laughing horse.

According to Natalie Curtis Burlin in her translation of the Song of the Horse, the Navajos sing:

(continued on following page)

How joyous his neigh!
Lo, the Turquoise Horse of Johano-ai,
　　How joyous his neigh!
There on precious hides outspreadeth standeth he;
　　How joyous his neigh!
There on tips of fair fresh flowers feedeth he;
　　How joyous his neigh!
These of mingled waters holy drinketh he;
　　How joyous his neigh!
There he spurneth dust of glittering grains;
　　How joyous his neigh!
There in mist of sacred pollen hidden, all hidden he;
　　How joyous his neigh!
There his offspring many grow and thrive forever more;
　　How joyous his neigh!

So perhaps the Navajo legend is the truer one, being
older; and perhaps the laughing horse is derisive only
when he looks too long into a city street or an institution
of learning. When he goes about his business, he is only
"making the sun-noise," I suppose.

But then, no one really knows.

In the spirit of its new range in the Southwest, *Laughing Horse*
began to publish work by writers whose poetry and prose reflects
the best of the regionalist spirit—a celebration of the vitality
and character of the land and its varied peoples. Over the years
these contributions, some of which are gathered at the end of

this chapter under the collective term *New Mexicana*, suggest the breadth of that era's literary expression.

By 1927, *Laughing Horse* seemed to have found a permanent home in Taos, after ramblings in Berkeley (issues one through seven), Mexico (eight), Santa Fe (nine through twelve), and New York (thirteen). Beginning with issue fourteen it was published in Taos, under Spud's own roof, on his tiny Kelsey foot-powered press. One notable exception occurred in 1930, when Spud, spending a month working at the *Santa Fe New Mexican*, decided to issue a special number around the issue of censorship.

ACTING UP:
THE *Horse* VS. THE ESTABLISHMENT

Ever since the obscenity skirmish with the University of California eight years earlier, *Laughing Horse* had stood firmly against censorship. Now two pressing events were at hand. An amendment to a tariff bill pending in the United States Senate called for censorship by customs officers of imported books. This meant, among other things, that D. H. Lawrence's new novel *Lady Chatterley's Lover* would be prohibited from entering the United States. As a friend of Lawrence's, Spud was opposed to such restriction. But on a larger scale, he opposed censorship on principle, as did most members of the literary community. He decided to launch a campaign in support of New Mexico Senator Bronson Cutting, whom he had persuaded to oppose the proposed censorship regulations.

In the *Santa Fe New Mexican* Spud announced his plans for a hurried symposium on censorship in *Laughing Horse*:

The censorship issue. . .is being rushed for immediate publication because of the timely element involved—the censorship clause in the tariff bill being a vital controversy in the United States senate which will probably come up for a deciding vote within the next few weeks. This issue of the Horse is of course a New Mexico gesture in support of Senator Cutting who has been responsible for the revival of the question in congress and who is making such a laudable fight for a sensible revision of the present law.[14]

Spud went to work at once, soliciting comments from poets, novelists, editors, and critics all over the country. Some sent closely reasoned arguments against censorship; others dashed off telegrams to meet the publication deadline. By the end of February Spud had assembled a compendium of opinion from twenty-nine prominent Americans; this he published as *Laughing Horse*, no. 17. The special number was introduced by his own comments:

The Present Situation in the Senate

We wish we could reprint the Hon. Bronson Cutting's speech in the Senate of Thursday, October 10th, 1929, as it appears in the Congressional Record along with the comments of Senators Tydings, Dill, Smoot, et al. Or we wish we could enclose with this issue of the *Laughing Horse* copies of the Record itself, that particular issue having been far more readable and interesting than any we have seen for a long time.

But since we cannot, perhaps a brief summary of the situation will be apropos:

The Tariff Law of 1842 excluded indecent and obscene prints, paintings, lithographs and transparencies, and gave clerks of the Bureau of Customs the power of Censor.

The 1890 Act added obscene books, pamphlets, etc., instruments of an immoral nature, and contraceptive matter. This is the law at present and clerks of the Bureau of Customs still have the power of Censor.

The House of Representatives and the Senate Finance Committee, in presenting the new tariff bill last fall, added an amendment to the censorship clause concerning matter advocating treason, insurrection and the like; and in that form it was presented to the Senate.

Senator Cutting at first tried to have the whole thing stricken out, and so he presented his first amendment; and after this had failed, he modified it still further. In this

(continued on following pages)

form, permitting books to enter in spite of alleged inde-
cency and also in spite of alleged treasonable or insurrec-
tionary matter, but excluding matter "urging forcible
resistance to any law of the United States, or containing
any threat to take the life of or inflict bodily harm upon
any person in the United States," it passed by the narrow
margin of 38 to 36.

Many people have assumed that writers like Engels and
Karl Marx will, under the present reading, still have to
pass the approval of customs inspectors; but it is unlikely
that the wording of the amendment as passed can bear any
such construction. Few books in the world could actually
be excluded under a fair interpretation of the present
amendment. Of course if it is unfairly interpreted, that is
the time to make a fresh fight.

A real danger at present, then, is that in the new contest
the ground that has already been gained may be lost again,
so that emphasis should be laid on keeping the amendment as it now stands, rather than on any attempt to alter
it more drastically. That has already been tried.

The main point, as Mr. Will Irwin has so ably pointed
out, is that twenty-five-dollar-a-week customs clerks
should not be allowed to sit as court of final judgment on
Voltaire—or, indeed, on anybody else!

CARL SANDBURG

(Poet)

Until censorship shows more intelligence, we should have
less of it.

JOHN DEWEY

(Professor of Philosophy, Columbia University)

I am glad to hear that you are taking up the matter of Censorship. It is especially timely in view of the efforts of Senator Cutting to liberate us from the burden of customs censorship. It is ridiculous that the foreign literature that comes to the American nation should be subject to restrictions imposed by a group of officials whose business is concerned with economic affairs. If the American people submits to this imposition, it is a proof that it has lost its love of liberty and self-government.

It is a reflection upon the eastern states that boast of superior culture that the leadership in this fight should come from New Mexico, and it is most encouraging to know that Senator Cutting has you behind him in his fight for historic American liberties. I wish you all success.

ARTHUR DAVISON FICKE
(Poet)

A DEFINITION OF CENSORSHIP
(Quoted, by permission, from the Twenty-fourth Edition of the Encyclopaedia Britannica.)

CENSORSHIP—A degrading form of unnatural sexual vice, publicly practiced in some parts of the world by certain undeveloped and ignorant types of savages. Modern scientific research has made it entirely clear that the tendency toward this vice does not exist in healthy, normal organisms, but is solely the result of disintegration of that important series of nerves which connects the cortex with the reproductive organs.

No cure has so far been discovered. In civilized societies, habitual victims of the disease are usually committed to institutions for the care of the insane, where, as a rule, they receive the sympathetic attention which their misfortune merits.

Any mention of the subject, in refined circles, is regarded as somewhat indelicate.

(See also: Dementia Praecox, Impotence, Bestiality, and Delusions of Grandeur.)

—A. D. FICKE, M.D.
Director of the Laboratory of
Abnormal Psychology, Hardhack University.

SHERWOOD ANDERSON

(Novelist)

You may be dead sure that I am in sympathy with the intelligent fight being made against a senseless censorship by Senator Cutting and with your effort to back him up.

WITTER BYNNER

(Poet)

'An American Tragedy'

Each morning in the newspapers
Our estimables read
O human life and gulp down crime,
Part of their daily feed
Their children, lapping it up as well,
Could open the parents' eyes
As to murder, rape and birth-control;
But oh, so good and wise
Our estimables have to be
That when an artist speaks
The open truth about our lives
And seriously seeks
To find some explanation,
Some reason or some cure,
The parents, smugger in their vice,
Believe the books impure.
No wisdom, heartiness or wit,
No sympathy, no sense,
But just a Wall Street willingness
And moral impotence
Is what our estimables choose
As proper for the young—
No flesh and bone, no heart and soul,
But dishwater and dung.

LINCOLN STEFFENS

(Ex-Liberal)

You can't enact liberty, any more than you can morality, or democracy, or justice. We have tried it; read our constitution, all the amendments. Convinced of this, I may not— no ex-liberal should appear to sponsor any such move as this that interests you. It is all very well for you liberals; it is still wiser for legislators, lawyers and chambers of commerce to pass liberal laws. They are safe; literal liberty itself is perfectly harmless, but liberal laws are both safe and misleading.

You know, as any writer and talker knows by experience, that free words don't do anything and free actions, like strikes and insurrections, can't get anywhere in this country. Were our rulers as cunning as we think them to be, they would pass laws making freedom complete and absolute. That would spread among the people a sense of self-respect, contentment and pride, which would make them—well, let us say—work better. It would be a false sense, of course. If an emergency should arise, a hopeful strike or a dangerous revolt or even a flaming speech, our courts could be trusted to interpret and the police to club their way through the laws to common sense and good order.

No. Your proposition is one for the reactionaries to support, if they are intelligent enough to see the point; it is not for those of us who need suppression, discontent, emotion into which to instill the perception that political, social and personal liberty must be founded on economic freedom and fearlessness.

But maybe the *Laughing Horse* is only laughing again.

ALFRED A. KNOPF

(New York Publisher)

I would like to take this opportunity of contradicting the belief that seems to be wide-spread, that publishers welcome censorship because books sell better when the censors attack them. This is usually the contrary of the truth. Assuming a publisher to have published deliberately a book that he felt was under the law obscene, and assuming that he had published it because he felt that its obscene or pseudo-obscene qualities would increase its sale, then it may be true that that publisher would favor the present censorship laws. But I do not think I am flattering my colleagues by stating that when they find themselves up against censorship laws, it is usually over books that they sincerely do not believe to be obscene even under the present law.

They are then faced by the unpleasant fact that however innocent the book is, once it has been publicly attacked by the censors, it becomes, in the eyes of most people who might buy it, an obscene book, and the publisher finds himself all but unable to exploit it in a dignified and decent way. So, most of the time, he stops exploiting the book altogether, surely with no beneficial financial result to himself.

Mabel Dodge Luhan

(Writer)

Power to you in your extremely righteous campaign against stupidity.

Upton Sinclair

(Social Reformer)

I think I should be inclined to favor some kinds of censorship, except for the fact that the censors almost invariably prove themselves stupid and reactionary. On this account I almost always find myself opposing censors; and sometimes the censors have been opposed to me.

Several cartoons were solicited to accompany the written comments, one by Ward Lockwood and one from Will Shuster. Ironically, Shuster's cartoon was itself suppressed by the mayor of Santa Fe, to whom Johnson had entrusted the magazine copy for delivery to the printer. When he discovered that the mayor had removed the offending cartoon, Spud hastily penned an insert explaining to subscribers why the Shuster cartoon was missing and offering to mail it upon request:

FIGURE 37. Ward Lockwood cartoon, "Laughing Horse after reading certain issues of the Congressional Record," from *Laughing Horse*, no. 17.

FIGURE 38.
Will Shuster,
"Chronic
Appendicitis, of
course!" a cartoon
censored from
Laughing Horse,
no. 17, the issue on
censorship. Shuster
(1893–1969) painted
in Santa Fe from
1920. He was a
member of Los
Cinco Pintores and
inventor of Zozobra,
the effigy puppet of
the Santa Fe Fiesta.

A cartoon by Will Shuster, depicting a haloed censor and an innocent babe named Literature in the operating room of a hospital—a cartoon of the most innocuous and gentle kind, but a very funny one—which was to have appeared in this issue of *Laughing Horse,* has been "censored" and "suppressed" in a most strange and certainly an unfair manner by the man who was entrusted with the task of sending the cartoon to the engravers; a man who had no vestige of right to say what should or should not be printed in this magazine but who disapproved of the cartoon and could apparently (and, indeed, with reason) think of no way to prevent its inclusion except to keep the drawing in his desk drawer until the edition was about to go to press and it was too late to have the cliche manufactured.

We are humiliated, albeit somewhat amused, that in an issue devoted to the cause of fighting stupid censorship, we must acknowledge ourselves the victims of it; but we take pleasure in announcing that anyone desiring a copy of the cartoon, will be sent a print of it free of charge by simply returning this slip with his name and address.

THE EDITOR.

FIGURE 39. Spud Johnson's insert explaining the censorship of Will Shuster's cartoon from *Laughing Horse,* no. 17.

Despite the flap over the Shuster cartoon, Johnson was delighted with the final outcome of his anticensorship campaign. He had sent a copy of *Laughing Horse*, no. 17 to every U.S. senator, and support from all quarters of the country helped persuade them to vote against censorship. A jubilant Senator Cutting sent Spud a copy of the Congressional Record which contained his arguments. Appended to it was a note: "Dedicated to Spud Johnson, without whose inspiration this issue of the Congressional Record might have read otherwise. B. C. Cutting."

By this time *Laughing Horse* had become an annual publication, making its appearance when Johnson had accumulated enough material for another issue. Once in a while, though, events prompted him to put together a smaller offering, released as a supplementary pamphlet. The 1928 presidential election was such an occasion. Johnson was working in California, writing and assisting Lincoln Steffens with his autobiography, when he persuaded the famous writer to contribute an article for publication by *Laughing Horse*.

Steffens, the inveterate socialist reformer, had long since decided that corruption was the very essence of most political activity. But he was intrigued, at the same time, with the unconventional candidacy of Alfred E. (Al) Smith, skilled New York machine politician and the first Roman Catholic to be nominated for president. Smith, known as the "Happy Warrior," waged a lively campaign with his brown derby hat, cigar, and colorful speech. Opponent of prohibition, proponent of labor, crusader for social reform, Smith was intelligent enough to recognize the political conflicts—some wrenching, some merely absurd—that he would face as president. In this essay Steffens pokes fun openly at Smith, by implication at his stodgy

Republican opponent Herbert Hoover, and most of all at the absurdity of presidential politics. To all of it, Steffens suggests that a good horselaugh is the only appropriate reaction.

No, no! Not in the White House, No!

LINCOLN STEFFENS

Yes, but—admitting all that goes without saying—how would it look—I mean how would it sound to have laughter ringing in and out of the White House in broad daylight? There has been laughter there before. I have seen T. R. slap his leg and roar, but he put his other hand over his mouth and threw a crafty, respectful glance around at the closed doors. Some sense of decorum. And Harding laughed at me once there. I asked him to join with the governors of states in a general Amnesty for a lot of conscientious criminals who had done foul deeds for a good Labor cause and he said he would if I'd get his cabinet.

"No," he amended, "you get me two and I'll attend to the rest. Get Hoover and Wilson, the Secretary of Labor."

And when I came right back quick with the answer, Harding laughed one short snort which, however, he cut off in apparent fright. No one heard it but a clerk who ran in, looked, saw the president sitting up all dignified and

(continued on following pages)

sober, and so knew that he had been mistaken. No one knew, no honest man knows that anyone has ever laughed, heartily, in the White House; not the way Al Smith would laugh, not all over, with glee.

This I am sure of because once when I was in doubt about it——one time when a president was doing things he didn't want to do, but had to; when he was eating dirt and tasting it, I got hold of a menial in the permanent House service and I asked him whether a president didn't ever laugh. He said:

"Yes, they most all do, sometimes, but," he lowered his voice to a whisper, "they have a way of doing it. It's a secret; I mustn't tell you; if it leaked that I told, I'd be fired." And then he did what he ached to do: he told it.

"A President," he said, "after he's broke in, when he just has to bust——a President, he waits till it's bed-time, then he kneels down in his little nightie beside his little bed—— just like a poo' little child; he covers his face with his two hands, like he's praying, and buries his whole head in the bed-clothes, and——well, now, to be honest with you, I can't swear to what he does down there, but his shoulders shake and shake and when he rises up there is tears running down his countenance. Maybe he prays and maybe he weeps, but I think——our 'pinion is that he has been reviewing his day's work, and letting go what he's been holding in, and being honest to God with hisself just for a minute. Any way he's always cross, if he sees you, but he don't mean it. He feels better."

Now this witness was a colored man and colored folks tell white lies. His testimony may have been colored by his race sense of the pathetic. But, as I was saying, would Al Smith have the decency to do what the other, ordinary, presidents do? Let's suppose that he were elected and in the White House and found he had to do what he did not want to do. And, remember, a president just has to do what other men want him to do. You can't go back on the fellows that have contributed, among them, some millions of money to put you in the White House to save the country. You can not and Al Smith won't. Al may not do as much for as many of them as some presidents have done. He is a Tammany man, you know, and Tammany knows what graft is and what it isn't. A Tammany man never makes a mistake; all his errors are crimes because, dogonit, he is on. Some presidents can think themselves around to believing that a wrong is a right, and that's why they may be really praying when they kneel down at night and shake their shoulders. They have been to college and know how to think. But Al Smith can't. Al Smith is educated (right) and he is experienced (wrong); he is intelligent. The way he laughs, now, before he is elected, shows that.

And so, I ask you in all candor, what will Al smith do when he is President? What will he do when he finds he isn't the only man that is president? What will he do, when, a democrat, he has to hold up the tariff wall against cheap foreign labor? It isn't enough, you realize, to do that; you got to believe in it, and Al Smith can't swallow that sort of stuff and stay dignified. And what'll he do when he has to boost business and soak labor? And when he has to stand by fellows that swipe the Tea-pot Dome and other natural resources and turn them into power and campaign contributions? And then, when, against imperialism and out for world-peace and the limitation of armament, he tries to get all the other nations to agree to hold down their armies and navies to no more than we need to lick the weak, little, backward countries that we have to bring into our empire, what will Al Smith do then? And when he is remonstrating with good, old England and bad young Italy and obstinate, intelligent, logical France for their war plans at the very same time he has to be sending a few marines and bombing planes into Nicaragua to slay bandits there, how can he argue with them and keep a straight face? And Mexico, and Cuba, and the Philippines and—? And the American farmers? And the people?

I tell you President Smith will be apt to laugh. Out loud. In the day time. In the White House.

I tell you this and I warn you: if ever a President laughs, as Mr. Smith surely will laugh, so that the People and the Foreign powers hear him and see him and catch the contagion of it—as they might—then this whole political business will bust, the whole world will shake on its knees, and, worst of all, these United States will never be the same again. Never.

WINDING DOWN:
A KINDER, GENTLER HORSE

After issue nineteen appeared in 1931, *Laughing Horse* was put out to pasture for seven years, while its editor struggled through the years of the depression. Only in 1938 did Johnson decide to revive the *Horse*, prompted by the acquisition of some new material. The centerpiece of issue twenty would be a fragment of a D. H. Lawrence play written in Taos years before, caricaturing a number of well-known New Mexicans, including Spud himself. (See D. H. Lawrence section.) Johnson asked his good friend Gina Knee to illustrate the Lawrence piece and secured other woodblock prints, poems and essays.

Laughing Horse, no. 21, published in 1939, would be the little magazine's last appearance. Its most accomplished piece was a series of four prose sketches by a thirty-seven-year-old Colorado-born writer, Frank Waters. From his forthcoming book *The Dust Within the Rock* Waters excerpted "Spring," Summer," "Autumn," and "Winter," each of which Spud arranged to have illustrated by a companion print. Gene Kloss provided "Spring," Ila McAfee "Summer"; Helen Blumenschein "Autumn," and Ward Lockwood "Winter." Frieda Lawrence contributed a block print as well.

There was no announcement, no hint that number twenty-one would be the last-ever issue of *Laughing Horse*. One suspects that Spud himself had no sense of its finality. Ever since he had suspended annual publication eight years earlier, Johnson had consigned the *Horse* to the unhurried pace of life in Taos. When something was ready, it was ready. Besides, he had other publishing commitments with newspapers in the region.

The cover price of twenty-five cents had remained constant since the *Horse*'s first appearance in 1922. In later years the press

FIGURE 40.
Ila McAfee (b. 1897),
"Summer" from
Laughing Horse, no.
21 (1939).

FIGURE 41. Ward Lockwood (1894–1963), "Winter" from
Laughing Horse 21 (1939).

run was only 200, but even that was a tedious job on Johnson's seven-by-eleven-inch turn-of-the-century Kelsey press. With vigorous pumping of its foot pedal, the little machine could approach an output of 500 sheets an hour—probably more than Johnson's spindly legs could manage. Often he persuaded friends to drop by and help with folding, stapling, and delivery.

Over the years there were many printing problems. Spud recalled that in the preparation of the Lawrence number at Ossining, New York, "one of the printers—a parolee from Sing-Sing, left out three pages of an article so that the whole edition had to be unstapled, pages added, and then restapled." Once back in New Mexico, other memorable printing mishaps occurred:

> . . .when the editor later set up issues by hand, a page at a time, and printed them by foot-power on his own minute press, first in a bedroom, then in a kitchen, finally in his own print shop with the roof always threatening to cave in. At one crucial moment I remember that the jaws of the press locked (tetanus?) and I was helpless until John Evans [Mabel Dodge Luhan's son] ingeniously gave it a sharp rap with a sledge-hammer and it immediately came unlocked and worked better than it ever had before.[15]

With its cheap, highly acidic paper, a typeface that required a deep impress to be readable, and the printer's limited skill, *Laughing Horse* never won any prizes for printing quality. But that wasn't Johnson's chief concern. Particularly alongside the rough-hewn quality of the block prints, he felt that a certain hand-crafted look was suitable for the pages of text as well. Or at least that's what he said in issue fourteen, the first printed on his own press at Taos. Therein, probably to forestall anticipated complaints by authors or subscribers, he set forth his bemused *mea culpa* for editorial and printing faults:

 Apology of the Editor

The Editor (himself—not a movie, though truly a moving picture) having set up and printed this issue of the Laughing Horse "by hand", as the phrase goes, although in this case also by foot, since the press is propelled like a sewing machine, he feels it necessary to apologize for all its typographical shortcomings.

For instance, if hypocrisies is spelled with an "a" on page three in your copy, that is because it looks all right that way to the editor and not because Mr. Bynner does not know how to spell. And if certain pages are very pale grey in effect and others very dark with viscous black ink, that is partly because some of the printing was done at night and looked quite well by candle light, partly because the paper seems to be a species of blotter, partly because there is no automatic ink-feed on the Laughing Horse Press, partly because this is the printer's first job and partly because. . .

However, don't let him seem to be making excuses. After all, if it were perfect, it might just as well be machine-made, whereas we are sure that the "artist's" hand is evident on every page—in the shape, if in no other way, of inky finger prints.

Meager advertising revenues during the depression and a cover price that remained at twenty-five cents provided a negligible return for Spud's considerable labors. Too, the financial balance sheet helps to explain Spud's disinclination to publish frequently. One wonders why he did not raise the price to offset his costs and the labor-intensive process of birthing each new issue. It is a mystery, until one realizes that publishing *Laughing Horse* was never intended as a money-making venture; it was always a labor of love.

CONCLUSION:
THE ROLE AND LEGACY
OF *Laughing Horse*

From its first appearance at Berkeley, the little magazine was an experiment in publishing, with intentions both aesthetic and political. Like other avant-garde little magazines of the era, *Laughing Horse* wanted to explode conventional society's complacency and challenge unexamined values that tied America to its past. As Margaret Anderson, editor of the *Little Review* explained, "Anarchism and art are in the world for exactly the same kind of reason."

Over time, even though *Laughing Horse* published many political pieces, its emphasis was increasingly on artistic and cultural concerns rather than social policy. Particularly when the magazine moved to New Mexico, with a short detour via Mexico, it adopted a distinctly American, specifically southwestern aesthetic. Other American little magazines of the twenties, such as *Broom* and the *Dial* published avant-garde literature and art, both American and European. But those publications were especially concerned with defining American style as it developed, then diverged from, European antecedents. While the *Dial* specialized in publishing work by European celebrities, often in translation, *Broom* examined a new trend: the growing European enthusiasm for New World culture. In fact, as Wanda Corn points out, *Broom's* editor Harold Loeb "lashed out at writers such as Van Wyck Brooks, Waldo Frank, and Paul Rosenfeld [frequent contributors to the *Dial*] who 'hammer the country for its emptiness of beauty' and encourage 'the imitation of European art.'"[16]

In the 1920s, then, Americans were searching for a new identity, and its little magazines offered avenues for finding it. One path posited an American aesthetic based on commercial culture; another led to what Wanda Corn has termed the soil-spirit school, in which artist and place were joined in a self-conscious, solemn merger.[17] It is the latter paradigm that comes closest to the achievement of *Laughing Horse*, though in a distinctly regional variation.

Instead of examining urban America's relationship with Europe, the *Horse* set itself the task of analyzing the particular place of the Southwest in a newly self-conscious American culture. True, the *Horse* did feature celebrity contributors like Lawrence, whose European connections gave the little periodical a certain cachet. But Lawrence had lived in New Mexico and wrote of it fondly after his departure; his contributions to *Laughing Horse* are mostly about that American sojourn and his views of southwestern culture and character. So his writings really reinforce the periodical's attempts to define a southwestern consciousness.

Turning away from Europe as a constant point of reference, Spud Johnson and his contributors looked for other cultural standards against which to measure American achievements. For those living in New Mexico, their southern neighbor provided a handy alternative. Exotic but close, Mexico demonstrated endless contrasts to American ways of thinking. Johnson discovered this as early as 1923 and repeatedly in subsequent trips south. Over the years he persuaded many writers to contribute their perspectives—in essays, poems, and stories—on the rich cultural links between Mexico and the United States. Joined by more than history, divided by more than a border, these two regions had much to teach each other, Spud believed. On the pages of *Laughing Horse* he established a lively, long-term cultural dialogue between the two areas.

But Mexico was not the only source of multicultural connections for *Laughing Horse*. Many Euro-American writers and artists working in New Mexico, an area that lacked most of the visible 1920s markers of mainstream American culture—skyscrapers, factories, Coney Island, grain elevators, and jazz—looked to the Native American and Hispanic populations for authentic alternatives to the increasingly materialist values in American life.

Grounded in their connection with the earth, the ancient lifeways seemed to represent America's real past. Certainly some of the modern Euro-American observers colored what they saw with a rosy tint of romanticism; they glorified a "primitivism" based as often on their own fantasies as on observed reality. But other writers presented a more balanced view. Johnson's publication of dozens of pieces on Indian culture presented a range of opinion, but always gave strong support to legislation that would help to sustain native lifeways. Especially in the work of Mary Austin, Witter Bynner, John Collier, and Mabel Dodge Luhan, the indigenous peoples found strong advocates. One could argue that whatever deleterious effects might have come from over-romanticization were offset by the net result: that American consciousness and American identity were expanded to include the culture of southwestern indigenous peoples. In this too, *Laughing Horse* played an important part.

One of the ironies of *Laughing Horse* and America's other little magazines has been their role in institutionalizing the avant-garde. From their original positions in opposition to established cultural values and traditions, they ultimately embedded their advanced ideas into the very society they set out to criticize. Armed with Americans' shared regard for the idea of innovation (already part of the consumers' world view), artists, writers, and editors saw ways to persuade middle-class audiences to absorb the novel styles of the avant-garde. Eventually their readers not only accepted novelty, they demanded it.

This is not to say that *Laughing Horse* was a beacon for modernist revolt. Rather, it was an eclectic, progressive publication reflecting its editor's openness to change and its readers' interests. Those readers were a highly mixed group. A few, on the East Coast and in the circle around Mabel Dodge Luhan, were interested in the most experimental and contemporary arts. Others could fairly be called dilettantes. Most, however, were somewhere in between. Like Johnson, they had not been to Europe, though they read European writers; they knew about experimental painting and music, but they didn't often buy it or hear it. In short, they were knowledgeable people who looked forward to the intellectual and aesthetic stings—not jolts—that awaited them on the pages of each new *Horse*.

Whatever his editorial failings, Spud Johnson kept one conviction firmly in mind: that poetry, criticism, fiction, and the visual arts are vital elements of a lively, humane culture. In the

FIGURE 42. Endpiece from *Laughing Horse*, no. 14 (1927).

pages of *Laughing Horse*, he showed a generous and intelligent concern for all kinds of artistic expression. Like imaginative publications everywhere, the *Horse* spoke eloquently of its time and place; it preserves, even today, an abiding legacy of both.

New Mexicana

Mary Austin, whose idealization of Native Americans appears in many of her writings, contributed short retellings of Indian stories for *Laughing Horse*:

One Smoke Stories

MARY AUSTIN

The corn husk cigarettes which, for ceremonial purposes at least, are still used south of the Green River and west of the Rio Grande, last only a little while. Since they are made chiefly of the biting native 'tabac', this is, perhaps, not to be regretted.

You select your husk from the heap and gather your pinch of the weed from the dark bowl as it passes the ancient ceremonial road from east to north by west to south, and holding the dry roll delicately between your lips endeavor to dispatch the salutatory puffs to the six, or, if you happen to be among the Tewa or the Navajo, the four world quarters.

Then, holding the crisp cylinder between thumb and finger tip, first one and then another of the company begins, always gravely, and holds on for the space of one smoke, tales as deft, as finished in themselves as a ceremonial cigarette. Or, if not a tale, then a clean round out of the speaker's experience that in our kind of society might turn up a sonnet or an etching. The essence of such stories

(continued on following pages)

is that they should be located somewhere in the inner ear of the audience, unencumbered by what in our more discursive method is known as background. For your true desert dweller travels light. He makes even of his experience a handy package. Just before the end, like the rattle that warns that the story is about to strike, comes the fang of the experience, oftenest in the shape of a wise saying. Then the speaker resumes the soul-consoling smoke, while another takes up the dropped stitch of narrative and weaves it into the pattern of the talk.

The one-smoke story draws from all the ways of thinking and knowing that the Red Man has. So that if those I render, fumbling for the native quality, seem all of one philosophic key, that is merely a matter of personal choice. Some of those I have heard can not be retold with propriety in our tongue, and some are too profound for our understanding. The best that can be hoped from my retelling is that nothing is added to or taken from them in my hands.

The Coyote Song

Hear a telling of the Song the Coyote gave to Cinoave and took away again, in the days when every man had his own song, and no one might sing a man's own song without his permission. Thus it was among our fathers' fathers. When his son was born, when he had killed his enemy or first made a woman to know him as a man, out of his great moment he made a song and sang it on his own occasions.

Sometimes it was a song for the people, which he left as a legacy when he died. There were also songs to be sung while he was dying, by himself if he were able, or the friends who stood around him; or it might be the song was so secret that it passed only between the singer and his God.

But Cinoave had no song. When the tribe came together for the dance of the Marriageable Maidens, or for the feast of the Pinon Harvest, Cinoave would busy himself gathering brushwood for the fire. Or he would sit apart from the others pretending to mend a pipe or sharpen an arrow, hoping not to hear the tribesmen whisper to one another, "There is Cinoave, the man without a song."

This to Cinoave was sadness. For without a proper song how can a man win favor of the gods or women? Thus say the fathers. Then, one day when he was digging tule roots by the river, the Coyote came by and said, "What will you take for your sweet roots, Cinoave?"

Said Cinoave, "I will take a song." For is not the Coyote the father of songmaking?

"What kind of a song?" said the Coyote, for though he meant to strike a bargain, he wished to hold out as long as possible. Cinoave considered within himself.

"A song that will warm the hearts of the tribe and stir up their thoughts within them," said Cinoave. This was a good asking. When the heart is warm and the thoughts deeply stirred, one ascends without difficulty to the Friend-of-the-Soul-of-Man and all things accord with our interests. "I wish a song so pleasing," said Cinoave, "that all men hearing it will say, 'Surely this is a Coyote song!'"

This was said in flattery, for he knew, having thrown him a tule root to taste, that Old Man Coyote would not go away without his belly full. Also he wished to make sure that it would not prove a Coyote giving.

That is a saying of our fathers for a gift that is taken back again when the giver is so minded. Cinoave threw him a fat, sweet root and when it was eaten he said, "Swear to me it will not be a Coyote giving."

The Coyote swore by the pelt of his mother, "So long as the song is used for what it is given, to warm the hearts of the Tribe and stir up their thoughts within them, it will not be taken away." Then Cinoave threw him the bag of roots and they were well pleased with the bargain.

That year at the feast of the Pinon Harvest when the tribes came together, Cinoave sang his song and the people were astonished, saying, "Surely this is a Coyote song?" In every camp there was talk of it, and the pride of Cinoave swelled like a young gourd in the rain. Everywhere he went singing it, their hearts were warmed and their thoughts stirred up within them. So it went until the feast of The-Grass-on-the-Mountain. Then the tribes and the sub-tribes came together at the place called Corn Water and there was no one who could sing equal to Cinoave. They had him sing his Coyote Song over and over, and as he listened to the talk and the hand clapping he changed the words of the song so that those who heard it should say, "This is the song of Cinoave."

It was now some months since he had bought the song of the Coyote, and the song and the praise of it had entered into his bones. He thought of nothing but being praised and remembered for the power of his singing. So he sang it until he and the people were all wearied, and fell into the deep sleep of exhaustion. But because he had forgotten that the song could only be sung for the purpose for which it was given, Old Man Coyote came in the night and stole the song away. When the people awoke it was discovered that not one of them could remember a word of it.

Thus it has become a custom among the Piautes, when it is remarked that a man warms the hearts of the tribe by his singing and stirs up their thoughts within them, we do not praise him much. For who knows but it may turn out to be a Coyote Song? And when a song is used for other than the purpose of the giving, may not the Giver of it take it away?

The Woman Who Was Never Satisfied

There was a Navajo of the Chinlee country had a wife who, when she was in one place wished always to be in another. In everything else she was a good wife to him, but if they stayed at their summer hogan among the Peach Orchards, she thought of Shiprock, and at the lambing pens of Tseghi she longed for the open country. Her husband, to please her, traded his horses for sheep, so that it should be in the way of his work to be always moving from place to place; but no matter how good the pastures, the woman was sure they were never so fattening as the place where they would be tomorrow or the one they had just left.

"I think," said her husband good naturedly, "that even in the Underworld you would not be satisfied!" But that was unlucky, to speak of the death of a living person as a thing already accomplished. For, within a year or two, his wife sickened, and though he had a White doctor from Shiprock there was no saving her.

She was buried in the place of the Peach Orchards, and the next day the Navajo began to move his flock toward Moencopie. It was the one place where they had not been together, and he hoped by this means to avoid thinking of his wife, whom he had loved greatly. But on the fourth day between the day and dusk she came back. Her husband found her sitting by the fire as he came in from the feeding ground, and he was glad to see her, though as a wife she was no more than seeming. Nevertheless, he could not forbear to say to her, "I hope this time, my dear, you will be satisfied." So for a time it seemed she would be, and whenever her husband saw that she was getting restless, he moved the flock.

Thus they traveled across the Moencopie country and struck into their old round. They met friends, who were astonished to find that the woman had come back. They spoke her kindly, but they would not sit at her hearth, and if she came to theirs they remembered errands that they had elsewhere, for it is feared among the Navajo that if the dead return it is not for any good purpose. It was about this time that her husband, as he walked with the flock, would have glimpses of her hurrying on the trails, or wandering about the open country like a child that is lost. Every now and then she would strike into a trail and would run along it as if by swiftness to overtake that which was sought, and when it ended in a spring or an abandoned camp, she would come circling like a dog to pick up a viewless track. Whenever her husband came up with her she would whimper and whisper, "I can not find it, I can not find it," and he would point her the way back to their camp, though he knew very well that that was not what she was looking for.

To ease her, the Navajo shifted his feeding ground toward Chaco, for there are many trails of our Ancients in that place, and "chindee hogan."*—Who knows where the trail of the Underworld begins, or if, like the torneo, it may not come twisting to find us? On the way to Kin Klazhin they found a White man with his pack beside a dripping spring, far gone with the breathing sickness, so that blood came out of his mouth with his breath. Many such come into the Navajo country, but this one had come too late; also he had lost his way and had wearied himself past enduring. This the Navajo saw as he stooped to ease the man of his sickness, and as he looked toward his wife to convey his thought, for he wished not to have the man hear him, he saw that her eyes glittered suddenly, and begged, like a dog's. He was silent for a deep breath taking, in which the White man was not remembered, for the Navajo saw what was in her mind, and, loving her greatly, he wished that she might be satisfied. "You must be very sure, my dear, this time," he said, "these partings wrench the heart." But he thought this time, perhaps, she would be.

For three days the Navajo disposed his flock as he best could, for there was not much grass in that country, while with his wife he nursed the White man. This was not easy, for when it was necessary for the sick man to be moved, though the woman put her hands on him, it was the Navajo who lifted, for there was no power in her, and it was hoped that the White man would not notice.

Nevertheless he may have known, for often there is inknowing in those whose trail of life is ending, and if he knew the way he was about to go, he may have been glad of company. He was not deceived about his sickness, for he told the Navajo what to do with his pack and a letter he had written.

It was toward morning of the third night that the Navajo heard his wife call him, for with the flock to keep, and all, he could no wise do without sleeping. He answered to her voice and saw that her eyes were shining. The White man struggled to rise from his blankets, and as the Navajo stooped to lift him, blood came with his breath. As the Navajo was easing him to his side, the sick man made a little noise toward the woman, as he did when he wanted her, which was afterward a great comfort to the Navajo to remember, for as he raised himself from stooping over the dead man he was aware suddenly that he was alone with himself. Beside the dogs and the flock there was nothing with him. For those who go to Sippapu go like the torneo, wrapping their trail around them.

"I hope," said the Navajo, "that this time she will be satisfied."

* Haunted houses.

The Man Who Walked With The Trues

In the days of the New, there was a man who walked with the Trues and heard what they said. He had lifted the curtain of dark cloud at the doorway of the Dawn, and talked with the Thunder; he walked with the Lightning, and talked with the Twins of War and Chance face to face. No man who has lived since, has understood so much of the Trues, and of their ways with men.

He saw how the Trues wove with men as it were the pattern of a blanket. Of the different sorts of men they wove different patterns, red and yellow and blue, as they had dipped them. But what the pattern would be no man could say until it was finished. According as the Trues had need of men, they took them, and the happiest where those who understood no more than that they were being used. But whether they understood or not, the Trues kept on weaving. This is how they were seen by the man who walked in the days of the New with the people of the Middle Heaven. As he saw, so he taught, so that the people might know themselves in the hands of the Trues and work with them to their own advantage. There was no tribe in those days that prospered more than that tribe, and the man who walked with the Trues was their chief and their Sun Priest of Souls, receiving honor.

Then there came a day when the Trues planned that their pattern should show how men of great wisdom and inknowing thought could conduct themselves in extremity, and cast about for an example. "Lo," said the Twins of War and Chance, "here is this man who has walked with us." So the Trues reached out and took him. The Sun Priest of Souls, being in great anguish, for the cords of the weaving cut even to the marrow, cried out, "Lords, what have I done to deserve this handling?"

"Did you suppose," said the Trues, "that you were not also a part of the pattern?"

Lone Tree

Hogan hated the Lone Tree in the same way and for much the same reasons that men occasionally hate their wives.

There was something exasperatingly feminine in the very meagerness of its appeal as it stood tiptoe above Dripping Rock, as inconsequential and as unrelated to the vast empty land as a woman would have been.

Hogan was doing assessment work on the Palimbino for a wage that would set him free for months of prospecting for himself on the streaked flanks of the Carrizal. Hogan had a hunch. Somewhere in that disordered drove of hills he felt gold calling, "Come and find me!" Consequently he hated everything connected with the necessity that held him to the Palimbino. He hated the pale sand with the black rock snaking through it, hated the sun and the moon glare and the clink of his own pick on the country rock; and because it was the only sizeable, living thing on the horizon, he hated the Lone Tree.

Times when he came back to camp, heat crazed and thirsting at every pore of his big body, Hogan could have slapped the little tree for the way it balanced and fluttered in the desert blast, offering its old-maidish, insufficient shade. It had a very woman's trick of spreading its roots about the ledge from under which the water seeped, as though its frail fibers were all that held Dripping Rock in place, and a woman's air of dispensing the spring, which was the only water in a half day's journey, with hospitality. But since in the desert there is a sort of companionship, even in hate, Hogan suffered the Lone Tree until the day that he finished his assessment.

Then he served it as men occasionally do serve a woman whom they have used merely because she is convenient, and not because they have appreciated her. He stuck his pick into the slender trunk, just above the roots, and gave it a savage, dragging pull till the sand and gravel began to come down with it. Then he went away, as men go, without looking back at the Lone Tree leaning over Dripping Rock with all its limbs aghast and its leaves drooped, like a woman fainting.

Hogan prospected the Carrizal according to his hunch. He worked and starved and worked again, for two years. Then with his pockets full of ore he started for Tucson to file on a claim that left him giddy with its promise.

He went by the Palimbino trail where there was water every half day, with three days rations in his pack. But it is three days and a half to Tucson, and Hogan's mind was more occupied with his strike than with the landmarks. At the end of the second day he found himself forty miles out of reckoning.

The season was half way between wet and dry, and off to the south a sand storm sent up threatening, tall, yellow banners. Hogan knew perfectly well what he had to do, which was to keep parallel to the storm and strike across below Dripping Rock to the main trail. He thought if he could make the Rock he would lie up there until the storm blew over. His food was gone by this time, but with water he could manage.

He began to think affectionately of the little Lone Tree, without any recollection of what he had done to it.

By noon the storm swung across his track; a flying wall of sand that blinded and stung and smothered. In such a storm the whole face of the desert is altered, carried aloft and redistributed by the wind. Hogan kept moving in the right direction, chiefly by the creature instinct. For the first six hours he thought of his claim and all it would buy him—the best reason he knew to keep a man moving. The last four he thought only of the Lone Tree and the water under the Dripping Rock. By this time his own mother would not have known him, staggering, swollen with the stinging sand and his thirst, but the tree would know him. He was so sure of this that when between blindness and exhaustion, he was finally down on all fours, he kept on crawling. He struck the ledge of Palimbino and his old trail to Dripping Rock; but when he came the last hundred yards, creeping at the bottom of the yellow lurk, he found that the roots that held the rock had been torn away by the falling tree, so that it had dropped into the sources of the spring. Across the sand choked basin lay the withered stock of the Lone Tree, but it was three years before anybody came that way to find the bones of Hogan mixed with its stark branches.

The Land of Journey's Ending

Between the Rio Colorado and the upper course of the Rio Grande, lies the Land of Journey's Ending.

No such natural boundaries define it north and south, only the limit of habitableness. About the sources of its enclosing rivers the ranges of the continental axis draw to a head in the Colorado Rockies. Southward they scatter, like travellers who have lost their heads in terror of desertness, among the vast unwatered plateaus of Old Mexico. But all the country east of the Grand Canon, west and north of the Journada del Muerte, is like the middle life of a strong man, splendidly ordered. This is the first sense of the land striking home to the traveller who gives himself up to it. Go far enough on any of its trails and you begin to see how the world was made. In such a manner mountains are thrust up; there stands the cone from which this river of black rock was cast out; around this flat valley rises unbroken the rim of its ancient lake; by this earthquake rent the torrent was led that drained it. What man in some measure understands, he is no longer afraid of: the next step is mastery.

That this is the first and lasting effect of the country comprised in the western half of New Mexico and the whole of Arizona, may be discovered, if from no other source, from the faces of the men who made it habitable. In any collection of pioneer portraits you will find one type of physiognomy predominating, full browed, wide between the eyes, and in spite of the fierce mustachios and long curls of the period, a look of mildness. Superior to the immediate fear of great space, or the lack of water or the raiding savage, there was a subtle content at work. Seeing ever so short a way into the method of the land's making men became reconciled to its nature.

There can be no adequate discussion of a country, any more than there can be of a woman, that leaves out this inexplicable effect produced by it on the people that live with it. To say that the Southwest has had a significant past and will have a magnificent future because it is a superb wealth producer, is to miss the fact that several generations of men wasted themselves upon it happily without taking any measure of its vast material resources. The nineteenth century assault which found California a lady of comparatively easy virtue, quailed before the austere virginity of Arizona, but the better men among them served her without recompense. If the Southwest is becoming known as an unrivaled food producer, still, food producing is one of the things man has taught the land to do since he has lived in it. There was nothing that betrayed its crop capacity to the untutored sense of the Amerind savage and the unlettered American pioneer. Both of these married the land because they loved it, and afterwards made it bear. If more lines of natural development converged here, between the bracketing rivers, more streams of human energy came to rest than any where else within

what is now the United States, it was because man felt
there the nameless content of the creative spirit in the
presence of its proper instrument.

FIGURE 43. William Penhallow Henderson (1877–1943), "El Leñador,"
woodblock print from *Laughing Horse*, no. 9 (1923).

Native Americans, their lifeways, their music, and their literature, became the most frequently represented of southwestern subjects in *Laughing Horse.*

Navajo Song

MAYNARD DIXON

Azlé, Azlé, you who have clambered the mountains, Azlé,
    Where is the little juniper growing up green?
    Over the band of blue mesas,
    Out of the yellow edges of dawn;
Come on the curled-up toe of your moccasin, Azlé.

Azle, you who have wandered the hill-trails, Azlé,
    Where does the little fawn come down from the rim?
    Over the line of red mesas,
    The Turquoise hollow of noon
Touch with the softness of white corn-tassels, Azlé.

Azle, you who have followed the canyons, Azlé,
    Where does the he-bear come at evening to drink?
    Over the wall of black mesas,
    Into the velvet of night
Go, stepping soft in your star-buttoned moccasins, Azlé.

Discovered — An American Gentleman

ROBERT HERRICK

I may well be the only white person in the state of New Mexico who is not interested in the Indian, never has been and never will be. Not interested in him financially or sentimentally, or aesthetically or morally or socially, or in any way that a stranger can become interested in a race. Who does not hope to exploit him either pecuniarily or artistically! Nor am I interested in his Cause. I have troubles of my own, many. Moreover, since 1914 I have been identified with so many lost causes that when I hear the words Honor, Justice, the Right, I have an attack of nerves from wondering what peculiarly monstrous evil is about to be perpetrated in those sacred names. I have learned, what the coming generation is apparently born already knowing, that justice is the last tormenting illusion dropped by the gods on this earth to torture man. So I refuse to become interested in the fate of the Indian.

I am a migratory bird of passage in this austere land. I accept the Indian simply as a fact along with his ancient mountains, the silent desert, the low brown walls of mud houses. Nevertheless, when I pass through one of the Indian settlements, see the Indian women husking corn and making bread, the men at work or silently communing among themselves; when I pass a finely featured Indian on the road driving a wagon laden with wood, I

(continued on following pages)

recognize between myself and this dark being with braided hair something much more akin than between myself and the Mexican or the tin-motor-car tourist from Kansas or Rhode Island. Why? I loiter in their pueblos listening to their low, sculptured tones, observing the harmony in which they live with one another, in close quarters, the gentleness and kindliness of their communal life, and I remember McDougal street or Halstead street where a communal life of a sort is also lived, but that more like jackals. And I wonder. I said "communal", which would seem to describe most fittingly the kind of living together in peace and harmony, the sharing together of labor and produce, which the Indian of the Pueblo has worked out for himself in the course of hundreds of years. But hush! hush! Lest some Indian agent should chance to read these words and have sufficient intelligence to apply them. Uncle Sam's spoiled darlings communists! Followers of the devil Lenin? Spirit of Hughes and Hoover to the rescue! Put them safely in tin-roofed bungalows of the Oklahoma type and build a high fence between each family so that they may learn the joys of competition and theft—according to the lovely civilization of the dollar . . . . But there is no danger while the flowing red tape of a government bureau in the ordinary process of its function provides for the welfare of its wards. For in the ordinary process of a government bureau we shall all become communists or worse before anybody with authority to do anything recognizes an Idea.

All the same, as far as I can see, as a bird of passage, the Indian has beautifully adapted some of the ideas of communism and has made of Lenin's harsh doctrine (or it has made of him) a very rare product—a gentleman. One who is not primarily concerned with the process of living, but has time and emotion for life itself. One who is kindly and takes long views, who remembers the past and is not afraid of the future. The peculiar suavity of the gentleman's spirit rises unmistakably out of the Indian pueblo. (Therefore, the pueblo would be an admirable training place for youth, much better than Groton or West Point!) This suavity of Indian life was emphatically manifested the other day at the Fiesta in Taos, when several tin-car tourists from Colorado, Oklahoma, California, etc., etc., their origin blazoned on their cars and on their faces,—red Ku-Klux-Klan or American-Legion-Protective faces hacked out of rather muddy clay—and their unspeakable women—drove into the plaza of the pueblo and did their best with their jokes and their honking and their stinking machines—chiefly by their vulgarizing presence—to destroy the simplicity and charm of the little festival. The Indian took them in the only way in which a gentleman can protect himself from a hoodlum, by silence, by ignoring their presence. And it came over me, standing there in the afternoon light, while this citizen of the pueblo practiced the rites and the games of his fathers that here in the face of the white mob was the only real gentleman this continent had ever seen—or possibly would see . . . .

FIGURE 44. Olive Rush (1873–1966), "Pueblo Mission," from *Laughing Horse*, no. 9 (1923). Indiana-born Rush studied art in New York and Paris, settling in Santa Fe in the 1920s. She was both an easel painter and a muralist.

The Indian Poet and His Song

NELLIE BARNES

Anyone with a quick ear for music may sit near a pueblo bridge on a summer evening and learn the native rhythms and melodies by listening as the Indians sing to the soft obligato of the mountain stream which sweeps away to the arid lands below. But the venture of the student of music is easier than that of the student of poetry, whose discoveries are the rare, if precious, essence of Indian thought; for these evening songs are likely to be without words, the mere pulsing of "ah-hai ah-hai e-yah" through receding cadences. Song-poems are more often sung in the secret ceremonies, and must be learned from individual singers who have patience enough to act as tutors.

It is not strange that, in spite of the growing interest in American Indian music for several decades, there has been slight notice of Indian poetry for more than a single decade, perhaps, and that the Indian poet still remains an unknown figure to almost all those outside a small group of ethnologists. Nor is it strange that composers of lyrics should be less known than their works, reticent as they are regarding their beliefs. Yet among Indian singers there has been a courtesy which recognizes the name of the composer so long as tradition bears it, and always the name of the tribe from which a song comes.

As a white student taught by Indians, a last listener in

(continued on following pages)

the long sequence of tradition, I venture to speak of verse that has never been written down until now. A Pueblo Indian's remembered lore is his "five foot shelf"; hence the personal recognition which he grants to a singer is a kind of copyright. Since this recognition is everywhere to be found among the pueblos, one may conclude that Indian lyrics in this region are of individual, not of group origin.

Authorship is primarily individual, even of ceremonial songs which take the name of the clan. The best singer in a group is chosen to prepare a new song for an important occasion. He first composes his melody as he goes about his work, and sings it with vocables, "he-ye-ah," until it is complete. He then creates a poem suitable for the occasion, carefully fitting it to the rhythm and cadence of his melody; for the words must be pleasing when sung to the music, or "must 'carry on' with the tune", as Rafael once explained. When the lyric is completed, the composer then sings it before his fellows in order to receive their criticism. He modifies a word here, a phrase there, until the group considers the words and music entirely suited; and from the moment of acceptance, the song receives the name of the organization. This type of song alone ceases to bear the name of the individual poet-musician; and acknowledgment for its use must hence-forth be paid to the clan.

So strict was the courtesy of older times that a tribe or individual not only acknowledged authorship but also paid another for the privilege of learning a song. Ceremonial songs were obviously better protected than those of a secular nature; and tribal ownership of a ceremony might be acknowledged in a practical way. Not many years ago, one tribe found blight in the grain fields. It finally invited a neighboring pueblo to conduct a ceremonial to destroy the blight; and it is said the visitors were well paid for their successful performance.

The general practice of paying for the use of songs apparently has died out in the region of the Rio Grande; though Juan has told me of long nights by the mountain stream, when he taught his songs to Antonio as long as Antonio's gifts of tobacco held out. As a student with both these singers, I am inclined to think that Juan's story is true; for across a span of years, broken by my long absences, I have had some identical songs from the two. The strictest etiquette forbade me to tell one teacher what another had taught me; and caution forbade one man to tell another that he was revealing anything sacred to a white person. Then, too, Antonio was dead when Juan came to be my teacher.

As to all secular poetry, or even sacred verse of earlier times, these men were careful to give the sources. Both were proud that they had learned their best songs from the famous older singer Santiago, when they were nine or ten years old; and that time was, by the white man's count, not less than fifty years ago. Among other singers who have advised my studies of poetry was a relative of the famous Santiago, the greatest poet and musician within the tradition of his tribe. His only rival for fame, so far as I can discover, is the Hopi singer who is said to have composed seven hundred songs.

Besides these great poets, many a lesser known singer

has been recognized. Perhaps a returning warrior once came ahead of his tribesmen to announce their victory; and when he came to the crossroads outside his pueblo, he began his impromptu song for all the friends and kinsmen who had come to greet him. Living singers mention such an occasion with awe, though they only dimly remember the song and the name of the warrior.

In such a fashion, lyrics can be traced back definitely to composers who sang fifty to a hundred years ago; but there tradition begins to waver. The proudest boast is of the ceremonial songs taught to the tribe by the "Ancients" who planned their way of life wisely for mortals. These songs are timeless fragments of unremembered ceremonies; even the words are of a speech no longer heard in the pueblo. "The meaning is thought to be so—," the Indian tutor will say, and one cannot go back of that teaching—archaic words of almost forgotten songs. The poems are sacred and old. What better poets may be named than the gods themselves?

With all the lore that gathers around a song in its travels from one generation to another, there persists this effort to give recognition of original ownership or composition within the tribe—even to the first fathers, as I have shown—and of origin in another tribe, if the song is borrowed. But even then the song, or dance, is acknowledged as the property of the person who learned it and brought it home. If other men wish to use it, they join the performer; but, out of courtesy, do not resort to it otherwise.

In time, to be sure, tradition loses the name of the composer; but it retains the story of the origin, or the occasion out of which the song grew—some high moment of personal experience or an heroic tale of the hunt or of battle.

So far have customs broken down that a visiting Indian singer was permitted to join the chorus at a recent Corn Dance. Indeed, the recollection of both occasions and composers is fading today; because transmission among the younger men is now by "listening in," not by gifts in the old way, as some well known singer performs. In the evening, the Indian Homer will stretch out half reclining on the floor, or sit by the fire singing his lyrics again and again. His listeners follow until they, too, can sing with the composer. Songs spread through many tribes in this manner; and the new singer acknowledges only the tribal origin, rather than the individual composer of his latest song "hit". So it happens that the student will find in his collection songs of related dialects; and the definite traditional record is lost, too often even of phrase and of rhythm.

The effect of this loss of personal recognition upon the Indian poet will be interesting to follow. One can only hope that he will eventually consent to the publication of his work; since the young Indian potter, weaver, and painter will find everywhere in the museums rare antique collections of their arts—but the new poet will find little of his ancient heritage of verse preserved.

Some of the older men think that publication must be withheld until pueblo lands are allotted in severalty; for the way of the progressive Indian is unbelievably hard when he seeks to record the lore of his people. The more ignorant and superstitious of his tribe cannot understand his purpose in recording a ceremony or song that it may be preserved accurately for later generations of Indians. The result is persecution of the "disloyal" individual who is likely to be one of the most intelligent and best informed of the group. There can be no growth of the tribe under such conditions.

In some pueblos, it is reported that no new ceremonial songs, whatever, are being composed and that there have been none for a very long time. This stage marks, then, the end of the old creative period. What of the new? Unquestionably the old ceremonial songs are the most beautiful Indian poems. The young Indian singer can never compose his best work in the white man's way. He must use the imagery, the symbolism, and the rhythm of his own people, and develop in the noblest Indian fashion to produce real poetry.

But with tradition losing ground, where shall the composer find direction? Unfortunately, many of the progressive young Indians have recognized no value in the old songs and dances; because they have broken with the old ceremonial ways and beliefs on religious grounds and have not yet rediscovered them as artistic productions. Against such a hope of discovery, there should be gathered a store of traditional verse which will yield full honor to the Indian poets of earlier days and awakening to those of coming times.

The Indian's Book

(A Review of the new edition of Natalie Curtis' Volume)

INA SIZER CASSIDY

Harper Brothers have published a new edition of Natalie Curtis' "The Indian's Book," first published in 1907, with the parfleche cover in new striking colors. None of the old material has been omitted, but considerable new matter has been added. Those who are under the impression that the Pueblo Indian question is a new one should read "The Indian's Book" and see where Natalie Curtis, nearly twenty years ago made the same plea now being made for him and the preservation of his art, his songs and ceremonies. It was really due to her efforts that the young Indian of today in the Government schools is allowed to sing his own songs and to paint water colors of his ceremonies. Incredible as it seems, before she made her plea to the then President Theodore Roosevelt, it was forbidden the Indian to sing his own songs in school, and to do so even in the Pueblo was frowned upon by the authorities. The Pueblo Indian and his friends owe much to Natalie Curtis for this.

In her plea for the preservation of the Pueblo Indian and his art Miss Curtis quotes an earlier authority John Fiske, the historian who says: "Among the Red Men of America the social life of ages more remote than the lake villages of Switzerland is in many particulars preserved for us today, and when we study it we realize as never before the conti-

(continued on following page)

nuity of human development, its enormous duration and the almost infinite accumulation of slow efforts by which progress has been made. The Pueblos of New Mexico and Arizona are among the most interesting structures of the world."

Natalie Curtis' self imposed task was to write, not what she thought of the Indian, nor what she thought should be done for him, but to record and preserve his own thoughts, his outlook on life, his beliefs and aspirations for the benefit of the Anglo-Saxon world of literature, music and art; and to preserve these for the young Indian as well, the Indian of today and tomorrow who is fast losing his pure Indian traditions in absorbing the traditions and culture of the white race.

It is unfortunate for all that the life of this gifted young woman should have ended before she had completed her task. Her death occurred in Paris two years ago, just as she was about to return to Santa Fe where she owned an attractive studio home, to continue her work. But she leaves a record in "The Indian's Book" which has already become, and no doubt will continue to be, a valuable reference book for all those interested in aboriginal culture.

Men and Gods

PHILIP STEVENSON

*(Corn Ceremony, Pueblo of
Santo Domingo, New Mexico)*

Drum-beats waver on the heated air, sound dull mono-
tones against flat solid houses, beat upon iron ground, and
rise in brazen waves above pale plumes of cedar smoke.
The pulse of voices chanting pushes up above the dancers,
mingles deep growls with the monotone of drum, soars
and trembles high in arid light. Earthen walls reflect the
sun—sun-heat, sun-light—earth-walls of houses cut
square yellow pedestals upon blue-painted sky. Stiff statues
stand in broken lines on pyramided pedestals of sun-baked
earth: statues watching, solemn, still, streaked with
coloured headbands—touched with purple, green, cerise
and scarlet; statues bright with silken scarves, blue with
turquoise, dark with black squaw-dresses, black hair, black
eyes, flashing with silver-conched belts and silver beads.
Drum-beats rebound from burnished breasts and bronze
brows, tremble in bands of colour, flash in silver beads and
belts. Hot-baked adobes waver in yellow light, shake with
the monotone of drum, absorb the chant, and lift pale
cedar incense to the sun.

Beat-and-Beat-and-Beat—the rhythm stumbles, falls, …
but quickens back to life on a higher wild triumphant key
that sings a thousand bodies joyful, springing joyful, free
and seeking, seeking plenty, seeking beauty filtered
through the incandescent air.

(continued on following pages)

Bodies

In double line approaching fifty dancers tread the dust.
Rigid bodies dare the sun; proud legs hammer the ground;
stoic faces fix the sky; wiry arms are jingling, chugging,
spattering sound from silver bracelets, tortoise rattles, peb-
bled gourds. Dangling skins of fox fringe pendulous from
girdled loins, panels black with streaming hair, ripple
rhythmic waves in quivering heat. Slowly, slowly, inch by
inch, the ground is trampled, shaken, flattened.
Moccasined feet of active men, velvet soles of passive
women, tread the ground and conquer it. Faces proud-
impassive, rigid arms right-angled, deny the rising-falling
chant, defy the blood-beat of the drum; are one with
chant, with drum, with earth and torrid sky.

The Pattern

Man—woman; man—woman; man—woman; down two
tramping lines to boy—girl; boy—girl; and child. Behind,
the old men stamp and sing—sing Haya-ha-ya-hey!—and
raise the branching pinon to the sun. High the symbol-
pennant bends its feathered head; lean up-thrusted pennant bends and moves above the dancers, scattering spirit-
plenty; bends, waves, and shivers in the air. Haya-haya-
hey-ey-oh! Tall, straight the drummer planted, lifted chin,
one foot advanced. The maddened drumstick plies his
hand, shakes his body, swings the bright brass earrings
pendant from a crimson scarf, but leaves the face its brazen
dignity. Corn-crowned koshari weave their striped and
spotted forms among the lines—break patterns, break

step—with upward gesture poised on single foot, break chant with rippled high Haaaaaaah!; leap, cry, and wheeeeeedle laughter from high roof-statues; stamp and pry between the rigid lines. Man—woman; man—woman; man . . . and corn-tufted clown.

Lines melt, break, confused, and mingle in wheeling slow advance. Shug-sha-shug-sha-shug. Stamp. Shug-sha-shug-sha-shug. Heavy women, buxom-breasted, infant shod, trip-tip trip-trip after men; delicate brown and up-toed feet go timid-softly pad-pad-pad behind the heavy-stamping rigid-elbowed men shapes rattling gourds. Shug-Sha-shug-sha-shug.

Haaaaaaaaaah! lines reform to rigid stamping, endless, heartless, tireless thumping stern unflinching confident command. O bring the rain, rain, rain. Rain will come; corn will leap. See, see, O You Above, the branched cedar-boughs are waving. High the tufted pennant shivers, scattering plenty, bending over these Your children, making fruitful earth and man. Send rain! Send rain! Rain will come—Haaaaaaaaaaaaah! Rain will come! Corn will spring! Stamp-and-Stamp-and-Stamp. Shug-sha-shug-sha-shug. Haya-haya-hey-ey-oh! Haya-haya-hey!

The Test

On—on—on. Bronze bodies beat the earth, stamp their will upon the ground, shout commands to a painted sky, forge a prayer on beauty's anvil. Stiffened sun-heat bends and wilts in purpled shadow. Clouds. Clouds! Haaaaaaaaaaaaah! Grim koshari grin, turn, gesture, poise, and point to endless distance. Clouds. Clouds! Wind will come, will come, and bring the rain! Haya-haya-hey-n—hey-n!

Tawny column-clouds are looming; clouds are creeping, marching, rushing. Maddened drumstick drums more angry, angry and loud. Whistle and roar of whirlwind, long-swept from arid sun-hammered plain, screams a warning as it come: "Sti-i-i-ill! Be-wa-a-a-are! I sweep a-a-all before me!" Lean tawny wind, opaque, streaks hungry down the long plaza, swoops to absorb the dancers, hisses a savage glee in limitless strength. sounds are lost, engulfed, danced upon by a demon-spirit's wrath. Statues flex and melt to viscous eddied brown. The blue of turquoise, yellow and cerise of headbands, bronze and black of brows and hair, koshari stripes and spots, pennant, lines, chorus, slip and fall to semi-solid whirls of stinging sand . . . .

It passes. Sounds first reappear through din of wind—soft sounds—Shug-sha-shug—Haya-hey-ey!—then blurry shapes of dancers, chorus, pennant, clowns reassemble in fading mist of brown. Faces still impassive. Lines as straight. Feet as proud. Rhythm of chant, of drum, of gourds, as one.

Beat-and-Beat-and-Beat. Stamp. Shug-sha-shug-sha-shug.

The wind is waiting. Broods.

Again a thunder-throated cloud hurls venom-hatred, swaddling hammered rhythms in long wind-moans of sifting sand. It grinds the tamped plaza-lane into tongues that lick the smoothness from solid houses, sucking the earth into long up-reaching ropes of dust. Faint, faint the drum,

FIGURE 45. Loren Mozley, "Faces proud-impassive, rigid arms right-angled. . ." from *Laughing Horse*, no 16 (1929). Mozley (b. 1905) was a painter, printmaker, muralist, and writer active in Taos in the late 1920s and 1930s. Professionally trained in France and New Mexico, his print shows a gift for simplifying form and a sure sense of balanced value relationships in his composition.

the chugging stamp of stoic feet scarce visible in arabesques of dirty brown. Higher the tempest mounts, louder the scream and moan of wind, sharper the sting of scudding twigs and pebbles, deeper drowned the prayer of dance and song.

The roar attains a peak, waits, gathers, and springs again till all the earth is a bacchanale of brown revolving furies.

Fitfully seen, the dancers are suspended beings, treading not the solid ground, but spurning lean, up-reaching arms of angry power. High among the clouds and stars they trample down brown hurricane shapes, methodically beating down long hands that clutch at calm. Oblivious to the rise and fall of storm, they tread, untouched, above, in tranquil triumph.

Time rests. . . .

Peace

The tired wind droops. With a last breath it blows away the veil. Dust floats slowly, softly off to earth, and the reappearing sun soaks up the purple vestige of shadow . . . .

Drum-beats waver on the heated air. The pulse of chanting voices lifts above square, solid houses, barren now of statues, lifts and quickens to new life on a higher wild triumphant key. Koshari grin, turn, and wheedle laugher from the air. Haaaaaaaaaaaaaah! They weave and pry among the dancers—break patterns, break step—lift hands in scornful gesture. Man—woman; man—woman; boy—girl; and child;—fifty forms in stiff alignment, straight and square as drummers' rhythms, chug the gourd, wave the green, spurn the caked ground. Churning knees of men, timid pad-pad-padding feet of women, rigid elbows, torsos, faces, rippling fox-skins, fringe and hair. Shug-sha-shug-sha-shug. Stamp. Shug-sha-shug-sha-shug. Ancients of the chorus lift majestic masks of deep seams and green-white hair, lift grand old faces to sunlight, thrusting the branched pinon toward the east. Haya-haya-hey-ey-oh! Haya-haya-hey! Rain will come. Corn will leap. Stamp-and-Stamp-and-Stamp.

Drum-beats bounding from burnished breasts and yellow-hot adobe walls sing a thousand bodies joyful, springing joyful, free and seeking, seeking plenty, seeking beauty filtered through the incandescent air.

FIGURE 46. Dorothy Brett, "Koshares," from *Laughing Horse*, no. 18 (1930).

Fiesta

ELIZABETH SHEPLEY SERGEANT

Under white hooped tops of prairie schooners come dark Pueblos, bearing plenty over desert ridges.

Heads bound with purple, like the seers, they stare from wrinkled Eastern masks and smile with tilted eyes.

I glimpse black pots and deep, benignant breasts of women in the hay, while thatch-haired young reach out for yellow melons.

Here jolt Pueblos, smiling through a sheen of dust. Corn growers, amigos of the Rain Gods, who make swift showers fall in drops that pit the sand.

FIGURE 47. Andrew Dasburg, "Indian Pueblo," from *Laughing Horse*, no. 12 (1925). Dasburg (1887–1979) was a highly influential teacher and one of the chief proponents of modernist painting in New Mexico.

Laughing Horse celebrated the cultural mix of the Southwest in poetry, prose and visual representations notably free of racism and sexism. If there was a cultural bias at all, it was against the Anglo-come-lately, whose affectations and boorish tourist behavior were repeated *Laughing Horse* targets.

FIGURE 48.
Ward Lockwood,
"Oh, Lookat!" from
Laughing Horse, no.
12 (1930). Noted as a
modernist landscape
painter, Lockwood
here shows a talent
for caricature in sati-
rizing the ubiquitous
New Mexico tourists.

Among the Southwest's legendary characters, even the cowboy was given his due, here in a poem whose author resists the
frequently cliched cowboy imagery:

Cow Ponies

MAURICE LESEMANN

After we'd turned in they gathered round
Nosing our blankets and stepping about our
    feet
Carefully . . . Then they nosed
Their soft cool muzzles over the bags for
    something to eat,
And stood for a while, and dozed . . .

They switched their tails, remembering the
    long day
They'd carried us . . . and the flies . . .
They stared into the fire and rubbed their heads
    together—
Raised them with startled eyes
At the strange nicker far off in the sage—
                              Nostrils wide,
Bay heads, white noses tossed back from the dark.
The sound died . . . The fire licked out and died.

They drooped their ears and pawed, and nosed
The bags again, lipped a few scattered grains,
Then wandered away and dozed . . .
Watched each other in the moonlight,
    shuddered, and sighed,
And stood to sleep . . . The wind drifted their
    manes.

And we too turned to sleep, and all night long
We knew that they were round us while we
   slept,
And they—they knew it too . . .
                Heads turned and tossed.
We swore across their dreams, they nosed in
   ours.
Above the corral the moon crept
And made a useless moon-dial of the snubbing
   post.

FIGURE 49. Frank Applegate, "Old Chisholm Trail," from *Laughing Horse*, no. 9 (1923).

On the other hand, Johnson loved caricaturing his friends. W. Herbert "Buck" Dunton was a Taos painter and outdoorsman given to rugged western dress, hunting and a vigorous outdoor life—the antithesis, in other words, of the somewhat effete Johnson. In a spirit of fun, Johnson humorously described Dunton's run-in with a real New Mexico "desperado" and then invited the painter to publish his own version of the events:

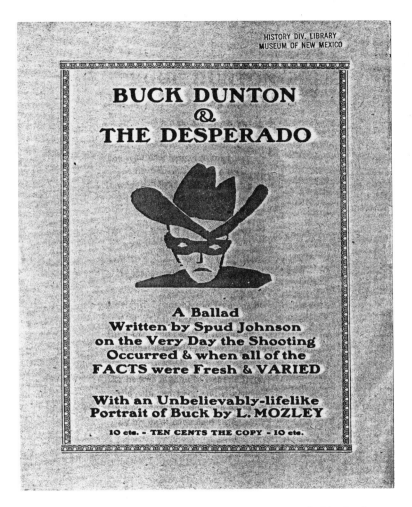

FIGURE 50. Cover page from "Buck Dunton & the Desperado," by Spud Johnson, from *Laughing Horse* supplementary pamphlet, 1929.

Buck Dunton & The Desperado

A Ballad

SPUD JOHNSON

Which was the proudest ever won
By artist pale or tan,
For he was christened by John Dunn
As "The Cowboy Painter Man."

He scarce had spoke, when out the night
A bold bad man stepped spryly.
"Hands up!" he said, "And don't show fight;
This ain't no bloody baile!"

Always a gentleman and true,
Buck Dunton raised his hat;
But when the man said "Goddamn you!"
Buck Dunton raised his gat.

"Gimme your money, or I'll shoot!"
The man spoke not in fun,
For he was out for golden loot,
And didn't see Buck's gun.

Buck groaned again, but took his aim
Straight at the bandit's heart;
And 'though he staggered and was lame,
He knew his hero part.

Buck shot him once, he shot him twice,
He said, "You dirty toad!"
The bandit fell and wriggled thrice,
Then laid there in the road.

A rancher nearby heard the fray;
He rescued Dunton quick,
And took them both to Santa Fe,
For Herbert sure was sick.

He swore he would relinguish pay
And even give up painting,
If God would take his pain away
And keep his heart from fainting.

As for the villain, he was too,
With a bullet in his mug.
The prison doctor pulled him through,
But left him in the jug.

Now Buck lies quiet in his cot
At old St. Vincent's San.
They operated.—And we've still got
Our Cowboy Painter Man!

What Really Happened

BUCK DUNTON

(On special request, Herbert Dunton has furnished the true detail of what happened in the Rio Grande canyon last week, varied stories having appeared in different papers. In justice to "Buck" the real statement covering the event, is published as follows:)

On Monday, June 10th, I planned to leave Taos the following a.m. for Albuquerque. I packed my grips and placed same in car before retiring; awoke twice during the night and each time on awakening my thoughts were on my six shooter; something told me to take with me a 45 Colt 6 gun.

I awoke and dressed sometime about 4:30, slipped gun and scabbard from belt (5 cartridges were always kept in cylinder) and placed them in the pocket on the right door of car and departed. Met first car this side of Ranchos. Met no more until I came to Embudo River just this side of the long narrow bridge.

Had driven about 14 miles when I said to myself, "Some place to have gun in case of need!" I took gun and scabbard from pocket and placed same between seats by my right side.

Was driving new Chevrolet coach, front windows open. Was sitting "catty cornered," my left elbow hanging over left window sill, and was keeping up a steady pace of 30 miles per hour and hugging inside of road.

(continued on following pages)

Had proceeded I should say a mile further when I approached a lone rock on left side and close to road. Got with in to above 50 feet or so of it when a man (somewhere around 30) short, thick set, dressed in very shabby, rusty brown coat and trousers and dirty shirt, jumped from behind the rock with hands raised and yelled, "Stop!" His face was very white and his eyes looked as if he were desperate-crazy. But I also noted at once the new Smith and Wesson 6 shooter tucked in his belt, Walnut grip slanting toward right side. I felt at once he was a "hop-hound" doped up for the occasion. I knew also that he was there to kill me, rob me, and depart with my car.

When he yelled "Stop," I grabbed wheel with my left hand, drew gun with my right hand and threw down outside window close to the windshield. The man had no sooner jumped than he evidently saw I would run him down. He turned instantly and leaped back. As he did so he turned his pallid face toward me and his right hand was dropping toward his gun when, as my gun swung down to his head, I cut loose. On its report, he clapped both hands to his right cheek, his face was convulsed in pain and I saw blood gush out and spread between his fingers. The blow of the bullet threw him back toward the road for a second; his cap sailed away like a clay pigeon to my left. Car was perhaps 10 or 12 feet from him by now, still at about 30 miles per hour. By this time had thrown down again. As I fired 2nd shot (tire must have hit a rock) he wheeled, half crouching and clapped his hands to his right leg above the knee. Almost instantly my left front tire hit him, spun him around toward me again, and he fell on his back oppo-

site the left window. By this time I had thrown down
again (still keeping up speed and the muzzle of my gun
was not more than 4 feet from his chest. I intended to kill
him. I was laughing at him (I recalled afterwards of yelling
to him at the time, "You're a hell of a stick up man!") I
noted that my second shot had cut a perfect hole in his
trousers leg but I saw no blood, it probably scratched the
skin. I also noted at once his helpless position and pathetic
condition. So I shot a ball into the ground from about 6 to
12 inches from his left cheek, spraying his head and neck
with dust. I passed the rock, and on glancing back, I saw
the man had gotten up and was running around in circles
like a rattled cottontail. Suddenly he started to run up the
slope, but turned back, grabbed his cap, and started back
up through the sage and rocks. I never saw him again.
About a hundred yards further on I stopped, stepped out
of the car, and looked back to see if I had any witnesses.
Not a soul was in sight. I then climbed back into the car
and in throwing out shells, found I'd shot all 5 shots
instead of 3.

I drove on, stopping to phone Taos officers at the next
town. No phone, but Mr. Vigil wanted to get the details so
he could warn tourists. Reported incident at 5:30 as he
requested my name and the time. At Embudo I routed out
Wallace who told me I should have killed the man. I
phoned the officers in Taos but they could not understand
me nor I them until I finally got mad and hung up.

When I arrived in Santa Fe, I reported to officer Holmes
at city Marshal's office, and gave a full description of the
man and later related the incident in full. I also phoned

Gov. Dillon and asked him for a permit to carry a gun in traveling to protect myself and property.

In the Albuquerque Journal of June 13th the article relating to the occurrence said, "Dunton, who was going to Albuquerque, stopped in Santa Fe and reported to the sheriff that he had shot a man. He said the man was lying alongside the road." In justice to myself I must correct this statement. This is a serious error. The sheriff must have been misunderstood because I would not shoot at a poor man lying by the roadside.

That's all. It's now ancient history. Forget it.

The Hispanic culture of the Southwest was often the subject of poetry and prints in *Laughing Horse*, as in a piece from the well-known poet Norman Macleod. ("Echo of Darkness" LH 19):

> "Constrict the shadow of sun
> in the upturned shell of the desert
> and darkness runs a long hollow into the hills.
> Penitent crosses bear
> the black loam of the earth
> only in shadows."

FIGURE 5 1 . Artist unknown, "The Virgin of Guadalupe," from
Laughing Horse, no. I I (1924).

FIGURE 52. Carlos Vierra (1876–1937), "Old Spanish Santo," from
Laughing Horse, no. 11 (1924). Vierra arrived in New Mexico in 1904 seeking a
healthful climate. He is regarded as Santa Fe's first resident professional artist
and is remembered for his paintings of New Mexico mission churches and his
role in promoting the Pueblo Revival style in architecture.

Other examples of New Mexicana in *Laughing Horse* celebrate the harsh or tender beauties of the region and its seasons.

 Santa Fe Sonnets

LYNN RIGGS

Spring

I must go and look at marigolds again,
Or heal my brain in water quieter
Than a mountain stream. No lightning, no sharp rain
Hurting the earth, come near me! No stir
Of wind in the alfalfa, no flight of birds
Arrowing from the south—none of the things
I have been so shaken with in other Springs
Can give me peace again, not even words.

No, not the ones with gestures shadowy
Like dryads from a wood, nor those so spun
Their wings will shatter in the feeblest sun
Can ease me with their little ministry.
I must go and look at marigolds asleep
In water barely warm, and not too deep.

Summer

Autumn will come too soon, the snake-like bed
Of the river glisten under the fallen leaves.
Poplars will flame again; the lion head
Of the wind will roar among the alfalfa sheaves.
Go not, summer, with your trumpet sound

Of dawn lying golden in the locust trees!
Moths flatten at your windows; burro and hound
Sleep in your sun, hollyhocks in your peace.

Stay, summer! Go not, spring, with your delicate
Petals of the pear tree, and your lazy rain
Purring in the dust of the road—till your ultimate
Leaf is born, your last Christ risen again.

Autumn will come too soon, and winter's breath
Shrivel the meadow grass; and after death...............?

The Arid Land

LYNN RIGGS

There will be willows plunging
Their bloodless roots in air
And the hard crooked flying
Of buzzards circled there.

About the treeless wastes
No sand may ever heap
With water, nothing will run
And nothing creep.

Arid, desolate, defiant
Under its iron band
Of sky, we yet may love
This so sunny land.

Three Sketches

HANIEL LONG

Cienega

It is always time to speak of Cienega. To speak of that town is to remember a road winding down from a arid mesa into a valley where drought cannot follow. In a moment walls of blue rock rise beside the road, a singing acequia crosses and re-crosses it, and red fields appear, fields red as blood, red as fire. The fields are divided into squares by little dykes of mud, and acequias lined with osiers water them all. Perhaps it is in these osiers that the meadow-larks sing so liquidly.

Cienega is a valley of meadow-larks. On the road we pass shy dark youths, one after another, riding bare-back: the only kind of youths who could ride to and fro in a valley so filled with bird-song.

The orchards are in flower. And now we reach the red houses, the incredible red houses of Cienega, which lift themselves out of the red earth into the orchards of misty white. Low red walls surround them; in their neat patios stands a cottonwood or a locust. Immaculate paties and houses!

I see it all again . . And yet, can these houses be so red? And the dogs the children play with, can they be so white? And the Cerrillos hills seen through an arroyo going skyward, can they really be so blue and so ensorcelled?

Perhaps Cienega is a dream. And when one goes to it

(continued in following pages)

over that road where the rock is so blue and the earth so red, one may not really go to it at all, but rather dream a dream he has dreamt before. For no one is sure he has been to Cienega. People say to themselves:

"Was it illusion; or have I, some time or other, seen dusk in a valley like this?"

Santa Fe

Sometimes people motoring through Santa Fe to the east coast or the west coast, pause to inquire with the haggard eyes of tourists:

"What do you call this town?" ......

If they were to ask me, especially on a winter night when the wind howls over waste places, rattling windows in little houses, roaring like a sea in the withered leaves of the ailanthus trees in the old churchyard, I would answer:

"I call it Anathoth".

And I would not tell them what I meant. But I tell you. Once there was a city full of echoes and responses; and if a man stood in the square of that city and asked a question aloud, he received an answer. He was told what doors to open on what streets, and where to find the keys to open the doors.

Anathoth was a singular city, and the gardens within the double and the quadruple doors were more singular still, with their beauty of bird and blossom. If a man desired love, he found it in those gardens; if he desired death, it awaited him. If he cried out to know why he had been born, or why he must die, he learned the reason.

Santa Fe is another Anathoth, for it is a city of doors, only of doors. Sometimes I think that all the questions people ask may be reduced to two: AM I LIVING? or AM I DYING? And from the plaza of Santa Fe doors swing out which answer these questions clearly and for always. They swing out to the streets of Santa Fe itself, to the houses of mail boxes and telephones and radios: in them the bird of life is singing, and as if it were immortal. They swing out to the little Spanish villages of the mountains; lo, hear the bird of life in the yellow church yonder, where sits the Virgin in her niche. They swing out beyond, to the pueblos of the Rio Grande, where as in archaic times the bird of life sing in the violet shadow of adobes houses.

Yes, in the streets of communication, in the villages of the virgin, in the pueblos of the ceremonial dances, await answers to the only questions men ever ask, unless they be tourists.

Cerrillos Hills

Those cones of turquoise to the southwest draw my thoughts like a magnet. They never reveal themselves; the more I gaze at them, the more they clothe themselves in their mysterious garments. I am like the early Spaniards, enchanted by fairy-tales and by sirens with scales of gold. Yes, I am like the early Spaniards: I too forget that it is a craving in my own breast which lures me on, a craving for strange and precious metal, in dim regions of my own spirit.

All the fairy-tales are true, the sirens really exist (and

one should have a special tenderness for them); but they do not exist outside of ourselves. The turquoise mounds yonder across the mesa are simply a gate through which I pass back into the breast of humanity, the unknown land where live the monsters, but where live also angels, madonnas, and heroes.

I have finished a charming novel, the author of which, like children and like poets, thinks of landscape as of something that has a life of its own, a strange and beautiful presence. But surely it is man's eye and man's mind which give the earth its beauty. How may images of heaven and earth be beautiful to us until our eyes have come to rest on them in love? And is not the spirit living in those far-off blue volcanic hills—those lovely symbolic cones—a spirit really in our own hearts, prophesying a loveliness to come?

The beauty of landscape, it seems to me, is one of the caresses by which the mother of men hopes to bring her children to fulfillment.

After a City Winter

HANIEL LONG

Hill-tops are forms of silence,
  And sunlight is like skin,
And every pine along the cliffs
  Hushes what I have been,
And what I have known. And the quiet
  Draws me to tingle and throb;
And a three-stemmed dogwood in blossom

Breaks from me like a sob.
There is nothing, and then still nothing
(Excepting everything)
And I vanish in many white sepals
And the blue curve of a wing.

FIGURE 53. Paul Horgan, "Spring Snow, Roswell," from *Laughing Horse*, no. 20 (1938). Horgan (b. 1903) is a Pulitzer Prize–winning author of fiction, history, poetry, and drama. Friend to visual artists, he ventures here into print-making with a competent rendering of a scene near his longtime Roswell home.

In prose and poetry Spud Johnson himself wrote of the land, the history, and the colorful peoples of the region, occasionally illustrating the pieces with his own prints.

Hades, N.M.

SPUD JOHNSON

"Oh, see the adenoids and tonsils," said a young lady on entering one of the great vaults of the cavern near Carlsbad, New Mexico, recently. Her lantern revealed an intricate pattern of pink limestone entrails on the wall in front of her.—And then she fainted when she suddenly collided with an enormous erect stalagmite.

This, say Walter Mruk and Will Shuster, is a typical experience of the cave: laughter at its weird, freakish beauty, laughter covering an emotion that blends quickly into fright. And they ought to know. Not only are they among the first to explore this recently discovered natural wonder, they are the first to record its strange magnificence with the more personal medium of paint. Photographers have flashed there with elaborate and expensive equipment; tourists and even scientists have described its cold, terrorizing interior; but these two adventurers are the first artists to visit and record these particular contortions of the earth's bowels.

Picture them in those mile-long corridors of darkness, separated at times, alone, each with a dim lantern, sketch-

(continued on following pages)

FIGURE 54. Will Shuster, "Interior of Carlsbad Cave," from *Laughing Horse*, no. 11 (1924).

ing the immediate, barely illuminated stalactites, imagin-
ing the infernal shapes beyond in the bottomless darkness:
Stygian pits, whole lakes of inky water, even starvation and
death should the lantern fail and the trail be lost.

And their experiences, translated into color on canvas,
will be an adventure for a large number of other people
very soon, when their many sketches and the paintings
they have made from them are exhibited here and in the
art galleries of other cities.

"The Carlsbad cave," said Mruk, "has taught me a great
deal about form. There I saw Nature invert a landscape
and paint it from a perverted, hellish, palett." And Shuster
echoed the same thought when he exclaimed, "The cave
has made a cubist, vorticist, and post-impressionist of me
against my will. If Dante had been along, he would have
rewritten the Inferno in the manner of E. E. Cummings
and Yvor Winters."

FIGURE 55.
Walter Mruk,
"Hades, N.M.," from
Laughing Horse, no.
11 (1924).

Agua

WILLARD JOHNSON

"I should think," said a Harvard Professor's wife in Santa Fe the other day, "that water would be worshipped in this country." And so it is. Only two days before, the Indians at the pueblo of San Ildefonso had danced for rain—a ceremonial dance, ancient and beautiful; a living prayer for water.

The dance was held in a new plaza of the village, not yet beaten by the footfalls of years into an adobe floor. There was still much gravel, and the sun was so hot, the earth so dry that each glassy pebble was like a diminutive pyrex casserole which had just been removed from a hot oven. We, the spectators, sweltered in the shade of our motor-car, even though we had been cavorting in the shallow waters of an acequia but a half-hour previous, whereas the Indians before us had been dancing under the merciless rays of the desert sun since early morning.

And although the time was early June, we soon were given ample proof that the day was warmer than for any August dance we had ever witnessed. The men, naked but for short bright skirts and long fringed sashes, wore moccasins and danced with a religious fervor which ignored all physical discomforts. But the women, dressed modestly in long black dresses, with gay blue tablitas on their heads like bits of sky, were barefooted and soon began to show the agony they suffered—a very unusual proceeding. As a

(continued on following pages)

rule they seem an integral part of the desert themselves—
placid, broad-hipped, eyes downcast, feet barely moving in
syncopated rhythm with the more ecstatic, savage dance of
the men in front of them. But today they were miserable
and they could not hide the fact. They cringed, percepti-
bly. A school girl near the end of the long line hesitated,
broke the rhythm of her dance, almost halted and limped
pitiably. An old woman, the perspiration gathering in the
deep folds of her bronze skin, danced on stoically, but
presently dropped the evergreen branch she held in her
clenched hand, and danced upon its prickly green coolness
as a momentary respite from the heated pebbles. Others
followed her example with relieved glances of gratitude—
but presently each branch had to be retrieved as the dance
moved on across the yellow quadrangle of desert and the
feet of the women were blistered anew.

A few moments later three little girls hurried from their
place in the dance to the nearest house, running across the
intervening space on their heels to spare their burning
soles. A sympathetic murmur from the spectators greeted
this departure from rigid custom. But the feeling was evidently not shared by the elders of the village, for not a
minute later the little girls came running back to their
places, frightened but still suffering from the burning
sands. An old man, probably the governor, was chasing
them with a long whip. And we in the motor cars arose
excited when he approached the tardiest of the girls angri-
ly. She was walking painfully towards her place in the line,
still on her heels, and the old man's menacing gestures
were not empty threats, for he was incensed over the sacri-

legious impudence of the girl and sincerely indignant in meting out a fitting punishment. It was a dramatic moment, intensified by a low rumble of thunder.

ᐟ We looked up into the sky, surprised and almost alarmed by this evidence of divine anger, and saw that some of the hot white clouds had been silently collecting over the mountains across the Rio Grande and that a black mass of them was carrying a shadow nearer and nearer across the plain toward us.

Then, miracle of miracles, another rumble of thunder broke the dark canopy into a million pieces and the merciful rain beat down into the blistering plaza and on the glistening bodies of the rapturous dancers for rain, with a thrill of coolness that stopped even our hearts for a breathless moment!

And the Indians are not the only people who pray for rain—although they may be the only ones who dance for it—and get it so suddenly and effectively. During dry years the interests of every inhabitant of the Southwest are intimately concerned with the lack of water. "The year the old well went dry," "The year the trees died," or "The August it rained" are common expressions and mean much more than they say. When conditions become serious, even the conventional Protestant churches forego their discussions of prohibition, divorce, and the wrath of God, to devote special services to prayer for rain. And when a prosperous business man loses a building or a warehouse by fire as a result of lack of water to fight the flames—even he becomes concerned and comes down from his cool mountain cabin to discuss the horrific drought.

In the face of this it is strange that there is not among the "whites" more sympathetic understanding of the Indian attitude, and of the tribal ceremonies which are customary and continuous in the winter as well as in the summer months. And yet their very prayers for rain are called "barbaric" and "heathenish." The common attitude has been well expressed by Witter Bynner in one of a series on sonnets called *Santa Fe*:§

"We couldn't tell you, but we had a dance,"
Francisco said in Santa Fe one morning,
Santo Domingo had been given warning,
Like all the Indian villages and clans
In the United States, to take the chance
That whiter people take, an order scorning
The paint and fur and feather tips adorning
Dances for rain. Rain is a circumstance.
A salesman heard him, called him, "Come here, Joe.
You been to school? Better go back again
And learn to put an end to heathen tricks
And be Americans, be modern men".
Francisco, breathing, was a crucifix:

"We make the rain for you and you don't know." They dance stoically through the heat of summer, not only that they themselves may have rain, but that all their neighbors, persecutors and conquerors may have the blessing as well. "But we don't know!"

Even where it is luxuriant and tropical in Old Mexico, you will hear the natives sing a hymn for rain. In the capital city itself, step into the patio of certain of the public schools in the early evening and listen for a moment. A lovely song may be heard, rising from the throats of roomfuls of boys and girls who labor in the factories all day. The tune is one of the loveliest they know, and the words are, *"Agua le pido a mi Dios."* Later you will hear these same voices with many others in the Great National Theatre in the heart of the city—and on a certain Sunday a chorus of a thousand workers will join in the refrain of this same song on a hillside under the trees in the palace gardens at Chapultepec: "Water we pray of Thee, O God!" And every blind singer in the Republic, in every tropical village—on the sea coast or on the shores of inland lakes—will sing it to you with broken voice for a penny.

Until recently there were elaborate religious processions and festivals in Mexico, as in the Latin countries of Europe. And these often were public demonstrations to offer up prayers during times of drought or other calamity. But since such out-of-door religious events have been forbidden by the Mexican government, New Mexico is almost the only place on this continent where they may be witnessed. On De Vargas Day, on the Fiesta of St. Francis, and on Corpus Cristi Day, the Catholics of the entire countryside gather at the cathedral in *La Ciudad de la Santa Fe de San Francisco de Assisi,* and form one of the most spectacular of religious processions.

Led by the Archbishop and other high officials of the church, clad in resplendent vestments and accompanied by acolytes in white lace who carry candles and lanterns, the procession follows a high canopied throne on which is borne the Virgin, St. Francis, or the Body of Christ. And even the least interesting portion of the mile-long cavalcade is a fascinating picture. All the little girls in white dresses; all the little boys, trooping like ants; Indians in colorful attire, but somehow subdued; hundreds of sad-eyed women in dark dresses and long black shawls like Witches of Endor; and the men of an old race, blood of the conquerors.

A few years ago when the rain had not wet the earth for weeks upon weeks, and when the crops had died and the land and the people suffered, such a religious procession was held as a special plea for relief: a pilgrimage of the multitude from the church to a holy shrine on the outskirts of the village. The throngs marched in the heat across the pavements and along the dust of the country road to the chapel and back—but no rain came. The procession was formed again. The faithful stoically traversed the heated Holy Way a second time. And no rain came.

It is related that the few men who carried the sacred throne and who were perhaps touched with the heat, dashed from the church-yard with angry shouts before anyone could prevent them, kidnapping the Virgin!

Her golden tinsel was strewn on the street. Her holy image was hurled into the sandy river-bed by the faithless cowards. And heaven was so agitated over the blasphemous affair, that it gathered its clouds, hurled its thunderbolts, and poured its rain down in torrents, bringing to an end one of the longest and most terrible droughts that had ever been known!

............"Rain is a circumstance."

§ One of these sonnets was published in *The New Republic*, Dec. 5, 1923, and two of them in the *Laughing Horse*, December 1923.

Patricio Came

WILLARD JOHNSON

There was a gay hello from the gateway as Patricio came across the yard, greeting me at the door-sill with a hug— and over my shoulder his Indian eye saw, instantly, our new black drum. As happy as a little child, but accepting a cigarette as he went straight for the new-stretched hide, he raised and fondled it, bright-eyed, thumping it gently to test the tone; then sat down and looked at me with an approving smile.

The measured eat, the throb, began as softly as a woodpecker on a distant tree at night. And when he sang, his voice, pitched strangely high at first, began a song of soft staccatto monosyllables that blended slowly into a melody as wild as that of a savage, giant bird.

It was difficult at first to reconcile the furniture to alien noises, and to forget that only the walls, a few houses, and a mile or two of street separated him from the deserts and hills that had heard his cry long before even a Spanish horse had echoed along the stony canyons. Slowly, slowly I eased out of my modern pose; gradually I responded to rhythms as old as earth and as fresh as new leaves. Over the desert rim I saw the clouds shadow the hills on the horizon, gather and thunder, then disperse, leaving the gleaming plain hotter that it was before. I saw a line of dark skinned men emerge from a yellow kiva; I saw them dancing for rain in fringes of costume that danced around their naked bodies a rhythm wilder than the rhythm of the song. And I felt the throb of a burning sun, the throb of a

FIGURE 56. Spud Johnson, "Boy with Guitar," from *Laughing Horse,* no. 11 (1924).

hundred feet, and the throb of blood in my ears, as the drum-beats quickened to a pitch of frenzy—then stopped.

And there was Patricio in a chair made in a factory a year ago; and there was I, strangely enough, in trousers and coat, between a typewriter and a telephone.

FIGURE 58. Howard Cook (1901–80), cover for *Laughing Horse*, no. 14 (1927). A versatile painter and printmaker, Cook was a longtime resident of Taos, specializing in scenes of the New Mexico landscape.

FIGURE 57. *(opposite)* B. J. O. Nordfeldt, cover for *Laughing Horse*, no. 11 (1924).

FIGURE 59. Miguel Covarrubias, cover for *Laughing Horse*, no. 16. Covarrubias (1904–57) was a Mexican painter, writer, and anthropologist, whose inventive caricatures appeared in many magazines and books. He was in Taos in 1929.

FIGURE 60. Gustave Baumann, cover for *Laughing Horse*, no. 18. German-born Baumann (1881–1971) was a Santa Fe painter, woodblock printmaker, and woodcarver. His horse design, more like one of his wooden puppets than the stallions or centaurs of other *Laughing Horse* covers, reflects Baumann's highly refined skill as a carver.

CHAPTER 3

Laughing Horse's
Major Literary Contributors

I: WITTER BYNNER

Witter Bynner (1881–1968) became one of New Mexico's most durable literary figures. Born into a New England family of means, he received an exemplary education, traveled widely, and mingled with the great writers of his generation. His eighteen volumes of published verse, as well as his translations and prose pieces, made his name as well known at one point in American poetry as those of Carl Sandburg, Vachel Lindsay, and Edna St. Vincent Millay.

Bynner's association with Spud Johnson, variable in its intensity, lasted nearly fifty years. They met when Bynner began teaching literature at the University of California at Berkeley. Johnson, enrolled as a student, became an admirer and protege, enlisting Bynner's participation in *Laughing Horse*.

Some of Bynner's poetry appeared under his own name in *Laughing Horse*, but he also used the journal as a vehicle for perpetuating the notorious Spectra hoax. Bynner and his friend Arthur Davison Ficke (both bored with current "schools" of poetry) purely as a lark invented a new school of poetry they called Spectrism, "which tried to see the spectre in our life and capture the varied light of the spectrum."[1] Critics, poets, and the public, all eager to catch the latest literary wave, took Spectrism seriously. Bynner, writing under the pen name Emanuel Morgan, and Ficke, as Anne Knish, were only too happy to comply with the demand for Spectrist poems. Many were published in *Laughing Horse*, and the hoax was maintained until Bynner deliberately revealed it a few years later during a lecture.

Two of Bynner's Spectrist poems from *Laughing Horse* are amusing tributes to the iconoclastic spirit of the little magazine:

Little Fly

(A HITHERTO UNPUBLISHED
SPECTRIC POEM BY EMANUEL MORGAN)

Little fly,
For making a marriage bed
of my bald head,
you had to die.

The other one,
The one that escaped—
Was it Paolo
Or Francesca?

*Exclusive rights to the verse of Emanuel Morgan, founder of the Spectric school of poetry, have recently been granted *The Laughing Horse*. Mr. Morgan is the author of Spectra, and Pins for Wings, the latter of which first appeared in Reedy's Mirror.

More Little Flies

EMANUEL MORGAN

They tried to shoo the Laughing Horse
Not knowing it had wings
And could turn in air upon his course
Above terrestrial things.

If they had locked him as they wished
And bridled him their way,
His tail could never once have swished
As it easily does today.

Brushing aside the little flies
That buzz around his flanks—
They would like to eat his very eyes
Without a word of thanks.

But the Laughing Horse has wings beyond
Stupidity and stalls,
And leaves the flies and the stagnant pond
With leaps like waterfalls!

FIGURE 61. Spud Johnson and Witter Bynner in Santa Fe, c. 1922.
Photography Collection, Harry Ransom Humanities Research Center,
University of Texas at Austin.

When Johnson joined Bynner in Santa Fe in the summer of
1922, the pair quickly found a welcome in the budding literary
community at Santa Fe (Fig. 61). Alice Corbin, Lynn Riggs, and
Haniel Long became their close friends, meeting informally to
discuss life and literature. As Johnson recalled,

> We seemed to lapse so often into a Rabelaisian mood, that
> soon we were referring to ourselves as the Rabelais Club,
> which was quickly altered, since that sounded much too
> stodgy, to the simple informality of The Rabble."[2]

Beginning in 1923, only a year after his arrival in New Mexico, Bynner began to address the pressures for change which had already begun to invade the sleepy streets and the old attitudes of Santa Fe. Questioning the negative impact of efforts to boost, pave, enlarge, and "Americanize" the town, Bynner feared that defining, important differences would be erased.

The City of the Holy Faith of St. Francis

WITTER BYNNER

II.
Lead home your flock, St. Francis, mile by mile.
Gather, in the shadow of the sweetened nave,
The sinning, pioneering ghosts who gave
The halo of your name, the touch of your smile,
To a mountain town. And welcome up the aisle
These later townspeople. Help them to save
Their souls from the Satan waiting to deprave
New Adams with his terrible apples of guile.

See where he stands in the doorway. Mark him well,
A Salesman selling a pattern. Stare him down,
St. Francis. Conquer him with your moccasins,
With your burros and guitars, before he wins
Even your town, like every other town,
To the excellent machineries of hell.

A City of Change

WITTER BYNNER

Now and then, since a decade ago, travellers who had been taking a little extra trouble had been telling me of their reward. They said that Santa Fe, lying eighteen miles off the main line, had held its own against man and his mechanisms, had remained a city different from the rest, had escaped the American cooky-cutter which turns out cities one after another in approximately the same pattern. I was conscious of the sad fact that New Orleans, San Antonio, San Francisco and even Charleston had been changing, had been taking on, more and more, the one likeness. And when, three years ago, I came to the little ancient Capital, I came in time.

To be sure, the great oblong Plaza reaching the Cathedral had long since been cut in twain: half of it, the Cathedral end, solidified now into a Grecian bank, a Middle West department store and a New Mexican post office. On three sides of the surviving plaza were the usual haphazard and hideous fronts of an American business street, but on the fourth side the old Governors' Palace, massive adobes, seasoned pillars and *vigas* still held its ground; its *portales,* like a public cloister, still shaded one sidewalk, as they had formerly and properly shaded all four: and its *patio* was still a garden-spot with trees. On Sunday evenings when the band played, youths would stream in one direction round the Plaza and in the oppo-

(continued on following pages)

site direction maidens, just as apart from one another and just as aware of one another as I have seen them in Mexican cities. Older women moved nunlike, on Sundays or weekdays, with soft black shawls over their heads, the fringe hanging down their dresses. Burros came daily in droves with round burdens of firewood, or with riders from the country whose heels bumped lazily from a jiggling trot. Though there was no longer an open market in the Plaza, there was one street left where wagons, from ranches or from Indian villages, held corn, tomatoes, apples, melons and other fresh produce to be bought directly from the dark-eyed drivers. On the roads radiating from town were many views and few signboards. In doorways, on streetcorners, were many groups speaking Spanish and few speaking English. In the Legislature were interpreters nimbly moving from one member to another and nimbly re-phrasing remarks into English or Spanish. On the outlying hills were venturous artists in sombreros, corduroys and bright neckerchiefs. When Holy Days came, there were bonfires and the Virgin or St. Francis was carried through the streets by walking worshippers. And round about the landscape, in their snug, earthen *pueblos,* were Indians, guarding the dignity of their race and instinctively living the beauty of their religion and their art, as they had been doing for hundreds of years.

I had come in time.

Soon I had found my own adobe, one of the oldest, with a broadbeamed roof to shed homely dirt on me in windy weather and primitive rain in wet. I was above the troubled world. I was washed clean of the war. I was given communion each night when sunset would elevate the host on the Sangre de Cristo mountains. I was writing to friends who lived on another planet. I had found something not to be found elsewhere in These States, a town too much itself to be feverishly imitating its neighbors. Nothing strained, nothing silly just an honest-to-God town, seasoned and simple, easily breathing its high air.

And now what?

We Americans from the outside have quickly made of Santa Fe the city of our discontent. It must be boosted, paved, enlarged, it must be Americanized. The streets which were rough and made us go slowly are smooth now and make us go fast. The native earth which used to touch our feet on the edge of the Plaza is being sealed out of sight, out of touch. These pavements may grow machines now, but not persons. The little adobe houses near the Plaza have cast down their grassy crowns before a bulk of garages, garages in the Santa Fe style, yes, but inviting blatant vehicles which hurry people's errands and harden their faces. Even the Virgin this year, because it rained, took her annual outing in a limousine. There is a red aeroplane in town. Will she come to that, if it rains next year? The Ascension of the Virgin! A faint ambition to restore the *portales* encounters practical objection from the shopkeepers; but it may in the end be realized, not because *portales* lend beauty but because they attract tourists. Someone built a movie house in the style of a Pueblo Mission; someone else hired it and closed it to prevent competition with a movie house built like an oven. The band still plays on Sunday evenings, but the boys and girls walk now as they like. There are fewer and fewer black shawls, fewer and fewer burro riders. The free market place opposite Burro Alley is a thing gone and forgotten; it was unfair to the grocers. There are no more Indian pots to be seen and advantageously bought in the patio of the New Museum: it was unfair to the curio-dealers. The outlying views are flecked and flanged now with billboards. There are camp-grounds for the tourists and the contourists. Spanish gives way to English on the streets and soon in the Legislature. Eagle-eyed artists have motors and gather visitors into exhibition-parlours. Even those who persist with the sombrero and the flying scarf serve, it seems, a commercial end. "At first," said an old resident, "we respectable people used to resent the freakish, free-and-easy clothes you artists wear about town; but we have found that it attracts and amuses the tourists; and if you can stand it, we can."

We are all doing it. We can not help ourselves. We are attracting people here. We are advertising. We are boosting. We can not care enough that, by professionalizing the apparent difference of Santa Fe, we are killing the real difference. We are crowding out the natives, to make room for improved houses with artificial warpings. We are changing our town from the city different to the city indifferent. Even the Indians are feeling us, are yielding to us. Being Americans, we have to manage our neighbors. And it is always for their good. A few years ago, the Pueblos conducted their own deliberations and maintained their own character. Because of their simplicity, they were threatened with unjust loss of their lands. Not only Santa Fe but the country at large came to their rescue, spurring

Congress to pass at last needful legislation. As to their lands, the Pueblos are much better off than they were a few years ago; but almost any month now, a non-Indian with a child-like face and a flowing tie may be found steam-rolling an Inter-Pueblo Council according to his whim and writing letters for them in imitation Indian. Other outsiders, to serve other ends, are following his example. And what shall it profit the Pueblos to win their land if they lose their way? We in Santa Fe, for the sake of their health and their lives, are persuading some of them, in spite of their medicine-men, to benefit by the services of a visiting nurse. And while we thus discourage a therapeutic element of their religion, the Protestant missionary, less tolerant than his Catholic brother, is urging the Indian bureau to discourage an aesthetic element. While our own white medicine-men are saying to the Navajo, "Come away from the former things, you cannot be a guest at the heathen sings and be a member of Christ's church in good standing," our archaeologists, artists and merchants are busily summoning Indians to Santa Fe and to Gallup for a theatrical presentation of the dances and ceremonies which have hitherto been a communal and at their best a spiritual exercise. Last year, for this friendly exploitation, we cut down trees in the patio of the Governors' Palace and made it bleak with bleachers.

To "attract and amuse the tourists," to make a show of our town, are we cutting down and withering its beauty? Are we killing and embalming the best qualities of Santa Fe, in order that a long line may come and look?

Enough of pessimism.

Not long ago, at a meeting in Santa Fe, when a project was broached that some of the ablest Indian painters be sent as art teachers to the Pueblos, a zealous collector of old pottery, objected on the ground that such teachers might spread among the villages designs which belonged from antiquity in one or another particular region and which should therefore be sequestered at the source. As though the source were not Montezuma or Kubla Khan or the sun itself!

And so it is with Santa Fe. I have been talking like a collector of old pottery, of old shards. I have been talking as our friend did at the meeting, when he concluded, "It is unfortunate but true that art grows."

Cities grow, for the worse and for the better. A motorcar will some day be as quaint a sight as the old wagon over Candelario's. And he who rode in that old wagon was doubtless a shrewd trader; he may have told Indians about the Gospel and corrupted their art with beads. The wagon in its time took man away from the touch of the earth, so that he transferred healthful exercise from his own legs to those of a horse. No wonder the skull of the horse is still laughing, alongside the motor-road.

Lovers and old women and artists and Indians! Why should youth forever follow an ancient and unnatural custom? Why should the boys and the girls pass on opposite ways of the street? Why should old women be draped funereal before the *velorio*? Why should artists, or merchants either, be grudged their livelihood? Why should Indians give their corn or their cattle for a song that fails to cure? Why should those dance faith who had rather dance jazz? Are unbelievers more dignified in a dance than they are in a pew—or are believers less dignified in Santo Domingo than they are in Washington? The Pueblos have long danced their dances before Catholic altars and added an older beauty to the beauty of the saints. Will it hurt them to bring some of that beauty into an American town, just as the Acoma Mission has come beautifully to town in the shape of the New Museum? Or will it hurt the town to take what it likes from the Indian, from the Spaniard, from the Greek, from the Mexican, from the Middle West? There are more kinds of vitality here after all than are dreamt of in a sentimental philosophy. It is an abode not only for a collector of pots but for a collector of life. And as Heracleitus noted long ago, and a collector of pots long after him, life changes.

Besides Santa Fe, Bynner's other favorite place of residence between 1923 and his death in 1968 was Chapala, Mexico. After a first visit with Spud and the Lawrences in 1923, he spent most winters and wrote some of his best poetry there (Fig. 62). Both his Mexican verse and prose pieces reflect a deeply held belief that Mexico was a needed antidote to the societal arrogance he saw north of its borders.

FIGURE 62.
Spud Johnson
photographed by
Witter Bynner at the
American Club,
Guadalajara, 1923.
Photography Collection,
Harry Ransom
Humanities Research
Center, University of
Texas at Austin.

In a Mexican Hospital

WITTER BYNNER

Am I sick then? Or blessedly dead
In the shadow of a pepper-tree?
But this is no stealthy funeral tread
Escorting me.

In the room next to mine a guitar,
A man singing verse after verse,
And now and then, softly joining in a bar,
A boy and a nurse.

Since life is as happy as this
And heaven may not be, nor hell,
Who but a fool would take it amiss
And refuse to be well!

Sad songs? Yes, I know,
For I learned from an old Chinese
Eternities of melodious woe
And aeons of ease.

There is a country north of here
In which I think of a room,
As rich and smooth and carven and drear
As a marble tomb.

Where never a voice could be raised
For raising of the dead.
If I were there—but, heaven be praised,
I'm here instead.

And near me the strings of the moon
Are humming in the sky,
And the doctor is singing some of the tune,
And so am I:

"Tomorrow again it will rain
And tomorrow again it will shine,
And so may the world be rid of pain
Like mine."

While the Train Pauses at Torreón

Frederico Gamboa, when a member of Huerta's cabinet, worsted Wilson's Secretary of State, Bryan, in an exchange of notes; but, better than that, he is a Mexican author.

I happen to be on the same train with him when he arrives at Torreón in the State of Chihuahua. At the station, an expert band is playing him welcome; and between banners which hail him as "la gloria de las letras Mexicanas," he is being led by officials, on a national holiday, into this town of cotton, flour and iron mills.

What such flowering of the spirit has my own country to offer amidst all the massive mechanics of its civilization?

When we Americans come to Mexico humbly, when we forget to criticize the railroads, the hotels, the clothes, the mechanical status of the country, when we open our hearts and minds to the conscious earth that resists vulgarities, to the courtesy, the innate intelligence, the quiet force, the ease, the quickness, the sensitiveness, the endurance, the smile of these people, we shall begin to appreciate the nearness to our borders of a natural university for our youth. Unfortunately, the nearer Mexicans come to the aforesaid borders, the more rapidly they learn the gist of what we to the north of them know and the more deplorably they forfeit both outer and inner grace.

All this is being jotted down while the train still pauses

(continued on following pages)

at Torreón, while Gamboa's gesture of appreciation is still in the air; but the record is no momentary impulse, it is the result of a year of months spent in Mexico during 1923 and 1925.

Be it said at once that I am for the most part puzzled by Mexican aristocracy and officialdom and by the bourgeoisie. These classes seem in many ways unworthy of their supposed inferiors. With notable exceptions, they turn to Europe or to the United States for inspiration or example, when, obviously, they need to trust and cultivate the basic qualities of their own race. It is the Mexican Indians who challenge and deserve homage: human beings as graceful and rewarding as corn, as self-sustaining and self-defending as cactus, as violent and quick to change as Mexican sky, as firm and slow to change as Mexican mountains. From them be it hoped, comes future Mexico. From them comes a spirit of civilization strange to motorists. From them come wisdom and laughter, a proportioned sense of the values of life, a power to work when work is necessary, a power to endure when endurance is necessary, a power to oppose when opposition is necessary, to smile and live and fight at happy intervals and to loaf magnificently when the earth commands.

Yes, these are qualities under the sun and moon. But under government, under the economic harness in which the world is driven, how are they then, these Mexicans? How are these estimable Indians as officials, as governmental instruments? They are like the Chinese. They are often enough honest grafters. They speak hypocrisies on occasion, but they also take occasion to wink. They fill the heart, the stomach and the pocket as conveniently as they can, but almost always they exercise therewith the morality of humor. They are not like Anglo-Saxons, "weaned on pickles," grimly swallowing scruples and using a Christian cookbook to explain unholy diet. Our American humor is too frequently a humor of fear lest the other fellow laugh first, a defensive humor lest we be thought slow or stupid or sensitive or tender or decent or just. Mexican humor, humor among the Mexican Indians is more natural, more vital, more imaginative. The Mexican Indian is often obscene, but with the earth's obscenity, often cruel, but with the earth's cruelty; lest he might succeed in becoming pompous or pretentious or greedy, in ways false to his bit of substance with the earth.

Besides his sense of humor, he has an awareness that, in the long run and in the large sense, justice is inevitable. Revolutions may have helped in the lesson. He may close one eye, but he seldom closes both eyes.

It has been said of Señor Calles, President of the Republic, that he manipulates the national law to indulge his own career and pocket and of Señor Zuno, recently Governor of Jalisco, that he put the Guadalajara streetcars out of business because he controlled the supply of buses; just as it has been said of Mr. Coolidge, President of the United States, that he would have preferred to retain rascals in his cabinet and of Mr. Mellon, Secretary of our Treasury, that because he and his family are major beneficiaries of the aluminum trust, he grossly favors it.

Let us assume, for purposes of comparison, that these charges are true, both in Mexico and in the United States.

In Mexico there is an important offset. The public, the consumer, may in both countries be robbed with the left hand. Obregon and Fall may both own ranches which they never earned by service to the state. Yet in America, the aggrandizement at the moment is all one way. President Coolidge removes from this and that public commission members who might act as watchdogs for public interest against private interest. He has given, otherwise, ample evidence of believing that there is no public interest of the many, except through the preferred private interest of the few. His disregard of the ordinary citizen's welfare is implacable, whole-souled and complete. In Mexico a few important pockets may be neatly and unduly lined, but on the whole the ordinary citizen looms higher and higher as a conscious and considerable decider of Mexican destiny. The Mexican laborer is being handed the beginnings of a real education, not merely pious bunk but the facts of economics and the satisfactions of art; land has been given him, and now he is to receive the water and the tools to make it yield; the professional military college is to be closed or curtailed and the workers of the country are to be depended upon for an army. In a word, the Mexican people, against temporary obstacles and confusion and outside interference, are more and more becoming the state. North of them, that state is more and more being substituted for the people. There may be more melancholy on the Mexican Main Street than on ours; there is also more happiness, more awareness of lasting values in other things than oil. And though America may officially protest to Mexico that its appropriation of moneys for educational purposes is excessive, Mexico insists upon teaching its own people in its own way.

It is conceivable that Gamboa was being welcomed to Torreón as a politician; but it is not inconceivable that the banners meant what they said, that he was being welcomed as a man of letters. It is conceivable that ex-Governor Zuno of Jalisco may not have been averse to his own welfare; it is incontestable that, besides easing and bettering the life of Jalisco laborers, he has reopened the University of Guadalajara after its long desuetude and has even offered a free Mexican trip to the winner of an American poetry contest. American Governors please notice.

There are bandits in the United States as well as in Mexico. There is oil in Mexico as well as in the United States. There is civilization in both countries, each after its kind and each complementary, though not always complimentary, to the other.

II: MABEL DODGE LUHAN

Complex, talented, difficult, Mabel Dodge Luhan (1879–1962) became one of the best known of the many memorable characters who populated Taos (Fig. 63). In the course of a forty-year friendship, she and Spud Johnson came to know each other intimately. Mabel was his hostess, employer, literary contributor, and confidante, though the relationship (as with most of Mabel's associates) was stormy from time to time.

While still at Berkeley Spud began to hear from Bynner about the notorious Taos doyenne. They met during the summer of 1922 when Bynner and Johnson spent a good part of July at Los Gallos, Mabel's Taos home (Fig. 64). During that time and in the following years she befriended Spud, eventually luring him away from Bynner to work as her secretary.

While Bynner and Luhan feuded, competing with each other for prominence on the literary turf of New Mexico, Johnson took pains to remain on good terms with both of them. Once established at Taos, he typed Mabel's manuscripts and correspondence, gave her literary advice, and wrote about his new patron. Over the next thirty-five years he did much to enhance Mabel's literary reputation. As her biographer, Lois Palken Rudnick, writes,

The popular image that established Mabel as a cross between Madame de Stael and George Sand had much to do with the public relations work of Spud Johnson. . . .In a typical article, Spud wrote of her as "a woman who has left her mark on her century. . . . One of the first salonniers of her time, an international figure, she has known most of

FIGURE 63. Mabel Dodge Luhan, c. 1930s. Photography Collection, Harry Ransom Humanities Research Center, University of Texas at Austin.

FIGURE 64. Portal, Mabel Dodge Luhan house, Taos. Photography Collection, Harry Ransom Humanities Research Center, University of Texas at Austin.

the world's creative artists of the twentieth century, fostered and influenced not a few."[3]

Published between 1923 and 1931, Mabel's six articles for *Laughing Horse* reflect her growing attachment to the Southwest. "Beware the Grip of Paganism!," originally published in the *New York American*, was written in the first flush of her enthusiasm at being in New Mexico. Based on her visit to a Santo Domingo Corn Dance, it reflects a highly romantic, primitivist view of Pueblo life. Johnson reprinted it in *Laughing Horse,* no. 16 (1929), calling it "too good to be lost in the back files of a metropolitan daily."

"Beware the Grip of Paganism!"

"Bosh? Don't be too sure. For if Santo Domingo's Indian drummer gets you under his spell—well, you'll surrender in spite of yourself and become a savage dancer, too!" —Original Caption.

MABEL DODGE

The sun is pouring down and taking the night chill from the air. The sun and the air alone make life sufficiently rich. The sky reaches down to the round horizon, from the darkest cobalt to a light turquoise blue where the purple hills, shaven clear of trees, makes a rippling edge to the great earthen bowl that holds us.

Santo Domingo, a village of a thousand of the oldest and most conservative Indians, lies completely at ease on the plain. The one-story mud houses are older than anyone living can know. The Spanish church—standing apart and facing the village like a father before his family—is comparatively modern, with its Sixteenth Century date.

The village lies in three long streets. A Kiva, or sacred dwelling for communal meetings and religious ceremonials, waits at each end.

(continued on following pages)

The houses are whitewashed inside; on the outside they are so exactly the color of the soil that they are only distinguishable by inky black shadows that they cast.

There is no green anywhere; this life is all red and magenta and blue and orange against a pink and tawny background. But sometimes a green of the sharpest emerald color cuts through the hot shades of an Indian dress.

It is very still here. The tempo is molto largo.

We can hear the ponies in the nearby corrals and a cock or two is crowing. Some woman is grinding corn between two stones; a group of young men are singing with heads close together; the blue smoke rises from a dozen chimneys against the pink brown earth. The sun pours and pours down until it has penetrated every damp and dreary place. There are no bad smells in this land; there are no ugly sounds here; there are no awkward ways of life.

All is serene—and ennobled by the sun.

Fifteen miles away we see two Indians moving like sticks across the hills: we can hear a woman laugh a mile away. A thousand souls are at ease here. There is sun—air—color—beauty—in space and time.

"Lord, we have done as thou hast commanded, and yet there is room."

A hundred white pigeons are circling around and around over the Pueblo.

We go into the houses with their white walls and heavy beamed ceilings. The beds are mattresses around the walls, and are covered with bright blankets in the daytime. The most biting magenta and vermilion blankets and scarves hang on a rope across one end, the saddles are polished and hung on posts. Near the end of the room hangs a picture of a bleeding Christ—and next it is painted a triumphant sun symbol.

Everywhere Indians are leaning against the sun-soaked walls. They are wrapped in striped blankets and with red handkerchiefs tying back their black hair. They salute gravely: "How."

Here comes a row of six men, singing. They walk in a rhythmical beat up one street and down the next and up the last. They sing, announcing to all that the corn dance will begin soon. They pass from sun to shade and sun to shade: sometimes they are against the turquoise sky— black haired, red skinned and flaming dressed. In the shadow they are black like Spanish painted things.

The people gather on their roofs, a long line of color against the burning blue; the sun shines in their eyes: they cover their mouths with their blankets, sitting and standing immovable.

Soon we hear the drum throbbing. This is the most exciting sound ever heard. It is like hearing the sun beat. It goes right through one in waves—heating one. All around is the dark immobile race, waiting while the drum beats the sun through them in waves of hot sound. They make a living vessel to contain the dancers—they hold the dancers in living walls—pulsating but motionless.

A hundred men are beating out the dance, it is a dance of the sun energy converted into a man form. Millions of feathers and bells and shells fly and ring on a hundred men, the feet caress the earth or stamp fiercely.

They sing and sing and turn and bend; the sun-beats of

the drum support and carry them; they are not separate from each other or from the sun. They are all one, and the earthen houses and silent watchers are one with them.

The hour goes on; the sun climbs in the blue. It is noon. The pigeons circle around. It seems to us that we are losing our identity; we are becoming one with the sound and the sun-beats. The movement has become one with the movement of our breathing—we float in it; we are living in rhythm—we are rhythm. There is no more you or me, or hot or cold, or dark or light. There is only sun-beat.

The Spanish bell in the church tower sounds with shivering agitation . . . We look up from the bottom of our bowl and see two Indian youths pummeling the bell with leather mallets. It is noon. The sun has reached the limit of its climbing, and the dancers slow down, and gradually the waves of sound and heat diminish, letting it easily die. The dancers leave, trotting; the people disappear into their houses. They will eat and rest now.

Only the sun is left in the village street—only the black shadows and the burning sun. The sun behind the sun has retired; the life of the sun will rest now.

In the afternoon we climb the hill until we reach the tableland, up the narrow trail we go till we come to great plains above our bowl. Here we can see for miles and miles. Here we can see how happy Santo Domingo is— lying in the bowl, resting. No movement comes from it save the blue chimney smoke. We lie on the hot earth of the hill and rest too. The dancers have beaten out our latent sun life—we flowed with them in a hundred million sun waves. They have danced for us until we are empty of our sun stored life . . they have danced us and all the watchers weary. . . we are empty now. We will be filled again if we lie in the sun on the hill and let it fill us with a fresh abundance. So we become refreshed and renewed and gather a new energy. So the women can let life pour through them as they become beaten into the dance on the waves of sun sound. So the men remain strong and fierce— always filled with the sun life.

In the evening the warm moon streams on the Pueblo. We go down the street whispering. Everyone speaks low. Lights shine out of all the houses, for groups of dancers will visit every house.

We follow the feathered dancers:—the leader squats on the ground and beats the drum while seven young men move together as one and sing a strong song. The babies are asleep in perfect security. All the people gleam and glow like coals in the light from the open fire—they are hot and glowing and happy. Soon it is finished and we follow them out to the next house.

But in the street we see a group of black naked bodies shining like ebony in the moonshine. These are warriors with emerald green helmets and turquoise jewels. They are bound with branches of fir. They are painted black and carry notched clubs. They are very fierce, for they have evoked in themselves the sleeping madness and cruelty of men. They are panting from their own darkness and wildness—they issue forth from their inner fastnesses as they sing and dance the war rhythm. They are letting loose all the buried life of hate. As they go from house to house, they leave a new trail behind them. On this trail float out old days and old antagonisms. The air smolders and grows heavy—the eyes are gleaming now, the brows are scowling.

Here come three jokers. Three half-nude boys in masks are singing now in the heavy air. They are imitating the Mexican traders and soon everyone laughs and rocks with amusement. The air clears. All becomes very gay and light again. "Noch, noch!" ("Again, again!") everybody begs, and they repeat their imitation again and again.

Happy! Happy!

"Let us stay outside in the moonlight, Gregorio."

"Yes, we sit here."

So we sit close together on the plaster wall of the porch and watch the coming and going. To north and south and east and west drums beat and groups of singers chant the life of the people to the people. The singers and the listeners are one—it is in common.

The moon cuts the streets into black angles. Silent men move up and down. The night air is cold, but intensely alive. Here is real living.

All around the pointed hills leap up to join the moon. The light is so intense that purple triangles mark their deep indentures.

The moon has reached its centre now. It has come to where we saw the sun twelve hours ago. It is time to rest again. Gregorio points to the centred moon.

"You sleepy?"

"Yes. Now we sleep."

The streets are nearly empty now. The lights go out one by one.

We move away in the sandy street.
Everyone sleeps.

Mabel's essay "The Door of the Spirit" appeared in *Laughing Horse* in 1923, the year she married Tony Luhan. By that time she was much more familiar with Pueblo life but was still trying to understand the subtleties of their social dynamic. In this article she follows the process of decision-making in the Pueblo, responding to the poetic life-force she finds in their architecture, dress, and voices.

The Door of the Spirit

MABEL LUHAN

The councilmen were meeting in the governor's house to talk about a door.

Now, you know, Taos Pueblo builds up irregularly in clock houses and forms two great community houses of pyramidal shape with the river coming down the mountain and running between them. The Indians cross from one side to the other over two foot-bridges made of logs thrown across, and on one very good wagon-bridge.

These low, rambling houses look like pyramids from whichever direction one sees them. They rise five stories high and spread out a good deal at the bottom. From a dis-

(continued on following pages)

tance of five miles or more out in the desert, they point up like two breasts—and looking down upon them from the steep side of the Pueblo mountain that broods forever over them, they draw up like two of its foot-hills, earth-colored. They were reared there out of the land that forms them, and there they endure unchanging. That they have kept their pyramid shape through thousands of years, with the Indians living and dying and being born again and building more rooms on every year as old ones fall down, is a thing that everyone wonders about; but I don't wonder about it any more after this night of which I am going to tell you.

I was waiting there outside because Tony was in the council. The door the Indians were meeting to talk about was in the neighbor's house next to his mother's, so he had to be there, too. All I knew about it was that this neighbor wanted to move his door from the east side of his house to the north side. To do this he needed the consideration and approval of the governor and his whole council of old men: the Cacique, who has, by heredity, almost unlimited power, and the war-chief with his lieutenants. No one in the Pueblo is able to add to his house, or build a new house or even build an oven outside somewhere without all these people meeting together to talk it over and pass judgment on it—maintaining the form!

Why do they want to keep the pyramid form, anyway? I don't know why. And maybe they don't know, either, for it was judged necessary to build it that way so very long ago that perhaps the reason is forgotten and it is up to them merely to conserve. Well, they do it. Passionately, persistently, and with the fire of the spirit. When this fire of spirit is still in men to preserve something, it endures.

This night that I was out there was one of those still moon-lit evenings when everything seems changed into something else. You know how it is—one loses one's customary sense of things, and yet the reality before one is no less intense than the one at home in the fire-lit room—it is perhaps more intense for not being so familiar, yet seeming so crystal-clear and full of significance.

The governor's house has one small window without glass, for there is no glass in pueblo windows except in the church. Once I asked Tony why they allowed glass there if not in their houses, and he replied: "But that is a different religion, you see." The governor's door was narrow, and from where I was I could watch it swing open and let in one shrouded figure after another, passing into the broad beam of light thrown out by the unshaded oil lamp and the fire.

The moonlight fell so that half the house was in black shadow, including the door corner; and the rest of the adobe walls were softly glowing. The window cut out a high yellow square from the blackness. It was so very simple, that picture, no detail. A square house jutting out from the dark mass of the whole structure, the little yellow lighted window and the moon-lit wall, the door opening and shutting in the shadow, throwing out a path of warm light as, one after another, the Indians silently opened it and passed within, an air of serious celebration and a something withdrawn, inwardly concentrated, about each figure. They wear their blankets until they are soft with repeated washings so that they mould the body easily, clinging to the head, and flowing back over the left shoulder. Some wear white and some pale grey, and a few of the blankets are brilliant and patterned.

The room filled. They gathered there quickly after the war-chief called them from the roof of his house, his voice reaching all through the Pueblo into dim out-of-the-way rooms and farthest corners. The Indians always hear these calls, announcements, summons, no matter where they are in the Pueblo. They don't stop talking and listen or stop in their work, but they all hear and understand, and obey. And the crier on the house knows how to throw his voice so that it will reach the one who hides as easily as the one next door.

All the old men were gathered within. The door was left open and their voices flowed out gentle and vibrant like the beam of light. At first they were merely chatting together as they assembled, seating themselves on low white-covered couches around the walls, smoking and laughing a little.

But when they were all there a silence came. Then a single voice in some kind of prayer or exhortation arose, calm, contained, a majesty in it; and after that all the voices, murmuring. Then the young men came, singly and in twos and threes, padding on quiet moccasins out of the gloom, swathed in white wrappings, only their eyes showing. They stopped below the window to overhear what was going on inside. There is no secret diplomacy in the Pueblo regime. Everything is open.

The light from the window fell on the white figures. These people know instinctively how to move, how to stand. Their attitudes at that hour and in that light seemed to betoken a mysterious participation in some ceremony unknown to me. Anyway, beautiful, beautiful, the whole atmosphere beautiful and strange and significant beyond usual things, and a queer chill crept over me as I watched, for I felt the beauty and the strangeness, and I wondered. "Tis the beauty, not the terror, turns the traveler's heart to stone."

Inside the room the old men's voices murmured together, rising and falling in that cosmic sound. Sometimes one voice would rise over the others in a priestly note of exhortation or warning, but it was always measured, rhythmic.

The white figures in the group below would melt away, others would take their places. These spoke no word to each other but, approaching, would stare in silence into each other's quiet eyes trying to fathom the identity, not touching, not moving, as each searched and raked the soul confronting him. Then satisfied that he had penetrated the personality in the other's eyes, one would make way. They respect, utterly, the anonymity of the night.

The old men's voices flowed on, a river of sound, and the rhythm emerged to the listener. This was, somehow, cosmic music. Over on the bridges the young boys sang happy songs in the moonlight. Against the wise and secure old men's voices, the young voices soared like lark-music. Contrapuntal. And how enhanced by the river water! How many thousands of years have the Indians known that voices over water make their songs lovelier?

The night was very quiet, as if it listened too. The moon sailed on, smiling. The old men wove their spell.

Once my companion moved to the window during a

momentary absence of listeners there, and beckoned me to come and look in. "Tony is right opposite the window and is amazing." I went to the window and saw on Tony's face a look of exaltation. It was vivid and illumined, his eyes raised to the wall opposite him.

The hours crept by and yet they did not seem long. They did not seem like hours, anyway. Time was unbound. And from that roomful of old men a revivifying spirit issued, refreshing and restoring the psyche.

Sometime near midnight there was a pause. Several Indians came out, and Tony came up to the place where I sat. "Are you all right? Not cold?" he asked. "No, but Tony, what are they talking about?" I whispered eagerly. "About that door," he answered, and returned to the house.

Again that cosmic murmur filled the air and passed into one's deeper consciousness and did something good for one. Then, all at once, I had a realization. "It's not that *door* that it's all about," I said to myself. "That's only a point of focus. But there's something else underlying what they are doing. This is a tribal expression, they are making something, continuing something that is alive. They themselves live by their creation. This is *their kind* of 'creative work.' Altogether they are projecting some essential life-giving energy and each one gives and each one receives of it."

A council meeting? Then I though of our council meetings our committee meetings, our Leagues of Nations, and I wondered if they, too, have an underlying life of their own that is spun out all unconsciously, while we *think* we're meeting to carry on grave discussions of this and that. But our meetings don't animate us and refresh us. Why not?

At about two o'clock I gave in to a feeling for sleep and went home. Tony stayed there until early morning and finally came back looking intensified and strengthened.

"Well, did they decide to move that door from east to north?" I asked him.

"Oh, yes," he said, "The meeting was to decide that."

In a similarly romantic manner Mabel wrote in "From the Source" (1924) of the Indian's position at the center of existence, a theme she would return to repeatedly in her writings. Here she calls for Euro-Americans to stop trying to impose time and change on the people she calls the "first and oldest receivers of human life":

From the Source

MABEL LUHAN

"What a wise old face on that Indian! Is he looking at us and reflecting on the difference between him and ourselves? Is he thinking perhaps how queer we are?"

No, for Indians do not reflect very much. That is not their way. They do not think and analyze and contrast things. But there is a reflection in his face. The reflection of a deep undisclosed, unconscious process that rises and becomes the static map that is his face. His face is the crystallized reflection of his being: your face is the perpetual changing surface of your consciousness.

No, he does not *think* you are queer. Indians do not think very much except in groups. Yet they *know*. Indians utter truth sometimes unreflectively, quietly, like bubbles rising to the surface of a lake.

One day an Indian said to me: "God put all the little animals on the earth each in his own place and with his own way of doing. The birds in the air, the fishes in the water and things moving on dry land. And they all stayed where He told them to stay. Everything wants to stay in itself. God told them not to change.

"Then after the animals He put the Indians on this earth, and after that the white people. But they were separated by something. By time. Indians have no time. They have never had any time. Now the white people He told them to change. And so *changing* began when the white

(continued on following pages)

people came in the world. But He had told the Indians to be themselves, not to change. He never put change in the Indians. The white people have to change; that is their way, so they must try and change everything. They take God's animals and change them from one thing to another. And even they want to change peoples and nations and will not let them be. All their religion is in machinery to change things, and now they want to change the Indians —even though God has told them to stay Indian."

"And in what is the religion of the Indian?" I asked him.

"To get life and keep life," he answered.

Receptors, maybe. Reservoirs. That there is a bubbling, ever new life in them, no one denies. They are close to the source. We are at the periphery of the circle of life—dangerously widening it, perhaps—but the Indians have stayed at the centre. Why should we try and draw them away from that centre?

Does any other race in the world today receive life at its immediate, pristine source? If we draw them away from that center, who, then, will fulfill their part in the whole? They are the first and oldest receivers of human life, and from them it passes in widening circles until it reaches us. It does not seem credible that power passes *back and forth* from race to race; it is more likely that it goes *forth* only, in an unbroken, lawful succession.

History begins when succession in time begins and the Indians are in a real, literal sense pre-historic, pre-time, ahead of time, so to speak. Are they not the guarantors of our endeavors? Because they are not coming or going, but abiding only, passing on the power of life that we may become the "time binders" and supermen. Because the oldest, ever pristine race remains faithful, the new age may be born.

We think and feel outwards, as light leaves the sun in arrowy rays. The oriental thinks and feels inward, as arrows to the sun. But the Indian remains at the sun's heart—neither thinking nor feeling. Worshipping...... receiving.

So they call him static. Because he does not move outwards nor inwards. He is pure motion without direction. And that we may travel as light travels, the Indian must remain motionless at the centre, transmitting the power to move.

In 1924 Mabel's poem "The Ballad of a Bad Girl" appeared in *Laughing Horse*, no. 10. She described it to her friend Carl Van Vechten as "an earnest appeal to women to leave off trying to steal the world away from men."[4] The "very, very angry man/With blue, blue eyes and a red, red crest" is clearly D. H. Lawrence, who had spent a turbulent period as her guest in Taos in 1922 and 1923. Following a winter in England, he returned to New Mexico in the spring of 1924. Determined to please him better than she had during his first stay, Mabel wrote this poem, paralleling her real-life flight from an unhappy childhood to seek an identity in the larger world and in esoteric knowledge. Behind the parodic lines of the poem are her own efforts to find and challenge a male divinity, only to be rebuffed by God [Lawrence in the poem] and kicked rudely back to earth.

Women, she concludes, are made for mothering and must give up the vain search for patriarchal control. Was Lawrence pleased at Mabel's overtly submissive gesture? No specific response is recorded, except for the illustration Lawrence provided to accompany the poem in *Laughing Horse*.

The Ballad of a Bad Girl

MABEL LUHAN

When I was a baby Mother pushed me from my cradle.
But I didn't fall! Oh no, sir? Tho' it's odd, odd, odd.
I snatched up in the hall Father's silver-headed walking-stick
And a-straddle it I hastened after God, God, God.

I flew, flew, flew on the silver-headed cane.
Little girls and women were gaping down below,
Higher, higher, higher, past the Higherarchy.
(Mother didn't know of it till Father told her so.
But she didn't care!)

I passed the seven cycles of the old, old men,
All the ancient mariners were gathered safe in rows,
Safely making magic to keep the world a-going,
And from them I found out things no other woman knows.

I passed the ducky angels all busy with their songs,
No way to tell the boys from the girls, girls, girls,
Together they were making the music of the spheres,
And they all wore dresses and they all wore curls.

(continued on following pages)

In these airy regions it was fun, fun, fun!
Honey-cake and ether was a sweet, sweet fare,
And every day I higher went among the secret-masters,
(I'd left my doll below but I didn't care.)

I was lost among the stars and I was glad I was lost.
For I was learning things I'd have never learned in school;
Higher mathematics is to put it very mildly!
(The last thing I'd learned on earth was called the
      Golden Rule.

THE BAD GIRL IN THE PANSY BED   by D.H.L.

But I forgot that up there.)
For eons and eons I spiralled thro' the heavens
Father died raving, and Mother? Mother married again.
And sometimes, very queerly, in the middle of a secret,

Way down below upon the earth I felt a little pain.
But that was not important. I kept going, going, going,
Pushing past all barriers and beyond locked gates.
I dodged three grey-haired ladies who all looked
          very knowing,
Somebody whispered: "Those are the Fates."

And then one day!......(Heavens, what a day for me!)
I pushed past a curtain to where God lay fast asleep.
I knew I'd finally found Him and forever, ever, ever.
And I knew He had the secret that it wasn't His to keep!

Very, very warily I stole to His shinning side
Ready to plunge my eager hand within his burning breast,
When out of His heart there up and jumped a very, very
          angry man.
With blue, blue eyes and a red, red crest.
"Quit that! Get out of here! Down, down, down you go!
Back, back to earth to where you belong.
This is no place for women here! Don't you know your
          business?
You took the wrong turning, and you're wrong, wrong,
          wrong!"

He pointed a freckled finger down, and I looked down there.
Down, down, down again? How could I go?
But all of a sudden I forgot my lovely secrets
For it ached me, it ached me, the little pain I'd left below.

But that man! He didn't care a bit! He raised a foot and
          threatened,

"You-clear-out-of-here! Get t' hell, hell, hell!"
I looked amazed and waited but he meant it, oh, he meant it!
While I looked he gave a kick and I fell, fell, fell!

Well, I fell, and I fell, and I fell, fell, fell.
Never any end to it at all, at all, at all.
On the way I learned a secret, the best one of any,
That a *Woman* can be saved by a fall, fall, fall!

Something made me sorry for what had taken place.
I took my father's silver cane and put it in the hall.
Then I lay down in the pansy bed and whispered:
   "Mother! mother me,
And teach me how to mother and that's all, all, all!"

Following the 1926 publication of *The Plumed Serpent*,
Lawrence's Mexican novel of power, love and transformation,
Mabel published an article—not a review, but a portrait of
Lawrence—in *Laughing Horse*. Knowing that she was a partial
model for one of Lawrence's characters, Mabel would have preferred that his book had been set in New Mexico rather than
Mexico, but she responded warmly to the book's theme: that
modern men and women might find salvation in the re-integra-
tion of individual and communal life through ritual.

The Plumed Serpent

MABEL DODGE LUHAN

". . . . . between two worlds; one dead, the other
powerless to be born."—MATTHEW ARNOLD

People read D. H. Lawrence's books and from them they
form their opinion of the man who wrote them. But they
do not generally recognize that an artist is not making a
portrait of himself in his work. No matter how hard he
may try to picture himself as he is, he is usually creating
himself as he is not, projecting his deep wish for perfec-
tion, rounding himself out, completing himself in his
work.

Take Cezanne, for instance, as an example of this creative instinct for self-production. Nowhere in modern
painting do we find such form, such stability, such a sense
of structure as in his paintings. He labored and sweated
blood to realize the solidity of his forms. The delicate
tones of his pigment represent to our vision real ponder-
able values. We can feel the weight of the objects he repre-
sents, we can touch and handle the apples, the vases and
the flowers. And the earth he has painted has depth that
reaches to China, while the houses have the textures of
stone, plaster and wood as they rest heavily and solidly on
the ground. In other words, Cezanne has realized form and
structure in his work.

But the man himself? Did his life have form, character,
structure? No, we know that Casein in his own nature was

(continued on following pages)

weak, vacillating, and shapeless. He had none of that responsible weightiness in his character that, when we see it, makes us exclaim: "There is a real man." He only achieved in his painting the dignity and the harmony that come from a true sense of form. He created for himself in paint the qualities that he felt were lacking in his nature. In this way, one may say, he attempted to complete himself.

All true artists are thus engaged in filling themselves out, and what they produce in doing so we call art. Real art has the man in it, the spirit, the wish, and the courage that spin out of himself those qualities he needs to satisfy the discontent in him, and the artist is the greatest of us all in these divine athletics of self-creation.

We remember the philosopher who was searching in the dark room for the black cat that was not there; and the mystic who went into the room and saw the cat! But it remains for the artist to go into the room and come out with the cat!

D. H. Lawrence is an artist who, in his work, is like one of those salmon upon whom he commented in one of his articles. He is swimming upstream against the current and nearing, each year, closer to the source. As he strains upward, the phenomena in the downward flowing streams of life flash past him and beckon him to give up his painful journey, but he rejects fiercely everything on both sides. He doesn't find many to companion him as he works himself along in the swift waters, for there are few real enemies of inertia.

The burden of genius is the heaviest one a man has to

carry. No other yoke is so hard to bear. Yet our destiny is to bear gods and the genius of our race seeks to embody divinity in the feeble flesh of men. How many of us realize or understand the anguish and the travail that breaks these artists? Can their lives be measured by the squares and their actions balanced in the scales that so neatly reveal the small dimensions of lesser individuals? Never. They are forever outside the usual conformities; they are subject to inner daemons that use them for the vast enterprises of a spiritual universe not even dreamed of by most of us.

Lawrence's books contain the substantial representations of a dying world that he himself furiously rejects. That imperfection and limitation implicit in all men and in himself as well, he shows up and with loathing he rejects it. He destroys as he goes. His touch upon decaying matter is that last, swift, sweeping break-up of dissolution, consigning all these out-worn forms and modes of our behaviour to dust and oblivion. In him is the fire that devours the rubbish, in him is the wind that scatters the ashes.

People, when they read his books, feel the passionate spirit in those pages, but they seldom realize, perhaps, that the living flame in them catches at their own faded lives and with nimble subtlety starts the little fire that will consume their dry-rot. They cannot be touched by Lawrence's spirit as it flares at them and come out of that contact unscathed. For your organism and mine, and for his own, he has a wily contempt; and for the surface of the world; for our society, our methods, and the foolish aims and foibles of our whole sorry scheme! He would burn it all to the ground in the hope that a new flower might come up from the root.

But the way of the destroyer is hard. There are many dangers lying in wait, ready, self-protectively, to overcome the flaming swords of genius. To tell the truth the world *hates* genius—and will always hate it, for genius is the living and lively revelation of the world's errors and failures, and we all love to abide by our mistakes.

Lawrence is a difficult person to write about. It would be comparatively simple to write of him as a "writer." or to "study" him as a man, but it would be hard to get the truth of him that way. I do not think anyone will ever get this one down pat. Can the behaviorists sum up this D. H. Lawrence by an observation of his acts? I do not think so. His outward life is simple and natural. He gets up early in the morning, lights the kitchen fire, makes breakfast for himself and his wife. Then, like many another, he does chores about he place. He cuts wood; he cleans ditches. He reads and he writes and he pays his bills. He washes his shirts when they need it. He quarrels, he grumbles, he laughs, and he does this one and that a good turn. He bakes bread if he needs bread. He bakes it for his neighbor if his neighbor needs it. He is hot-tempered and good-natured, loyal and disloyal, he is this and that . . .

But all this is merely the story of this and that—of his mortal frailty, his organic mechanism. But Lawrence himself is more than this and that—and yearly he increases. What he is, essentially, no one knows. It is doubtful if he knows himself.

But he is a man who has written:

"I am the Son of the Morning Star, and child of the deeps.

No man knows my Father, and I know Him not.

My Father is deep within the deeps, whence He sent me
  forth.
He sends the eagle of silence down on wide wings
To lean over my head and my neck and my breast
And fill them strong with the strength of wings.
He sends the serpent of power up my feet and my loins
So that strength wells up in me like water in hot
  springs.
But midmost shines as the Morning Star midmost
  shines
Between night and day, my Soul-star in one,
Which is my Father whom I know not.
I tell you, the day should not turn deep,
Save for the morning and evening stars, upon which
  they turn.
Night turns upon me, and Day, who am the star
  between.
Between your breast and belly is a star.
If it be not there
You are empty gourd-shells filled with dust and wind.
When you walk, the star walks with you, between your
  breast and your belly.
When you sleep, it softly shines.
When you speak true and true, it is bright on your lips
  and your teeth.
When you lift your hands in courage and bravery, its
  glow is clear in your palms.
When you turn to your wives as brave men turn to their
  women
The Morning Star and the Evening Star shine together.
For man is the Morning Star.

And woman is the Star of Evening.
I tell you, you are not men alone.
The star of the beyond is within you."

For Lawrence the word emancipation means deliverance. It means that somehow men and women shall deliver
themselves from the doom of perpetual organic repetition,
and no longer be under the necessity of reaction and reflex.
For self-will, which is merely of the nature of the beast, he
would substitute free-will, which is deliverance from it.

Someone said earnestly the other day: "Strictly speaking, we are worms." And Lawrence, with unending feroci-
ty, rejects this limited worm-like mechanism of man that,
left to itself, turns in a circle and devours its own tail. In
himself and in his neighbors he despises the automatic
reactions of mere organism. His apparent disloyalty to
men is his rejection of the machinery of man—of the ego-
tistic robot that is known as the finest flower of evolution.

Everything that natural evolution has been able to produce is not enough for Lawrence. He spits on it. In himself
and in the rest of mankind he sees persisting the old Adam
of the heart, mind and the instincts that is so out-worn, so
demode and that must put off, at last, the body of this
death, lest this humanity spin itself ut in a stale repetition
of organic imperatives. The yogi, the saint, the ascetic
alike, are no better, for him, than the harlot or the acrobat,
since each only continues a circular movement of some
special centre in this same mechanism that nature has
brought to pass.

"Not *that* nor *that* nor merely more of *that*," he seems to
cry, "But a change, a birth of something altogether new;

the real 'substance' of things hoped for. No further flowering of *this,* no added beauty, nor nobler gesture of *this*—there's been enough, ad nauseaum. . ."

And he rejects it all—and us all—and himself, too; and will have no more of these subtleties and varieties of our seemingly versatile but all too final human behavior.

"He had to meet them on another plane, where the contact was different; intangible, remote, and without *intimacy.* His soul was concerned elsewhere. So that the quick of him need not be bound to anybody. The quick of a man must turn to God alone: in some way or other.

"With Cipriano he was most sure. Cipriano and he, even when they embraced each other with passion, when they met after an absence, embraced in the recognition of each other's eternal and abiding loneliness; like the Morning Star. . .

"Men and women should know that they cannot, absolutely, meet on earth. In the closest kiss, the deepest touch, there is the small gulf which is none the less complete because it is so narrow, so *nearly* non-existent. They must bow and submit in reverence, to the gulf. Even though I eat the body and drink the blood of Christ, Christ is Christ and I am I, and the gulf is impassable. Though a woman be dearer to a man than his own life, yet he is he and she is she, and the gulf can never close up. Any attempt to close it is a violation, and the crime against the Holy Ghost.

"That which we get from the beyond, we get it alone. The final me I am, comes from the farthest off, from the Morning Star. The rest is assembled. All that of me which is assembled from the mighty cosmos can meet and touch all that is assembled in the beloved. But this is never the quick. Never can be.

"If we would meet in the quick, we must give up the assembled self, the daily I, and putting off ourselves one after the other, meet unconscious in the Morning Star. Body, soul and spirit can be transfigured into the Morning Star. But without transfiguration we shall never get there. We shall gnash at the leash.

We call him disloyal because we are self-satisfied and he is not. We find his refusal to shut his eyes upon the fact of our limitations to be a kind of going back on his gang. "He has," we tell each other, "no esprit de corps." No, indeed, he has no longer any esprit de corps—for things as they are. He waits for the new substance of things hoped for, he waits for the new mode. But even if his waiting be all in vain, he will not capitulate, in weariness, to the old modes, for he cannot if he would.

Something seeks to come to pass in him:

"For this, the only thing which is supreme above all power in a man, and at the same time is power; which far transcends knowledge; the strange Star. . . . "

During her early years with Tony Luhan, Mabel had tried to enter as far as she was able into the life cycle of the Pueblo people. As Rudnick explains, "She sported a Dutch bob so that she would look more Indian, wrapped herself in shawls, and spent several hours a day among the Tiwa women, trying to absorb their warmth and ease by imitating their orderly and soft-spoken ways."[5] By 1931 Mabel had found a way to move comfortably between the two worlds, though she retained much of her primitivist thinking. When a circus came to Taos, she described the excitement it stirred among the Pueblo, Anglo, and Hispanic residents, for whom the event became a communal rite of magic and dreams.

Circus in Taos

MABEL LUHAN

Robinson Brothers' Circus!

FOR A WEEK THERE WERE TWO little posters fastened up at the camp ground on the north side of the plaza, advertising the "Robinson Brothers' Circus".

In the centre of each was a great white clown's face, grinning in the foolish, friendly manner of all clowns, his little peaked cap perched on the side of his head. All around him were lesser pictures of ponies, dogs, a monkey and a bear, the ponies galloping, the dogs jumping through paper hoops, the monkey sitting, pensive, on a chair.

(continued on following pages)

And then today at noon a huge yellow van that looked like a giant's ice-box, motored into town with the word "Tickets" printed over a little window at the rear end, and "Robinson's Circus" painted on one side in big fancy, red letters.

In a flash, from nowhere in particular, twenty little boys in faded blue overalls were on the spot following the majestic truck as it motored slowly around the plaza before it pulled up on the camp ground.

Groups of little girls watched the alluring sight more timorously from the side of the road. The editor of our "Valley News" stood in the doorway of the Post Office smiling and rubbing his hands. Our doctor paused on the corner near the blacksmith shop to note the arrival and two or three men in broad-brimmed hats and high boots pulled up their horses under a cottonwood tree and observed the newcomer silently, their faces in deep shadow under their hat brims.

When would the circus begin? We went up and asked the driver of the van. "Choost venever de orders coom in," replied the blond-headed proprietor. "No ways to know ven dem orders get here. Mebby two o'clock. Mebby tree." He smiled and there was no doubt about the fact that he would be the clown!

No sign of life came from the interior of the yellow box. Little boys stared at it as though they would pierce the solid painted panels and wrench its secrets from it. Failing to do so, they scuttled again to look at the posters that they had already devoured several times a day with eager eyes, hungry for enchantment. Again they pointed out to each other the ponies, the dogs, the monkey. Above all they loved the smiling clown and they speculated passionately about his probabilities.

Indians gathered, silent too, in their white sheets, only their eyes showing dark in their swathings. They stood in little groups watching, motionless, absorbent. Then in bowled the second van, this one yellow, too, but covered over with a gay blue and yellow striped tarpaulin. Shrieks from the little boys as, like a flock of blue birds with but a single motive, they flew to the striped stranger and pattered behind it to accompany it as it swiftly circled the square and came to rest beside its mate. And now the merchants began to come to the doors of their stores to watch these rare arrivals. We do not see a circus in our town once in a blue moon.

The sun shone generously on all this life. The bright green leaves of May stippled the space about them, twinkling on their trees in the tiny park. The vista at the end of every road leading out of the place showed dark blue mountains against a burning blue sky, while from the south a procession of clouds like curling, white-crested waves rolled after each other. We all scanned the sky anxiously. Were they heralds of the evening thunder showers? Alas!

There was a feeling of anticipation in the air—of festivity—of entertainment. But it was noon and we had to go home to dinner. Even with the circus coming to town, one must eat.

But no one staid long at home today. During the afternoon everyone went back and forth to the village to watch

the progress of setting up the tent, and to count the animals as they appeared. And some people were even allowed
to help put the show together.

Four motor vans in all finally gathered together, and
Oh! Wonderful! There were three lions! Lions in cages.
Several little ponies travelled in one van, and what a hustle
and bustle went on getting everything unpacked and distributed. Iron spikes were driven into the ground, the tent
was hoisted on three poles and ropes fastened it firm and
taut to the spikes—and then, in the regular old time style,
all the little boys lay on their bellies and peeked under the
tent!

All the afternoon wagons full of Mexicans pulled slowly
into the plaza and stood their horses' heads at the wooden
railing around the park while they themselves strolled and
loitered about, the women in black shawls, the men in
faded pastelle shades of warm clothing. Indians cantered
gaily into town on their small ponies—and even the
Americans paced about observing everything, though not
intending to exhibit a too great appearance of interest.

The day wore on, but no show! There was too much to
do to have everything in readiness for an afternoon performance. But one was promised for half past seven. And
then when we were all at home again for supper in our different houses on our different hills, at that hour when the
spring breeze has quieted down and the sun has fallen
below the horizon, when the hesitant evening peace has
come into the air all rosy and glowing form the warm day,
at that exquisite hour the lions chose to roar! Lions roaring
in the tranquil Taos twilight!

Not a leaf stirred on the big cottonwoods, so quiet is was, and those lions could be heard for miles around. In every abode in a radius of two miles or three people came to their doors and listened incredulous to the unwonted sound. The mountains loomed blue-black against a sky the color of tea roses in the west and in the east the color of a jade bowl. Those lions roared and roared—and pretty soon far and wide all our live stock raised themselves indignantly from their first doze and protested. Horses neighed, burros he-hawed, geese cackled, and even the cocks in some alarm, began to crow in spirited tenor tremulos. The lions boomed on, forming the bass notes in this cacophony. Doubtless it was their hour for roaring, so they did so.

We could not stay away from the plaza. Who, indeed, could have remained at home? Everybody went,—why there must have been a couple of hundred people there! As we neared the spot, suddenly the calliope, the dear old cally-ope, began to keen in that homesick fashion we remember so well.

The tent was not dazzlingly lighted. A few oil lanterns were sufficient to reveal to us the wonders of the little canvas world that held a dancing bear, four shaggy ponies, some snappy dogs, a desperate looking monkey (was his name not Jocko?) and the lions in their cage.

But Oh! the acrobats—two of them in pink tights with dazzling smiles on their bold faces, the lady with the feathered hat and a whip in her hand, and the clown! All painted white, his face was, and such animation you never saw; such gaiety; such joking in his funny face.

The calliope moaned on; the lady snapped her whip and made the animals perform; the acrobats flexed and unflexed their muscles; the clown shouted and ran wildly here and there, falling down, pretending to be scared, pretending to be angry. Soon everybody on the narrow board seats became one with the show. They and the show were united together in that dusky tent where the lamps threw great flickering shadows about.

The women and the little girls knew what it was to be so brave and beautiful and to crack a whip and make the animals do strange, unanimal things. The men and the little boys became athletes every one, with fine, strong bodies made for fearless play. And something of the animals entered into it all too, something of the roaring lions, the stylish, racy dogs even the tragic monkey contributed a poignant flavor to the experience in which everyone participated, in that conglomerate gathering of an hour where all the essences were mingled and everybody drank of the magical potion in a strange communion. For this, you see, was an *entertainment*. This was a releading of the spirit into poetry and romance. *This* was a *circus*.

Inevitably one had to contrast it with the circus in the Madison Square Garden, that April pandemonium that this year reached its apogee, one supposes, with its five rings, its many bands, its multiplicity and its emptiness. There, for our enjoyment, they pooled the freaks of all the side shows in America, as well as the acrobats and the animals and the imitation Indians. There everything ran in dozens and in hundreds, and the electric power they utilized to illumine every performance was enough to run a good sized town. But was there any glamour? Was there any thrill at all? Did those baffled children, whose heads ached from the strain of trying to see four ways for Sunday and from trying to make out one clear strain of sound, did they expand and flow out in spirit and identify themselves with these abstractions in human form who twirled and twinkled in that blatant light?

Did they dream great dreams of beauty and power as they sat through those terrible maneuvers of efficient and mechanical exploitation? Will it never dawn on our people in cities that so far as *fun* goes, mere size doesn't count? That a dozen of anything is not more stimulating to the imagination than one of its kind? That large numbers of thrillers only lessen the capacity to experience any thrill?

Oh, Mr. Showman! Come to the circus in Taos and learn how to make a real circus if, indeed, that is your intention. You have assembled what you call with truth "The Biggest Show on Earth," but if you think it is an entertainment, Taos has something to teach you. For your affair in the Garden fails in its purpose. It stuns, it amazes, it exhausts, but it doesn't entertain.

Besides publishing her articles in *Laughing Horse*, Spud continued to work for Mabel during the 1930s and often joined the evening gatherings at Los Gallos. Like a theater in which she was at once the director and the star, life at the Luhan compound absorbed the imprint of all Mabel's past and present lives. Spud's portrait of her is "Poppies," published in his own volume of poetry, *Horizontal Yellow* (1935). It is a poem which could have been written only by one of her intimates, who observed with amusement the hostess and the guests she plucked, like poppies from her garden, to populate her living tableau.

Poppies
(A Portrait of Mabel)

SPUD JOHNSON

I. MORNING

All of the poppies are plucked
From the garden between the alfalfa
And the acequia where the clover blooms.
All of the poppies are arranged
In vases, all around the drawing rooms.
And the Virgin on the mantel-piece,
Looking like Helen of Troy,
Has poppies all around her hips
Instead of a fleet of battle-ships . . .

The Italian urn and the Indian pot,
The Mexican bowl and the Chinese jar,
On the piano and behind the desk,
Over the fireplace and beneath the Venetian mirror—
Poppies!

And then, since the stage is set,
She descends, a poppy herself,
Refreshed by what strange dew
No one knows; and taking
All her guests away from marmalade
To motor twenty miles across the desert
For a bath. . .

(continued on following pages)

II. AFTERNOON

The poppies hang their pink heads;
And so does she, on a pillow.
The house is a mausoleum of drowsiness.
A telephone rings; an automobile
Full of tourists circles the drive.
But nothing stirs, except the poppies
Philandering in their sleep
With the Italian bees. . .

Maggie, a last-year's ghost of Mabel,
In a dress she wore a season or two ago,
Brings in the tea and sputters
Half in Spanish, half in English,
Something no one would understand
And which only the furniture hears.

When she rings the patio bell, her back
Is Mabel's back; but her face
Is Maggie's; no petals grace
Its broad circumference.
She is a poppy-pod, brown.
And she rattles.

III. EVENING

In the garden, only the stars bloom.
And the poppies in the vases
Are no longer colored faces.
The petals cover the floor
In every corner, like confetti. . .

And Mabel smiles brightly
From her couch where the pillows
Are like larger poppy-petals—
But not so large as all the guests
Who seem to have wilted in their chairs,
Weary of all affairs,
Like the poppies.
Like confetti after a carnival.
Mabel's carnival. . .

Johnson's relaxed nature and willingness to drive made him an amiable traveling companion. More than once he drove Mabel to Carmel, and he made several trips with both Luhans over the years (Fig. 65). Like many New Mexicans during those years, they favored Mexico as a winter destination, and in 1932 Johnson joined them for a trip that included Puebla and Oaxaca, with many side trips. Johnson was an avid journal-keeper, especially while traveling. In moods that ranged from the poetic to the ethnological to the gossipy and petulant, he recorded the pleasures and discomforts of travel with Mabel and Tony. In the following excerpts from an unpublished manuscript he called "Fragments from a Mexican Journal," Johnson describes Mexican train travel, a visit with an archeologist to a recent excavation at Monte Alban, and—ever the bibliophile—his purchase of rare books in the market at Oaxaca.

When we got to the station, the dawn light was changing from its dull pink to yellow. As the train started, we glimpsed Popocatepetl and Ixtaccihuatl, off to the west, pale blue against a murky pink, the yellow in the east hav-

FIGURE 65. Spud at the wheel. Photograph by Shaffer Studio. Photography Collection, Harry Ransom Humanities Research Center, University of Texas at Austin.

ing pushed the rose color all the way across the sky from east to west.

As I looked at the two beautiful volcanoes, the very first finger of the sun touched their snowy peaks, and then the pink gradually slid down them like an unloosed garment, and they stood in all their naked glory in the sun.

Frost on the cars of sidings showed that the cold we felt was not imaginary; and rushing through fog, later, the day did not warm very rapidly. At each of our frequent stops I rushed hurriedly to get off the train and walk up and down the platforms briskly.

At noon, in Cuicatlan, we arrived in the midst of a political meeting. The fat men who talked endlessly all the way . . .turned out to be politicos. I should have guessed it before. Here at Cuicatlan there was an ovation, banners, crowds, "Viva Calles!" et cetera.[6] Many men came aboard and embraced our neighbors—only their fat bellies keeping them a respectable distance apart. More "Viva Calles." Then a man made a speech at the car window—and one of the least prepossessing of our travelling companions answered it, leaning out of the window next to me. Oddly enough, he was the one who slept most of the way with his mouth open, and yet he suddenly came to life and seemed to be quite eloquent in a flowery Spanish way. The train pulled out, rudely, as he was in the midst of his speech— to his obvious relief. Still more "Viva Calles," and the banners and crowds disappeared.

. . . .

Late in the afternoon, after unsuccessful attempts at sleep, curled up in a single seat, head on travelling bag, an extra second-class coach was put on in preparation for an expected crowd at some approaching town. It was empty between the point where it was picked up and the next stop, so Tony [Luhan] and I occupied it, stretched out full length on the long benches. It was a great relief, after the cramped plush seats in our car, even though it was hotter there, and dustier—if that is possible to imagine.

Arrived at Oaxaca about five or five-thirty. Found it cool, and not tropically hot as we had expected. Pleasant rooms at the hotel. I peered surreptitiously at the register and was disappointed to find that they had not been as imaginative as had our hosts in Puebla, who had us down in large letters as "Antonio Lujan y Cia." Antonio Lujan & Co.! I suppose they could not account for an American Indian complete with braids, without assuming that we were a perambulating theatrical troupe!

Tuesday, March 15 [Oaxaca]

This morning we started off early by Ford for Monte Alban with Emma Reh, her friend and Bazan, one of the archeologists who discovered the rich tomb where all the pearls and other jewels and objet d'art [sic] were unearthed recently.

We crawled into the famous tomb itself and sat on the dusty floor around a gasoline lantern, an Aztec boy and a baby squatting near us—looking for all the world like a Greenwich Village studio party!

Bazan talked in Spanish all about the discovery and the contents of the tomb, because Emma is here to write a book about it for Macmillan. For my benefit Emma translated as he paused for breath occasionally. So that I got but fragments.

The crystal bowl or cup (which I saw in the Museum Saturday) was one of the first things they saw, right on top of the heap of rubble. They discovered the tomb by going straight down through the mound from the exact center of the top. . . . After entering in this manner, they measured from the top, calculating where the entrance would be, then dug and found the real one, later replacing the huge stones of the supporting arch which they had displaced for their initial entrance.

The pearls they found (uneven and slightly discolored, as they still appear in the necklaces at the Museum) were first thought to be decayed teeth from mummies! But soon they found that the entire pile of debris sparkled with emerging fragments of the gold jewelry, and they realized that they had stumbled on an amazing treasure.

[Bazan] told us that in a few remote villages hereabouts (San Mateo?) the native Indians still bring sacrifices to the ancient gods—such strange modern sacrifices as cigarettes, tortillas, chocolate, and so forth. And they burn copal, just as they still do in the churches, in lieu of incense: thus vindicating Lawrence's fictitious revival of the prehistoric religions as described in *The Plumed Serpent*.

After we came out of the tomb into the blessed sunlight again, we dispersed, and I wandered alone among the ruins, exploring the mounds where the excavation work had not yet begun. The entire hill top was either a city or else an enormous temple or series of temples—a whole Vatican! The top of the small mountain had been leveled, making an enormous central court, completely encircled by the spacious staircases which either led to buildings above, or else were themselves pyramids.

. . . .

This afternoon I have been wandering in the streets and market. Bought some lovely little books, three of a set of the "Obras Completas de Buffon" printed in Barcelona in 1833, just a hundred years ago.[7] The text is Spanish, but the illustrations, hand-colored, are apparently the original French plates. The first volume I found was the one on monkeys, with sixteen pages of pictures—the funniest and most charming monkeys I ever saw—all for 30 centavos. One of the other volumes was on birds, with only two pages of illustrations left, and the third volume quadrupeds again, with a few pictures of zebras, deer, etc. The man promised to look among his reserve stock for other volumes of the set, so I shall go back tomorrow. How I managed to bargain and converse with him on the subject, with my few words of Spanish, I'm sure I don't know, but we seemed to understand one another perfectly.

FIGURE 66. The Taos skyline in winter. Photograph by Mildred Tolbert. Photography Collection, Harry Ransom Humanities Research Center, University of Texas at Austin.

In *Winter in Taos*, her finest literary work, Mabel constructed an idyllic evocation of the harmonious, quiet winter season at Taos (Fig. 66). It is a meditative book, laced with observations about her neighbors, her home, the landscape, and the people who shared her world at Taos. One of the most sympathetic passages describes Spud's three-room adobe house, a dwelling whose exterior is perfectly integrated into the snow-blanketed village (Fig. 67). Inside, however, Mabel sees a highly personalized world: three cozy, dirt-floored rooms spilling over with

FIGURE 67. Spud Johnson's house, Taos, c. 1930s. Photography Collection, Harry Ransom Humanities Research Center, University of Texas at Austin.

Spud's collections of rare books and horses sculpted in every imaginable material. It is an intimate glimpse at the domain of a man whose life was becoming increasingly quiet and ascetic, dominated by his devotion to literature and the printed word.

Winter in Taos

MABEL DODGE LUHAN

Spud's house stands just beyond and to the right of the bridge. The creek curves around his yard, and big trees border it. There is a hammock swung there in the summertime; and in the center of his place, between the little house and the little river, there is a sunken pool, lined with stones, with flax and iris blooming around it. The water runs close to the surface under these houses, and he only had to dig two or three feet to reach it.

He can open a gate and go through his Mexican neighbor's place and reach Miriam's alfalfa field; and her adobe house lies there near the Indian boundary, blond and pale like herself. There are several old apple trees in the front of it, and their trunks and branches shine red in the winter sunlight. There is a hammock hanging between two of them, but it is grey and rotted now, for Miriam went away for the winter and forgot to put it inside the house.

Behind Spud's house stands the house of a Mexican neighbor, and a small, beautiful chapel with a white painted, carved door. A tree-bordered road turns off the highway here and leads in over a cattle guard to a dear little cream-colored house that stands in a brown field, and whose windows and doors are bordered with pink. Big gray trees hang over it, and make a shelter, and it looks like a cottage in a fairy tale. It is an old house we bought and made over to lend or rent to friends, and it was there

(continued on following pages)

Tony raised so many pumpkins and squash last summer. Miriam has a right of way through the place where she drives in to her house.

These small *adobe* houses that different people have bought for comparatively small amounts of money, and whitewashed and painted and cleaned up, provide elements for a beautiful, simple life. With a few pieces of well-designed furniture, perhaps modeled upon the Spanish Colonial and made by clever Mexican boys in the village, and mixed with two or three genuine old tables and chairs and cupboards, and with lovely colored Mexican *serapes* strewn upon the painted boards, or on the hard mud floors, and with muslin or old-fashioned checkered or sprigged calico curtains in the small-paned windows, they are picture-book houses.

Every one of them has its group of old trees to shade it, its apples or its cottonwoods; and its flower-beds in the summertime are filled with sweet peas and hollyhocks and blue larkspur.

There on the edge of the Indian pasture, then, live a group of people whose life-pattern is so different from their Mexican or Indian neighbors that it scarcely overlaps at any point, yet there is something about this valley's spaciousness, as well as its beauty, that makes it possible for these separate races to live here in amity, fundamentally indifferent to each other, superficially friendly. There is, however, one real meeting-place, and that is in their love for Taos.

In the wintertime, many of the small, remodeled houses look lifeless or asleep. They nestle in the snow; the trees about them give the sole movement in their neighborhood when the wind stirs the bare branches. No smoke rises from their cold chimneys and their windows gather a gray film of cobwebs across them. Their occupants have gone away to cities, fearful of the quiet immobility of the snow-shrouded valley, or of the enduring cold.

In Placita, Spud's house never dies. Like his Mexican neighbors', his chimneys keep their warmth all winter. In the early morning, the cock that wakens Cortez, wakens him as well; and in the night the howling dog brings him to his door shouting a fierce "Shut up!" at the same time as Enrique, across the road, tumbles out of bed to call the beast into his warm kitchen.

The "back room" in Spud's house is Rembrandtesque: all brown and black and white, from the hand press and the trays of type, the stove, the benches, the loom (where some day, we suppose, *serapes* will be woven, fusing together into odd patterns against the white walls), the dim old ceiling made of ancient cedar strips laid on beams, which comes weightily close to one's head, and the dirt floor, which provides a constant veil of fine dust that softens every outline and subdues every surface. A few numbers of past "Laughing Horses" that were born in this room, rest on shelves in their assorted colors. The room has dark corners; it has warmth, vitality, and the sense of being that places have where someone works and likes it.

There are only two other little rooms in the house. The door opens directly upon Home. Here is the diminutive cookstove with two or three small skillets and pans hanging above it and a tiny woodbox beside it—all so neat and enjoyable. In the deep embrasure of the tall, narrow window, beside the stove, geraniums bloom. The dining table is on the other side of it, covered with a red and white checkered cloth, and books and horses and more plants.

Across from the stove, there is a day bed, leaning up against a bookcase that stands out from the wall, and behind it are the pitcher and bowl, the shaving things and such-like, and more horses along the top; horses from here, there and everywhere, for everyone sends Spud horses; horses of ivory and wood and straw, pottery horses, metal horses, laughing horses, or horses fierce and prancing, grotesque and exquisite.

Beside the door, a flashlight hangs on a nail, right at hand the moment he comes into the dark house at night. There is no electricity here, but yellow light from oil lamps that must be lighted when he comes in.

The next room, usually called the living room (though all three of these rooms are really lived in), has a tall mahogany desk with glass doors at the top and books behind them. It started, in my recollection, in my own room years ago in Buffalo, but I traded it to him for a Buffalo coat which he had, and which I wanted to give to Tony for Christmas!

There is a darling fireplace in here, of just the right size, and it has bookshelves on either side of it and horses ranging across the chimney-piece and along the tops over the books. Another tall bookcase with high glass doors, stands across the room. It came from his home, one of those things people have who have anything, that they drag along across mountains and rivers and set among the later accretions of living. The best books are in here. The sets. Spud collects books like he collects horses. He likes them for their paper, their covers, their printing and their contents. Every extra dollar he has goes for a book, and there they are, all over his three rooms. He never buys horses—they come to him—but for books he makes sacrifices.

There is another wide, low day bed in this inner room, and a drum stove that smolders all the time while he is away at the Printing Office in the village. When he comes home on a cold night, the house is warm, the lamp is soon burning, and a fresh log snapping on the embers. I have heard him describe, with the greatest sympathy in me, how cozy it is to warm up some milk and go to bed with a book and a mug of the hot drink, to feel so secure and content, alone at his ease with the wild winter shut out and nothing more to cope with till the next day!

III: D. H. LAWRENCE

For some literary critics, the most memorable thing about *Laughing Horse* was its publication of D. H. Lawrence.[8] Indeed, Lawrence's association with *Laughing Horse* spanned the complete run of the little magazine. It began in 1922 when Johnson asked the British author, summoned to Taos by Mabel Dodge Luhan, to write something for *Laughing Horse*. Lawrence complied, submitting a review for the fourth issue—a review of *Fantazius Mallare*, a new novel by Ben Hecht. Lawrence found the novel revolting and said so, using many four-letter words in its vilification. Of the incident, Johnson recalled years later,

"Lawrence's review we had printed with all the 'objectionable' four-letter words left out—but the presence of dashes made it seem even more 'obscene' than if we had left them in!"[9] The university community was deeply shocked; it seemed a clear act of provocation by Johnson and his co-editors, a move calculated to test, and perhaps embarrass, the administration, who instantly declared the letter "obscene" and suspended publication of the magazine. The suppression of *Laughing Horse* became a political issue, bringing notoriety to the publication and initiating its long-term engagement with issues of censorship. The publicity was just what the editors had hoped for, and thenceforth *Laughing Horse* bore the imprint of literary and social radicalism that placed it alongside better-known magazines like the *Dial*, *Blast* and *Little Review*.

Lawrence, whose poems had been published in the *Dial* starting in 1913, was already well known to avant-garde literary audiences in America. His passionate imagination, his irreverence, and his often conflicted attraction to and repulsion for things American appealed to editors and sophisticated audiences searching for a new postwar aesthetic. His intermittent contributions to *Laughing Horse*, published during and after his years in North America, brought the vigor and effrontery of modernism to its pages.

Johnson's personal acquaintance with Lawrence began the first day he and Frieda arrived in New Mexico. They had been invited to Taos by Mabel Dodge, who was convinced that Lawrence was the ideal person to interpret New Mexico and its Indians to the world. "She wants me to *write* this country up" was Lawrence's understanding of the invitation.[10] On September 10, 1922, the visitors were met at the Lamy train station by their hostess and Tony Luhan, soon to become her fourth hus-

FIGURE 68. Left to right: D. H. Lawrence, Frieda Lawrence, Spud Johnson in Mexico, 1923. Photograph courtesy the Harwood Foundation, Taos.

band. The trip to Taos was too long to begin late in the day, so Mabel had arranged for the group to spend the night at Bynner's house in Santa Fe. From all reports the quartet—Lawrence, Frieda, Bynner, and Johnson—were taken with each other, finding many commonalities in their literary interests, their somewhat jaded postwar sensibilities and their desire to find renewal in the ancient cultures of the Southwest.

After a winter in Taos, first under Mabel's controlling gaze at her adobe compound, later at her son's abandoned ranch seventeen miles north of town, the Lawrences were ready for the warmth of the southern sun. They decided to head for Mexico, inviting Bynner and Johnson to accompany them. It was a trip of revelation for all of them, as seen in their varied recollections of the journey (Fig. 68).

For Lawrence, the impressions were recorded in a steady stream, almost from the day of departure. Here, with evident cultural and racial bias, his short prose piece "Au Revoir, U.S.A." contrasts the "tension" he felt north of the border with the "exasperation" he felt in Mexico. The piece was included in *Laughing Horse*, number eight, the Mexican issue Johnson compiled during the months he spent with the Lawrences at Lake Chapala.

Au Revoir, U. S. A.

D. H. LAWRENCE

"Say au revoir
But not goodbye
This parting brings
A bitter sigh. . . ."

It really does, when you find yourself in an unkempt Pullman trailing through endless deserts, south of El Paso, fed on doubtful scraps at enormous charge and at the will of a rather shoddy smallpox-marked Mexican Pullman-boy who knows there's been a revolution and that his end is up. Then you remember the neat and nice nigger who

(continued on following pages)

looked after you as far as El Paso, before you crossed the Rio Grande into desert and chaos, and you sigh, if you have time before a curse chokes you.

Yet, U. S. A., you do put a strain on the nerves. Mexico puts a strain on the temper. Choose which you prefer. Mine's the latter. I'd rather be in a temper than be pulled taut. Which is what the U. S. A. did to me. Tight as a fiddle string, tense over the bridge of the solar plexus. Any how the solar plexus goes a bit loose and has a bit of play down here.

I still don't know why the U. S. A. pulls one so tight and makes one feel like a chicken that is being drawn. The people on the whole are quite as amenable as people any-where else. They don't pick your pocket, or even your personality. They're not unfriendly. It's not the people. Something in the air tightens one's nerves like fiddle strings, screws them up, squeak-squeak!. . . till one's nerves will give out nothing but a shrill fine shriek of overwroughtness. Why, in the name of heaven? Nobody knows. It's just the spirit of place.

You cross the Rio Grande, and change from tension into exasperation. You feel like hitting the impudent Pullman waiter with a beer-bottle. In the U. S. A. you don't even think of such a thing.

Of course, one might get used to a state of tension. And then one would pine for the United States. Meanwhile one merely snarls back at the dragons of San Juan Teotihuacan.

It's a queer continent——as much as I've seen of it. It's a fanged continent. It's got a rattle-snake coiled in its heart, has this democracy of the New World. It's a dangerous animal, once it lifts its head again. Meanwhile, the dove still nests in the coils of the rattlesnake, the stone coiled rattlesnake of Aztec eternity. The dove lays her eggs on his flat head.

The old people had a marvellous feeling for snakes and fangs, down here in Mexico. And after all, Mexico is only the sort of solar plexus of North America. The great pale-face overlay hasn't gone into the soil half an inch. The Spanish churches and palaces stagger, the most ricketty things imaginable, always just on the point of falling down. And the peon still grins his Indian grin behind the Cross. And there's quite a lively light in his eyes, much more so than in the eyes of the Northern Indian. He knows his gods.

These old civilizations down here, they never got any higher than Quetzalcoatl. And he's just a sort of feathered snake. Who needed the smoke of a little hearts-blood now and then, even he.

"Only the ugly is aesthetic now," said the young Mexican artist. Personally, he seems as gentle and self-effacing as the nicest of lambs. Yet his caricatures are hideous, hideous without mirth or whimsicality. Blood-hideous. Grim, earnest hideousness.

Like the Aztec things, the Aztec carvings. They all twist and bite. That's all they do. Twist and writhe and bite, or crouch in lumps. And coiled rattle-snakes, many, like dark heaps of excrement. And out at San Juan Teoti-huacan where are the great pyramids of a vanished, pre-Aztec people, as we are told—and the so-called Temple of Quetzalcoatl—there, behold you, huge gnashing heads jut

FIGURE 69.
Mexico, 1923.
Standing, left to right:
Frieda Lawrence, Spud
Johnson, unidentified
person, D. H. Lawrence.
Front: unidentified.
Photography collection,
Harry Ransom
Humanities Research
Center, University of
Texas at Austin.

out jagged from the wall-face of the low pyramid, and a huge snake stretches along the base, and one grasps at a carved fish, that swims in old stone and for once seems harmless. Actually a harmless fish!

But look out! The great stone heads snarl at you from the wall, trying to bite you:-and one great dark green blob of an obsidian eye, you never saw anything so blindly malevolent: and then white fangs. Great white fangs, smooth today, the white fangs, with tiny cracks in them. Enamelled. These bygone pyramid-building Americans, who were a dead-and-gone mystery even to the Aztecs, when the Spaniards arrived, they applied their highest art to the enamelling of the great fangs of these venomous stone heads, and there is the enamel today, white and smooth. You can stroke the great fang with your finger and see. And the blob of an obsidian eye looks down at you.

It's a queer continent. The anthropologists may make what prettiness they like out of myths. But come here, and you'll see that the gods bit. There is none of the phallic pre-occupation of the old Mediterranean. Here they hadn't got even as far as hotblooded sex. Fangs, and cold serpent folds, and bird-snakes with fierce cold blood and claws.

I admit that I feel bewildered. There is always something a bit amiably comic about Chinese dragons and contortions. There's nothing amiably comic in these ancient monsters. They're dead in earnest about biting and writhing, snake-blooded birds.

And the Spanish white superimposition, with rococo church-towers among pepper-trees and column cactuses,

seems so ricketty and temporary, the pyramids seem so
indigenous, rising like hills out of the earth itself. The one
goes down with a clatter, the other remains.

And this is what seems to me the difference between
Mexico and the United States. And this is why, it seems to
me, Mexico exasperates, whereas the U. S. A. puts an unbearable tension on one. Because here in Mexico the fangs
are still obvious. Everybody knows the gods are going to
bite within the next five minutes. While in the United
States, the gods have had their teeth pulled, and their
claws cut, and their tails docked, till they seem real mild
lambs. Yet all the time, inside it's the same old dragon's
blood. The same old aboriginal American dragon's blood.

And that discrepancy of course is a strain on the human
psyche.

Lawrence's literary output from the Mexico trip was prodi-
gious: poetry, articles, reviews, *Mornings in Mexico* (1927), and
his novel of Mexico, *The Plumed Serpent* (1926). The latter work,
the manuscript for which was typed by Johnson during the
weeks at Chapala, remained for its author "nearer my heart than
any other work of mine."[11] For Bynner, such remarks sealed an
animosity that had sprung up between Lawrence and himself
early in the trip—an animosity made worse by Bynner's unsym-
pathetic characterization as "Owen" in the novel. Johnson's character "Villiers" fared somewhat better, undoubtedly a reflection
of Lawrence's liking for the less-threatening younger man.

Johnson's vivid account of the Mexican sojourn, published
the year of Lawrence's death, captures the flavor of the creative

FIGURE 70. Mexico, 1923. Seated on boat at Lake Chapala, right to left: D. H. Lawrence, Frieda Lawrence, Idella Purnell (?), Spud Johnson. Others are unidentified. Photography Collection, Harry Ransom Humanities Research Center, University of Texas at Austin.

and personal tensions pervading the daily activities of the group and emphasizes the mediating role Johnson found himself performing (Fig. 70).

D. H. Lawrence
in Mexico

BUD VILLIERS

(SPUD JOHNSON)

I first met D. H. Lawrence and his wife when they came to the remote and isolated New Mexican village where Owen and I were staying, and finding the hotels crowded, quartered themselves upon us, moving in while I was seeing a Tom Mix show at the movie. We had only a little adobe hut, but we were pleased and flattered to have them. By giving up a bedroom and bunking in the studio, we could always make room for guests. This first informal acquaintance was responsible for another meeting the next spring, when there developed the spontaneous and excited plan for the four of us to go to Mexico together. Lawrence and his wife went on ahead, and Owen and I joined them in the City of Mexico.

Of the days we spent there, some are sharply etched in memory. First, of course, Easter, for which holiday we had hurried south, and which has been notably celebrated in *The Plumed Serpent*. That was the day of the bullfight, April 1, and Lawrence and Owen have said enough on that subject. Then there was the day we discovered Covarrubias in a sort of Greenwich Village café on the Calle de República de Cuba; and the day I went to the hospital followed by a shower of Lawrentian invectives for having drunk too much tequila; and the day Mrs. Lawrence discovered the

(continued on following pages)

strawberry shortcake at Sanborn's, and the day the Princess Bibesco arrived. . . . But the other outstanding day was May 1 and Lawrence wasn't there at all.

That was the time we saw the red flag hoisted above the statue of Christ on the Cathedral, the largest Christian edifice on the continent. That was the day Owen and I accompanied the proletariat to the Cathedral towers and tolled the bells with street-cleaners in honor of the Chicago martyrs for an eight-hour-day—while Mrs. Lawrence, deserted in the Plaza below, saw soldiers arrive and block the tower steps and pined for escorts and lunch. Lawrence had gone to Sayula to make a "preliminary investigation", and we joined him there the next day and began our real summer.

The Lawrences took a house—an el around an old garden, the outer sides even more effectively enclosed in a deep wood which marked the limit of the neighboring estate. It was up from the lake shore a bit on an unfrequented lane and had an enormous tree at its iron gate. The drawing-room was one of those cold, tiled, bare places with a high ceiling and stark chairs. I seem to remember Lawrence sitting in a sort of New England rocker, his feet drawn up onto the seat of the chair and his beard playing hide-and-seek around his knees as he denounced the Obregon government or discussed a Japanese play.

But I remember him again on his hands and knees on the tiled floor, like some strange animal scampering around one corner of a *serape* with a tape-measure. Perhaps that was when Owen got the idea for his "Studies in Unnatural History" in which he says that he does not know whether Lawrence is "a man wishing to be an animal, or an animal wishing to be a man."

At that time, however, Owen was similarly occupied on the other side of the *serape* and both of them were making strange notations on a slip of paper and later puttering with water-colors. They had discovered a weaver in a village at the end of the lake and were designing their own *serapes* to be made to order.

On such evenings Mrs. Lawrence sat in another New England rocker and knitted—and I merely sat, smoking black cigarettes. Perhaps those were the times when "there was in my eyes the curious basking apathy of a snake asleep", as he said of me in the first version of the *Serpent*.

Mostly, though, we sat on their little *portal* either on warm afternoons over tea, or in the evening when the moonlight made the garden beyond into mysterious shapes which Lawrence, I think, always fancied were bandits. There, also, was a tiled floor, but it was less forbidding than in the drawing-room. And on the wall there always hung a bright *serape* of green and red in which was woven the Mexican eagle standing on a gay cactus and waving a most enchanting snake in its beak.

It was on this cool, shadowy porch that many heated arguments took place between Owen and Lawrence. And it was here, too, that Lawrence was at his wittiest and best. He would imitate eccentric acquaintances who were "habitués or sons of habitués" of a certain London salon (he was a side-spitting mimic), and sometimes he would read poetry magazines or letters aloud, giving everything the most ludicrous interpretation until we were all roaring with laughter and in the best of humor.

Yet this mood would just as often be interrupted by a violent denunciation or a real tornado of wrath over some insignificant matter or carelessly dropped word.

Other times we walked on the beach of the lake or on the pier when week-end crowds gave a semblance of gayety. We laughed at the fifi-boys—or rather the others did, always with sly digs to the effect that I also was a fifi-boy, which injured my pride tremendously. But my reputation as such became fixed when it was known that I sometimes joined the dancers on the Sunday night sidewalks in front of the cafés. Lawrence loved the way the peons interrupted these week-end events by their imperturbable circumambulation of the plaza.

But this is not the story. There we were, Owen and I at the hotel which fronted the lake; the Lawrences in their tiny villa down the beach. Mornings we all worked, Lawrence generally down towards a little peninsula where tall trees grew near the water. He sat there, back against a tree, eyes often looking over the scene that was to be the background for his novel, and wrote in tiny, fast words in a thick, blue-bound blank book, the tale which he called *Quetzalcoatl*. Here also he read Mexican history and folklore and observed, almost unconsciously, the life that went on about him, and somehow got the spirit of the place.

There were the little boys who sold idols from the lake; the women who washed clothes at the waters' edge and dried them on the sands; there were the lone fishermen, white *calzones* pulled to their hips, bronze legs wading deep in the waters, fine nets catching the hundreds of tiny *charales*: boatmen steering their clumsy, beautiful craft around the peninsula; men and women going to market with baskets of *pitahayas* on their heads; lovers, even, wandering along the windy shore; goatherds; mothers bathing babies; sometimes a group of Mexican boys swimming nude off-shore instead of renting ugly bathing suits further down by the hotel. . . .

Afternoons we often had tea together or Lawrence and I walked along the mud flats below the village or along the cobbled country road around the Japanese hill—or up the hill itself. We discovered that botany had been a favorite study of both of us at school and took a friendly though more or less ignorant interest in the flora as we walked and talked. Lawrence talked most, of course.

And we swam, too. Owen generally went in for strenuous water-sports with the gang of boys who always awaited our appearance on the beach. And I dawdled in the water leisurely on the outskirts of the gang or lounged with them in the scalding sun as they tried to pick up English and as we struggled with the vernacular of Mexican Spanish. The Lawrences swam alone below the frequented stretch of beach—he looking, in white trunks, like an ivory "Ocean Christ" by Anatole France.

We lived strangely separate and yet strangely mingled lives. Separate because our inclinations were opposed. Mingled because there was an affectionate interest that bound all of us together and because, being the only English-speaking people in the town, we were dependent upon each other for companionship.

A strange setting for a strange drama. Lawrence and Owen really liked one another—and yet hated each other, too. Just as Lawrence liked me and I liked him, although he heartily disliked some of my American traits and I some of his English. It was the same sort of thing all around.

Lawrence and Owen talked about each other blasphemously when they were apart and although they were polite to each other when face to face—even then, in their political arguments or literary discussions, there was the bitterness of completely opposed ideas and a sharp intolerance not only of the absurdities but of the fundamental wrongness of the other's principles and conclusions.

The result, from my point of view, was highly amusing. Here's the way the thing worked out: I became the secretary and confidential companion to both of these writers who were making "copy" as fast as they could out of the situation. All summer long, I was the reservoir for the accumulated wrath of both in saga and song, in invective and confidential confession, in cold-blooded discussion and in hot-blooded reaction.

I don't mean to speak unkindly. They were not exploiting their emotions—it was simply their natural safety-valve they were using.

There they were: Lawrence sitting under a tree at one end of the village writing a novel in which Owen is made to appear as one of the characters; Owen sitting, stripped to the waist, on the Japanese hillside at the other end of town, acquiring his vacation tan and relieving his mind of all his ideas about Lawrence! And there was I at a typewriter on a balcony of the hotel overlooking the same lake on which both of them rested their eyes between paragraphs, the lake across which oriental sailboats flew. There was I, copying both manuscripts and chuckling quietly to myself—not at all worried over what both Lawrence and Owen were writing about me or, indeed, saying, as they buried their hatchets, occasionally, and went off on an excursion together.

"Owen had no soul, only a slow, soft caving-in at the center of him where soul should be," wrote Lawrence—and my fingers flew over the typewriter keys in my bird-like delight over the situation.

"Owen was empty and waiting for circumstances to fill him up," wrote Lawrence, again. "Swept with an American despair of having lived in vain, or of not having *really* lived. Having missed something. Which fearful misgiving would make him rush like mechanical steel filings to a magnet, towards any crowd in the street. And then all his poetry and philosophy gone with the cigarette-end he threw away, he would stand craning his neck in one more frantic effort to *see*—just to see. Whatever it was, he must see it. Or he might miss something. And then, after he'd seen an old ragged woman run over by a motor-car and bleeding on the floor, he'd come back pale at the gills, sick, bewildered, daunted, and yet, yes, glad he'd seen it. It was Life!"

In his turn, Owen should say:

"Lorenzo is a man without a soul!" And, vehemently, he would analyze this strange creature he had encountered over our absinthe at a table in the plaza where we were alone late in the evening. "I had not thought that anyone would wilfully choose the dark side of the world, would dig for the bitterest roots."

And I agreed gravely with both of them, in silent amazement over their marvelous concurrence on the subject.

That Lawrence was a kind of devil, a spirit of evil, was Owen's contention in both his prose and in the poems he wrote about him. And these, too, I pounded off on the machine with my "American delight over a new situation":

After wondering a long time, I know now
That you are no man at all. . . .
Only your reddish hair is you
And those narrowing eyes,
Eyes hostile to the flesh of people and to all their
     motions,
Eyes penetrating their thoughts to the old marrow of
     the beast,
Eyes wanting a mate and the starlight. . . .

You will always be smouldering against men;
And, after yielding slowly
The nine lives of a domestic cat,
You will be worshipped by the Egyptians. . . .

Then, perhaps the same day, having a beer with Lawrence, or walking with him along the lake, he would make almost exactly the same accusation against Owen:

"Owen with his humanitarianism! His all-embracing brotherly love! His Socialism—bah! His kind of love is death. Just death, really, and nothing else.

"Owen thinks he's a liberal, but isn't. He talks about Socialism but lives on capital. He can't conceive of definitely renouncing the world and his previous life as I have done, and making something new. He's hopelessly wallowing in the old sentimentalities, pampering his whims, catering to his own softness. He's a Playboy of the Western World, playing the rôle of patron of the arts. He's just kidding himself, as you say in America; playing to the public square; taking life as a cocktail before dinner. And that sort of thing is death—just death. One has to take hold of life and do something with it. One can't just go on accepting, turning the other cheek, loving, loving, loving-soft, saccharine, smirking love!"

Exhausted by this effort, he would suddenly realize what an outburst it had been, laugh in his highest pitch and then say gently, almost apologetically, and with an indubitably English inflection, accenting the first instead of the last word:

"Shall we have another glass?"

Always they were spitting fire behind each other's back, with each other's very words in their mouths! Then Owen, angry with me, would agree with Lawrence that "something ought to be done" about me. Or Mrs. Lawrence and I would confer and pour out our troubles. Or Owen and Mrs. Lawrence would discuss the outlandishness of a husband as only a bachelor and a married woman can. . . .

Oh, it was quite nice. And through it all, like a chorus to our song, were amicable birthday dinners and pleasant visits from Guadalajara friends and tropical moonlight nights when guitars and wandering singers from across the lake and love-lorn couples made music all night long.

Woven into the pattern of our days were motor-boat trips to this town and that in search of an old church, or a fiesta, or an ancient Indian dance combined with a Spanish miracle-play, or to purchase *serapes* or Toltec idols.

Until it suddenly came to an end with the realization of

a dream and its accompanying events. All summer long we had seen and worshipped from afar the great flat-bottomed boats with their immense, fat, bellying sails, which carried on the commerce of the lake region. One day we saw a brand new one, unencumbered with flies or dirt, empty of cargo, rather spacious in a simple twenty-five-foot way. And so we chartered it and its crew and launched out on the wide waters.

Our craft moved when the wind moved, and lay becalmed under myriad stares whole nights. She was poled into quaint old ports where we bought fruit and chickens, eggs and tortillas. She glided magnificently over gentle, choppy waves to islands where mangos and goats' milk replenished our larder—where sometimes a shepherd would kill a kid for our pirate appetites. We cooked most of the food ourselves over a charcoal stove made of an oil can.

Owen got sick and we shipped him back to port by steamer, but the Lawrences, the crew and I drifted on, slow as the little islands of water-hyacinths from the eastern end of the lake.

There was music on the roof of our one-room boat-house at night, all of us lying on the sloping boards in our night-clothes, Lawrence or myself astraddle the ridge-pole in pajamas, one of the crew posed like a Greek statue at the tiller, half-illumined by a candle or lantern below; maybe Daniel, an Aztec faun, standing beside the mast in silhouette against a rising moon. Then a guitar and Spanish songs. Or no guitar and Lawrence singing English ballads in the nasal falsetto of a country boy lost in the hills. . . .

No wonder we decided to make this the happy ending

to Mexico and to return to El Paso before another revolution or another battle between Lawrence and Owen should shatter our sea-voyage calm. No wonder we wanted this to be our final memory: "the great seething light of the lake, with the terrible blue-ribbed mountains of Mexico beyond."

From Mexico the Lawrences returned to England, where they spent a gloomy winter, ambivalent about future plans. In London, on January 8, 1924, Lawrence received a copy of *Laughing Horse*, number nine, designated a "Southwest Number." It contained Johnson's amused account of the laughing horse's relationship to the mythic Navajo turquoise horse (see Chapter Two).

Nostalgic for New Mexico and delighted with the mythologizing of the sardonic equine, Lawrence wrote back immediately to Johnson, who published the letter under the title "Dear Old Horse" in the next number of the magazine.

Dear Old Horse

A LONDON LETTER
FROM D. H. LAWRENCE

Yesterday came the Horse, capering a trifle woodenly, and today a fall of snow. Enough bright white snow on the ground to make a bit of daylight. I've been here exactly a month in London, and day has never broken all the time. A dull, heavy, mortified half-light that seems to take the place of day in London in winter. I can't stand it.

However, with a bit of snow-brightness in the air, and a bit of a rather wooden neigh from the Horse in my ears. I prick up and write you a London letter.

Dear old Azure Horse, Turquoise Horse, Hobby Horse, Trojan Horse with a few scared heroes in your belly; Horse, laughing your Horse Laugh, you do actually ramp in with a bit of horse sense. I'm all for horse sense, O Horsie! Come down to it, and it's the Centaur. Good old Horse, be patted, and be persuaded to grin and to be a Centaur getting your own back.

Even if you're only a hobby Horse, with a wooden head and a Spoodle on your broom-stick flanks, you're welcome just now. Very welcome. Here's an apple. Be tempted, like Adam, and take it. And for the sake of all horses, be braver than Adam, who only bit a bite out and dropped the main. Eat up the whole gaudy apple, O Horse. Let's have the centaur back.

(continued on following pages)

Dear old Horse, you'd never be azure or turquoise here in London. Ho, London is awful: so dark, so damp, so yellow-grey, so mouldering piecemeal. With crowds of people going about in a mouldering, damp, half-visible sort of way, as if they were all mouldering bits of rag that had fallen from an old garment. Horse, Horse, be as hobby as you like, but let me get on your back and ride away again to New Mexico. I don't care how frozen it is, how grey the desert, how cold the air, in Taos, in Lobo, in Santa Fe. It isn't choky, it is bright day at daytime, and bright dark night at night. And one isn't wrapped like a mummy in winding-sheet after winding sheet of yellow, damp, unclean, cloyed, ancient, breathed-to-death so-called air. Oh Horse, Horse, Horse, when you kick your heels you shatter an enclosure every time. And over here the horse is dead: he'll kick his heels no more, I don't know whether it's the Pale Galilean who has triumphed, or a paleness paler than the pallor even of Jesus. But a yellow and jaundiced paleness has triumphed over here, the Turquoise Horse has been long dead, and churned into sausages. I find it unbearable.

Let the horse laugh. I'm all for a horse that laughs. Though I don't care for him when he merely sniggers. I'm all for a horse. It's not even the Houyhnhnms. They aren't blue enough for me. It's a turquoise centaur who laughs, who laughs longest and who laughs last. I believe in him. I believe he's there, over the desert in the south-west. I believe if you'll cajole him with a bit of proper corn, he'll come down to Santa Fe and bite your noses off and then laugh at you again.

Two-legged man is no good. If he's going to stand steady, he must stand on four feet. Like the Centaur. When Jesus was born, the spirits wailed round the Mediterranean: Pan is dead. Great Pan is dead. And at the Renaissance the centaur gave a final groan, and expired. At least, I seem to remember him lamenting and about to expire, in the Uffizi.

It would be a terrible thing if the Horse in us died forever: as he seems to have died in Europe. How awful it would be, if at this present moment I sat in the yellow mummy-swathings of London atmosphere—the snow is melting—inside the dreadful mummy-sarcophagus of Europe, and didn't know that the blue horse was still kicking his heels and making a few sparks fly, across the tops of the Rockies. It would be a truly sad case for me.

As it is, I say to myself: Bah! In Lobo, in Taos, in Santa Fe the Turquoise Horse is waving snow out of his tail, and trotting gaily to the blue mountains of the far distance. And in Mexico his mane is bright yellow on his blue body, so streaming with sun, and he's lashing out again like the devil, till his hoofs are red. Good old Horse!

But talking seriously, Man must be centaur. This two-legged forked radish is going flabby.

The Centaur's Lament! Not at all. The laugh of the Turquoise Man-Horse. Let the forked radish do the lamenting.

In modern symbolism, the Horse is supposed to stand for the passions. Passions be blowed. What does the Centaur stand for, Chiron or any other of that quondam four-footed gentry. Sense! Horse Sense. Sound, powerful,

four-footed Sense, that's what the Horse stands for. Horse
sense, I tell you. That's the Centaur. That's the blue horse
of the ancient Mediterranean, before the pale Galilean or
the extra pale German or Nordic gentleman conquered.
First of all, Sense, Good Sense, Sound Sense, Horse Sense.
And then, a laugh, a loud, sensible Horse Laugh. After
that these same passions, glossy and dangerous in the
flanks. And after these again, hoofs, irresistible.
Splintering hoofs, that can kick the walls of the world
down.

Horse-sense, Horse-laughter, Horse-passion, Horse-
hoofs: ask the Indians if it is not so.

Tell me the Horse is dead? Tell me the Centaur has died
out? It may easily be so, in Europe here, since the
Renaissance. But in the wide blue skies of the southwest,
and faraway south over Mexico: over the grey deserts and
the red deserts beneath the Rockies and the Sierra Madre;
down the canyons and across the mesas and along the
depths of the barrancas goes the Turquoise Horse, uneasy,
bethinking himself, and just on the point of bursting into
a loud laugh, after all, laughing longest and laughing last.

Ask the Indian, if there isn't a little blue foal born every
year, in the pueblos, out of the old dark earth-colored mot-
tled mare. Tell me the centaur can't beget centaurs?—Ask
the Indian, ask the Navajo, ask the Mexican under his big
hat.

It's no good. I've got to ride on a laughing horse. The
forked radish has ceased to perambulate. I've got to ride a
laughing horse. And I whistle for him, call him, spread
corn for him, and hold out an apple to him here in

England. No go! No answer! The poor devil's dead and churned into Cambridge sausages. Flabby flaccid forked radishes, sausages, pairs of sausages in dead skins; these seem to drift about in the soup of the London air. There's no answer.

There's no blue cave to stable the Turquoise Horse, here. There's no dark earth-colored mare to bear his foals. There's no far-away blue distance for him to roam across. He's dead.

And yet I've got to ride, centaur, on a blue stallion.

So, thanks be to the oldest of Gods, comes a wooden little Laughing Horse sliding down from the blue air of the Rockies, riding on his hobby stick like a rocket, summoning me to mount and away.

Hurray! Hup-a-la! Up we go! Like a witch on a broomstick, riding west.

By March 1924 the Lawrences were back in Taos. In the ensuing months Lawrence began to write of his reactions to the surroundings at their little mountain ranch and to venture off to Indian ceremonials in the region. One such trip, in August, took Mabel and the Lawrences to see the Hopi Snake Dance at Hotevilla in northern Arizona. With some three thousand other visitors, the Lawrence-Luhan party rumbled across the thirty miles beyond Walpi to Third Mesa. Immediately following the exhausting ten-day trek Lawrence produced an article on the Hopi Snake Dance, a piece Johnson published in the September issue of *Laughing Horse*.

Just Back from the Snake-Dance—Tired Out

D. H. LAWRENCE

One wonders what one went for—what all those people went for. The Hopi country is hideous, a clayey pale grey desert with death-grey mesas, sticking up like broken pieces of ancient dry, grey beard. And the hell of a bumpy trail for forty miles. Yet car after car lurched and bobbed and ducked across the dismalness, on Sunday afternoon.

The Hopi country is some forty miles across, and three stale mesas jut up in its desert. The dance was on the last mesa, and on the furthest brim off the last mesa, in Hotevilla. The various Hopi Villages are like broken edges of bread crust, utterly grey and arid on the top of these mesas; and so you pass them; first Walpi, then unseen Chimopavi, then Oraibi, on the last mesa and beyond Oraibi on the same mesa, but on a still higher level of grey rag-rock, and away at the western brim, is Hotevilla.

The pueblos of little grey houses are largely in ruin, dry raggy bits of disheartening ruin. One wonders what dire necessity or what Cain-like stubbornness drove the Hopis to these dismal grey heights and extremities. Anyhow once they got there there was evidently no going back. But the pueblos are mostly ruin, and even then, very small.

Hotevilla is a scrap of a place with a plaza no bigger than a fair sized back yard; and the chief house on the

(continued on following pages)

square, a ruin. But into this plaza finally three thousand onlookers piled. A mile from the village was improvised the official camping ground, like a corral with hundreds of black motor cars. Across the death-grey desert, bump and lurch, came strings of more black cars, like a funeral cortege,—till everybody had come—about eight hundred bodies.

And all these bodies piled in the little oblong plaza, on the roofs, in the ruined windows, and much around on the sandy floor, under the old walls; a great crowd. There were Americans of all sorts, wild west and tame west, American women in pants, an extraordinary assortment of female breeches; and at least two women in skirts, relics of the last era. There were Navajo women in full skirts and velvet bodices; there were Hopi women in bright shawls; a negress in a low-cut blouse and black sailor hat; various half breeds and all the men to match. The ruined house had two wide square window holes; in the one was posed an apparently naked young lady with a little black hat on. She laid her naked handsome arm like a white anaconda along the sill and posed as Queen Semiramis, seated and waiting. Behind her, the heads of various Americans to match; perhaps movie people. In the next window hole, a poppy-show of Indian women in colored shawls and glistening long black fringe above their conventionally demure eyes. Two windows to the west!

And what had they all come to see?—come so far, over so weary a way, to camp uncomfortably? To see a little bit of a snake dance in a plaza no bigger than a back yard. Eight grey-daubed antelope priests (so-called) and a dozen

black-daubed snake-priests (so called). No drums, no
pageantry. A hollow muttering. And then six of the snake
priests hopping slowly round with the neck of a pale, bird-
like snake nipped between his teeth, while six elder priests
dusted the six younger, snake adorned priests with prayer
feathers, on the shoulders, hopping behind like a children's
game. Like a children's game. Old Rogers is dead and is
low in his grave! After a few little rounds, the man set his
snake on the sand, and away it steered, towards the mussed
spectators sitting around. And after it came a snake priest
with a snake stick, pitched it up with a flourish from the
shrinking crowd, and handed it to an antelope priest in the
background. The six young men renewed their snake as
the eagle his youth—sometimes the youngest, a boy of
fourteen or so, had a rattle snake ornamentally drooping
from his teeth, sometimes a racer, a thin whip snake,
sometimes a heavier bull-snake, which wrapped long end
round his knee like a garter, till he calmly undid it. More
snakes, till the priests at the back had little armfuls, like
armfuls of silk stockings that they were going to hand on
the line to dry.

When all the snakes had had their little ride in a man's
mouth, and had made their little excursion towards the
crowd, they were all gathered like a real lot of wet silk
stockings—say forty—or thirty—and let to wiggle all
together for a minute in meal, corn-meal, that the women
of the pueblos had laid down on the sand of the plaza.
Then, hey—presto! they were snatched up like fallen
washing, and the two priests ran away with them, west-
ward, down the mesa to set them free among the rocks at
the snake-shrine (so-called).

And it was over. Navajos began to ride to the sunset, black motor cars began to scuttle with their backs to the light. It was over.

And what had we come to see, all of us? Men with snakes in their mouths, like a circus? Nice clean snakes, all washed and cold creamed by the priests (so-called), like wet pale silk stockings. Snakes with little, naive, bird-like heads that bit nobody, but looked more harmless than doves? And funny men with blackened faces and whitened jaws, like a corpse band?

A show? But it was a tiny little show, for all that distance. Just a show! The southwest is the great playground of the White American. The desert isn't good for anything else. But it does make a fine national playground. And the Indian, with his long hair and his bits of pottery and blankets and clumsy home-made trinkets, he's a wonderful live toy to play with. More fun than keeping rabbits, and just as harmless. Wonderful, really, hopping round with a snake in his mouth. Lots of fun! Oh, the wild west is lots of fun: The Land of Enchantment. Like being right inside the circus-ring! Lots of sand, and painted savages jabbering and snakes and all that. Come on boys! Lots of fun!

The great South-West, the natural circus ground. Come on, boys! We've every bit as much right to it as anybody else. Lots of fun!

As for the hopping Indian with his queer muttering gibberish and his dangling snake—why, he sure is cute! He says he's dancing to make his corn grow. What price irrigation, Jimmy? He says the snakes are emissaries to his rain god, to tell him to send rain to the corn on the Hopi Reservation, so the Hopis will have lots of corn meal.

What price a spell of work on the railway, Jimmy? Get all the corn-meal you want with two dollars a day, anyhow.

But oh, dry up! Let every man have his own religion. And if there wasn't any snake dance we couldn't come to see it. Miss lots of fun. Good old Hopi, he sure is cute with a rattler between his teeth. You sure should see him, boy. If you don't, you miss a lot.

Watching the Snake Dance ritual—a dozen or so dancers whose every move was devoured by thousands of hungry eyes—Lawrence could not screen out the context to focus on the ceremony itself. Though he acknowledged the sacred ritualistic aspects of the ceremonial, his characterization of it as a "circus performance" infuriated Mabel, who asked him to rewrite the article. "He had written," she complained,

> a dreary terre à terre account of the long road to the Hopi village and of the dance, a mere realistic recital that might have been done by a tired, disgruntled business man. It had no vision, no insight, no appreciation of any kind....[12]

Apparently chagrined, Lawrence started over, producing a longer meditation on the Snake Dance. In milder tone he repeated his denunciation of the sideshow atmosphere. But he acknowledged that behind it, discernible to the seeker, lay an ageless animistic religion. From the dismissive, fatigue-driven first article, Lawrence produced one of his most sensitive responses to the Native American people.[13]

FIGURE 71.
Dorothy Brett,
"Lawrence and
Susan," woodblock
print from *Laughing
Horse*, no. 15 (1928).

During the summer of 1925, his last in New Mexico, Lawrence and Frieda remained in relative isolation on the ranch. He had been very ill during the winter in Mexico, fighting the tuberculosis that would kill him a few years later. They took special pleasure that summer in the simple tasks of life: feeding the chickens, gathering strawberries, and milking Susan, the black-eyed cow.

THE D.H. LAWRENCE ISSUE OF *Laughing Horse*

After the Lawrences' final departure from New Mexico in September 1925, Johnson decided to devote a whole issue of *Laughing Horse* to the writer. From Lawrence himself Spud solicited two poems, three prose pieces, and a drawing.

Two of his prose offerings, "Paris Letter" and "A Little Moonshine with Lemon," reveal his piercing nostalgia for the little ranch in the New Mexico mountains and his disenchantment with a writer's vagabond life. The third of Lawrence's prose pieces in the special Lawrence issue is "Europe Versus America"—a more complex, less sanguine reflection on his American experience. As he had observed of Mexico, Lawrence found Europe less tense, less desperate than the United States, where many people have a "strangle-hold" on themselves.

The special Lawrence issue was completed with portraits of him—in words, woodblock prints, and clay—by people who had known him in New Mexico. Especially vivid is the portrayal by Frederic W. Leighton.

Mediterranean In January

D. H. LAWRENCE

The blue anemone with a dark core
That has flowered before
Shows one bud more!

Far-off, far-off, in the hyacinth ages
It flowered, before men took to flowering for wages;
Flowers now, as we're crossing the dreary stages.

Today, when the sun is computed old
And Europe's tail-spin rolls still unrolled;
And bank-tellers tell the one tale that is told;
And bank-notes are poetry purer than gold;
When the end of the world we are told, is scrolled;
And a man, when he isn't bought, feels sold:

Out of the winter's silky fur
Buds a blue anemone, still bluer.

Nations beside the sea are old,
Folk-flowers have faded, men have grown cold.
Nothing remains now but mould unto mould,—
Ichabod! Ichabod! lo and behold!

Oh age! that is hoar as anemone buds!
Oh chew, old cows, at your ancient cuds!
Chew also, young heifers, your juicier cuds!

(continued on following pages)

The wisdom of ages droops! It is folly
To laugh when we're feeling melancholy!
Tears wrinkle our faces, like rain in the holly.
The wisdom of ages droops! Ain't it jolly!

The sea has its bud-lips smilingly curled,
What! Yet another bad end of the world!
Why, 'twas only yesterday every man twirled
His moustache with an elbow lifted, and hurled
Braggadaccios around the blue rims of the world!

Now the world is ending in dust and in sorrow.
The world is ending; let's hurry to borrow
Black for the funeral! Wow! waly! and worrow!

The age is a joke! and surely, tomorrow
We'll see the joke, and how funny is sorrow!

Yesterday, yes! is a tale that is told.
Tomorrow comes stealthily out of the mould
Like a bud from winter disguised in grey,
Hidden blue with the blueness of one more day.

When I see this sea looking shoddy and dead,
And this sun cease shining overhead,
And no more anemones rise from the dead,
And never another *per Bacco*! is said:
I shall come to New York, and live on Manhattan,
And deep in Central Park I'll fatten
My griefs, and on New York newspapers batten.

Till then, I like better this sea, I must say,
Which is blue with the blueness of one more day.
The which, since it coincides with my day
And will shine if I stay or I go away
Persuades me to stay, since stay I may. . .

Beyond the Rockies

D. H. LAWRENCE

There are people there, beyond the Rockies
As there are people here, on this side.

But the people there, beyond the Rockies
Seem always to be asking, asking something.

The new moon sets at sundown,
And there, beyond the sunset, quivers.

An Indian, walking wrapt in his winding sheet
Answers the question as he puts it, in his stride.

Mexicans, like people who have died
Ask, in the space of their eyes:
What have we lost?

What have we lost, in the west?
We who have gone west?
There is no answer.

In the land of the lost
Nothing but to make lost music.

On the rim of the desert
Round the lost man's camp fire
Watch the new moon
Curved, cut the last threads.

It is finished: the rest is afterwards
With grey on the floor of the desert,
And more space than in life.

Paris Letter

D. H. LAWRENCE

I promised to write a letter to you from Paris. Probably I should have forgotten, but I saw a little picture—or sculpture—in the Tuileries, of Hercules slaying the Centaur, and that reminded me. I had so much rather the Centaur had slain Hercules, and men had never developed souls. Seems to me they're the greatest ailment humanity ever had. However, they've got it.

Paris is still monumental and handsome. Along the river where its splendours are, there's no denying its man-made beauty. The poor, pale little Seine runs rapidly north to the sea, the sky is pale, pale jade overhead, greenish and Parisian, the trees of black wire stand in rows, and flourish their black wire brushes against a low sky of jade-pale cobwebs, and the huge dark-grey palaces rear up their masses of stone and slope off towards the sky still with a massive, satisfying suggestion of pyramids. There is something noble and man-made about it all.

My wife says she wishes that grandeur still squared its shoulders on the earth. She wishes she could sit sumptuously in the river windows of the Tuileries, and see a royal spouse—who wouldn't be me—cross the bridge at the head of a tossing, silk and silver cavalcade. She wishes she had a bevy of ladies-in-waiting around her, as a peacock has its tail, as she crossed the weary expanses of pavement in the Champs Elysees.

(continued on following pages)

Well, she can have it. At least, she can't. The world has
lost its faculty for splendour, and Paris is like an old, weary
peacock that sports a bunch of dirty twigs at its rump,
where it used to have a tail. Democracy has collapsed into
more and more democracy, and men, particularly
Frenchmen, have collapsed into little, rather insignificant,
rather wistful, rather nice and helplessly commonplace little fellows who rouse one's mother-instinct and make one
feet they should be tucked away in bed and left to sleep,
like Rip Van Winkle, till the rest of the storms rolled by.

It's a queer thing to sit in the Tuileries on a Sunday
afternoon and watch the crowd drag through the galleries.
Instead of a gay and wicked court, the weary, weary crowd,
that looks as if it had nothing at heart to keep it going. As
if the human creature had been dwindling and dwindling
through the processes of democracy, amid the ponderous
ridicule of the aristocratic setting, till soon he will dwin-
dle right away.

Oh, those galleries. Oh, those pictures and those statues
of nude, nude women: nude, nude, insistently and hopelessly nude. At last the eyes fall in absolute weariness, the
moment they catch sight of a bit of pink-and-white painting, or a pair of white marble fesses. It becomes an inquisi-
tion; like being *forced* to go on eating pink marzipan icing.
And yet there is a fat and very undistinguished bourgeois
with a little beard and a fat and hopelessly petit bour-
geoise wife and awful little girl, standing in front of a
huge heap of twisting marble, while he, with a goose-
grease unctuous simper, strokes the marble hip of the huge
marble female, and points out its niceness *to his wife*. She is

not in the least jealous. She knows, no doubt, that her own hip and the marble hip are the only ones he will stroke without paying various prices, one of which, and the last he could pay, would be the price of the spunk.

It seems to me the French are just worn out. And not nearly so much with the late great war as with the pink nudities of women. The men are just worn out, making offerings on the shrine of Aphrodite in elastic garters. And the women are worn out, keeping the men up to it. The rest is all nervous exasperation.

And the table. One shouldn't forget that other, four-legged mistress of man, more unwitherable than Cleopatra. The table. The good kindly tables of Paris, with Coquilles Saint Martin, and escargots and oysters and Chateaubriands and the good red wine. If they can afford it, the men sit and eat themselves pink. And no wonder. But the Aphrodite in a hard black hat opposite, when she has eaten herself also pink, is going to insist on further delights, to which somebody has got to play up. Weariness isn't the word for it.

May the Lord deliver us from our own enjoyments, we gasp at last.—And he won't. We actually have to deliver ourselves.

One goes out again from the restaurant comfortably fed and soothed with food and drink, to find the pale-jade sky of Paris crumbling in a wet dust of rain; motor-cars skidding till they turn clean around, and are facing south when they were going north: a boy on a bicycle coming smack, and picking himself up with his bicycle pump between his legs: and the men still fishing, as if it were a Sisyphus penalty, with long sticks fishing for invisible fishes in the Seine: and the huge buildings of the Louvre and the Tuileries standing ponderously, with their Parisian suggestion of pyramids.

And no, in the old style of grandeur I never want to be grand. That sort of regality, that builds itself up in piles of stone and masonry, and prides itself on living inside the monstrous heaps, once they're built is not for me. My wife asks why she can't live in the Petit Palais, while she's in Paris. Well, even if she might, she'd live alone.

I don't believe any more in democracy. But I can't believe in the old sort of aristocracy, either, nor can I wish it back, splendid as it was. What I believe in is the old Homeric aristocracy, when the grandeur was inside the man, and he lived in a simple wooden house. Then, the men that were grand inside themselves, like Ulysses, were the chieftains and the aristocrats by instinct and by choice. At least we'll hope so. And the Red Indians only knew the aristocrat by instinct. The leader was leader in his own being, not because he was somebody's son or had so much money.

It's got to be so again. They say it won't work. I say, why not? If men could once recognize the natural aristocrat when they set eyes on him, they can still. They can still choose him if they would.

But this business of dynasties is a weariness. House of Valois, House of Tudor! Who would want to be a House, or a bit of a House! Let a man be a man, and damn the House business. I'm absolutely a democrat as far as that goes.

But that men are all brothers and all equal is a greater lie than the other. Some men are always aristocrats. But it doesn't go by birth. A always contains B, but B is not contained in C.

Democracy, however, says that there is no such thing as an aristocrat. All men have two legs and one nose, ergo, they are all alike. Nosily and leggily, maybe. But otherwise, very different.

Democracy says that B is not contained in C, and neither is it contained in A. B, that is, the aristocrat, does not exist.

Now this is palpably a greater lie than the old dynastic lie. Aristocracy truly does not go by birth. But it still goes. And the tradition of aristocracy will help it a lot.

The aristocrats tried to fortify themselves inside these palaces and these splendours. Regal Paris built up the external evidences of her regality. But the two-limbed man inside these vast shells died, poor worm, of over-encumbrance.

The natural aristocrat has got to fortify himself inside his own will, according to his own strength. The moment he builds himself external evidences, like palaces, he builds himself in, and commits his own doom. The moment he depends on his jewels, he has lost his virtue.

It always seems to me that the next civilization won't want to raise these ponderous, massive, deadly buildings that refuse to crumble away with their epoch and weigh men helplessly down. Neither palaces nor cathedrals nor any other hugenesses. Material simplicity is after all the highest sign of civilization. Here in Paris one knows it finally. The ponderous and depressing museum that is regal Paris. And living humanity like poor worms struggling inside the shell of history, all of them inside the museum. The dead life and the living life, all one museum.

Monuments, museums, permanencies and ponderosities are all anathema. But brave men are forever born, and nothing else is worth having.

A Little Moonshine With Lemon

D. H. LAWRENCE

*"Ye Gods, he doth bestride the narrow world
Like a Colossus . . !"*

There is a bright moon, so that even the vines make a shadow, and the Mediterranean has a broad white shimmer between its dimness. By the shore, the lights of the old houses twinkle quietly, and out of the wall of the headland advances the glare of a locomotive's lamps. It is a feast day, St. Catherine's day, and the men are all sitting round the little tables, down below, drinking wine or vermouth.

And what about the ranch, the little ranch in New Mexico? The time is different there: but I too have drunk my glass to St. Catherine, so I can't be bothered to reckon.

(continued on following pages)

I consider that there, too, the moon is in the southeast, standing, as it were, over Santa Fe, beyond the bend of those mountains of Picoris.

Sono io! say the Italians. I am I! Which sounds simpler than it is.

Because which I am I, after all, now that I have drunk a glass also to St. Catherine, and the moon shines over the sea, and my thoughts, just because they are fleetingly occupied by the moon on the Mediterranean, and ringing with the last farewell: *Dunque, Signore! di nuovo!*—must needs follow the moon-track south-west, to the great South-west, where the ranch is.

They say: *in vino veritas.* Bah! They say so much! But in the wine of St. Catherine, my little ranch, and the three horses down among the timber. Or if it has snowed, the horses are gone away, and it is snow, and the moon shines on the alfalfa slope, between the pines, and the cabins are blind. There is nobody there. Everything shut up. Only the big pine-tree in front of the house, standing still and unconcerned, alive.

Perhaps when I have a *Weh* at all, my Heimweh is for the tree in front of the house, the overshadowing tree whose green top one never looks at. But on the trunk one hangs the various odds and ends of iron things. It is so near. One goes out of the door, and the tree-trunk is there, like a guardian angel.

The tree-trunk, and the long work table, and the fence! Then beyond, since it is night, and the moon shines, for me at least, away beyond is a light a Taos, or at Ranchos de Taos. Here, the castle of Noli is on the western sky-line.

But there, no doubt it has snowed, since even here the wind is cold. There it has snowed, and the nearly-full moon blazes wolf-life, as here it never blazes; risen like a were-wolf over the mountains. So there is a faint hoar shagginess of pine-trees, away at the foot of the alfalfa field, and a grey gleam of snow in the night, on the level desert, and a ruddy point of human light, in Ranchos de Taos.

And beyond, you see them even if you don't see them, the circling mountains, since there is a moon.

So, one hurries indoors, and throws more logs on the fire.

One doesn't either. One hears Giovanni calling from below, to say Goodnight! He is going down to the village for a spell. *Vado giu Signor Lorenzo! Buona notte!*

And the Mediterranean whispers in the distance, a sound like in a shell. And save that somebody is whistling, the night is very bright and still. The Mediterranean, so eternally young, the very symbol of youth! And Italy, so reputedly old, yet forever so childlike and naive! Never, never for a moment able to comprehend the wonderful, hoary age of America, the continent of the afterwards.

I wonder if I am here, or if I am just going to bed at the ranch. Perhaps looking in Montgomery Ward's catalogue for something for Christmas, and drinking moonshine and hot water, since it is cold. Go out and look if the chickens are shut up warm: if the horses are in sight: if Susan, the black cow, has gone to her nest among the trees, for the night. Cows don't eat much at night. But Susan will wander in the moon. The moon makes her uneasy. And the horses stamp around the cabins.

In a cold like this, the stars snap like distant coyotes, beyond the moon. And you'll see the shadow of actual coyotes, going across the alfalfa field. And the pine-trees make little noises, sudden and stealthy, as if they were walking about. And the place heaves with ghosts. That place, the ranch, heaves with ghosts. But when one has got used to one's own home-ghosts, be they never so many, and so potent, they are like one's own family, but nearer than the blood. It is the ghosts one misses most, the ghosts there, of the Rocky Mountains, that never go beyond the timber and that linger, like the animals round the water-spring. I know them, they know me: we go well together. But they reproach me for going away. They are resentful too.

Perhaps the snow is in tufts on the greasewood bushes. Perhaps the blue jays fall in a blue, metallic cloud out of the pine trees in front of the house, at dawn, in the terrific cold, when the dangerous light comes watchful over the mountains, and touches the desert far-off, far-off, beyond the Rio Grande.

And I, I give it up. There is a choice of vermouth, Marsala, red wine or white. At the ranch, tonight, because it is cold, I should have moonshine, not very good moonshine, but still warming: with hot water and lemon, and sugar, and a bit of cinnamon from one of those little red Schilling's tins. And I should light my little stove in the bedroom, and let it roar a bit, sucking the wind. Then dart to bed, with all the ghosts of the ranch cosily round me, and sleep till the very coldness of my emerged nose wakes me. Waking, I shall look at once through the glass panels of the bedroom door, and see the trunk of the great pine tree, like a person on guard, and a low star just coming over the mountain, very brilliant, like someone swinging an electric lantern.

Si vedra la primavera
Fiorann' le mandorline—

Ah, well, let it be vermouth, since there's no moonshine with lemon and cinnamon. Supposing I called Giovanni, and told him I wanted

"Un poco di chiar' di luna, con canella e limone. . . . ."

Europe Versus America

D. H. LAWRENCE

A young American said to me: "I am not very keen on Europe, but should like to see it, and have done with it." He is an ass. How can one "see" Europe and have done with it. One might as well say: I want to see the moon next week and have done with it. If one doesn't want to see the moon, he doesn't look. And if he doesn't want to see Europe, he doesn't look either. But neither of 'em will go away because he's not looking.

There's no "having done with it." Europe is here, and will be here, long after he has added a bit of dust to America. To me, I simply don't see the point of that American trick of saying one is "through with a thing," when the thing is a good deal bigger than oneself.

I can hear that young man saying: "Oh, I'm through with the moon, she's played out. She's a dead old planet anyhow, and was never more than a side issue." So was

(continued on following pages)

Eve, only a side issue. But when a man is through with her, he's through with most of his life.

It's the same with Europe. One may be sick of certain aspects of European civilisation. But they're in ourselves, rather than in Europe. As a matter of fact, coming back to Europe, I realise how much more *tense* the European civilisation is, in the Americans, than in the Europeans. The Europeans still have a vague idea that the universe is greater than they are, and isn't going to change very radically, not for all the telling of all men put together. But the Americans are tense, somewhere inside themselves, as if they felt that once they slackened, the world would really collapse. It wouldn't. If the American tension snapped tomorrow, only that bit of the world which is tense and American would come to an end. Nothing more.

How could I say: I am through with America? America is a great continent; it won't suddenly cease to be. Some part of me will always be conscious of America. But probably some part greater still in me will always be conscious of Europe, since I am a European.

As for Europe's being old, I find it much younger than America. Even these countries of the Mediterranean, which have known quite a bit of history, seem to me much, much younger even than Taos, not to mention Long Island, or Coney Island.

In the people here there is still, at the bottom, the old, young insouciance. It isn't that the young *don't care*: it is merely that, at the bottom of them there *isn't* care. Instead there is a sort of bubbling-in of life. It isn't till we grow old that we grip the very sources of our life with care, and strangle them.

And that seems to me the rough distinction between an American and a European. They are both of the same civilization, and all that. But the American grips himself, at the very sources of his consciousness, in a grip of care: and then, to so much of the rest of life, is indifferent. Whereas, the European hasn't got so much care in him, so he cares much more for life and living.

That phrase again of wanting to see Europe and have done with it, shows that strangle-hold so many Americans have got on themselves. Why don't they say: I'd like to see Europe, and then, if it means something to me, good! and if it doesn't mean much to me, so much the worse for both of us. Vogue la galere!

I've been a fool myself, saying: Europe is finished for me. —It wasn't Europe at all, it was myself, keeping a strangle-hold on myself. And that strangle-hold I carried over to America; as many a man, and woman worse still, has done before me.

Now, back in Europe, I feel a real relief. The past is too big, and too intimate, for one generation of men to get a strangle-hold on it. Europe is squeezing the life out of herself, with her mental education and her fixed ideas. But she hasn't got her hands round her own throat not half so far as America has hers; here the grip is already falling slack; and if the system collapses, it'll only be another system collapsed, of which there have been plenty. But in America, where men grip themselves so much more intensely and suicidally—the women worse—the system has its hold on the very sources of consciousness, so God knows what would happen, if the system broke.

No, it's a relief to be by the Mediterranean, and gradually let the tight coils inside oneself come slack. There is much more life in a deep insouciance, which really is the clue to faith, than in this frenzied, keyed-up care, which is characteristic of our civilization, but which is at its worst, or at least its intensest, in America.

The Bite of Mr. Lawrence

FREDERIC W. LEIGHTON

Some wit has remarked that Mexican politics is like an onion. It consists of innumerable layers each purporting to be the true body; yet always revealing when peeled another layer more plausible than the one discarded. At length, ripping the ultimate garment, one reaches the heart of the matter to discover—nothing, absolutely nothing. With its last peeling went the onion.

I have wondered if the case of authors is not similar. Critics are forever delving in the archaeological backyards of their prey searching letters, published works, table talk and reminiscences of childhood friends for clues to the inner spirit, the soul, the raison d'etre, that when dusted and given a proper museum mounting will show the world what after all was the heart and germ of the literary personage under consideration.

Possibly the critics are correct and authors, even mal-

(continued on following pages)

odorous ones, have hearts and cannot be compared to Mexican politics or onions. Nevertheless for me the comparison holds, so that what I say about Mr. D. H. Lawrence must be understood as a description of one or more of his layers and an attempt to convey the bit of the fumes which lurked amid peelings that I saw.

I met Mr. Lawrence in the City of Mexico and saw him later at the place he has called Sayula, by the shore of the lake of that name high in the mountains that guard the Mexican plateau. Mr. and Mrs. Lawrence were living in a comfortable villa whose inner portale opened upon a small patio graced with rose shrubs and a well. Mr. Lawrence was engaged upon the novel which has just been published. His spare time was spent in walks to Indian villages clustered along the lake shore, in voyages upon the lake in quaint square-sailed vessels that haul grain and wood across its surface, and in conversation with his American companions.

That was a play of personalities—Lawrence and his wife, "Owen" and "Villiers" (to use the names, again, of *The Plumed Serpent*). Have you ever watched a cat playing with a mouse—the cat poised, alert, motionless except for rapier paw thrusts, sadistically contemplating its prey; the mouse distracted, alert, alternately crouching in planful study and dashing in desperation to escape its tormentor, inwardly wailing at the thought of its comfortable refuge between the walls—so near at hand, so impossible to reach? If you will picture that scene and then visualize Lawrence contemplating Owen and Owen eyeing Lawrence, each inwardly feeling himself the cat and outwardly posing as the mouse; if you will imagine also Owen in a mouse mood feeling a vicarious concern for Mrs. Lawrence as a fellow mouse and Lawrence in a mouse mood feeling a similar pity for Villiers, you will recreate in your mind's eye what fell to my physical eye when I came to Sayula. The others can and possibly will sometimes, tell the more intimate details of this drama; for Lawrence and Owen both wrote about the mice they studied and Villiers took down their thoughts. . .

I saw only the outside—Lawrence caustic, opinionated and penetrating; Mrs. Lawrence smiling, patient, enthusiastic as a morning glory in the sun; Owen hearty, good natured, analytical; Villiers retentive, absorbing, quietly humorous. Truly a quartet of dramatic tensions!

That is what I saw there in Sayula; that is the setting of locality and personality which attended the birth and swaddling days of Mr. Lawrence's new novel.

What about Lawrence himself? What were the layers of him revealed to my gaze? They were numerous. Here I shall mention only one—the doctrine of cosmic superiority. In several talks we had he advanced the thesis that most men are burros fit only to be ridden and booted. Sprinkled among the cretin mass, as colored grains in an ear of yellow corn, was a select fraternity of ruling spirits. These spirits, though inhabiting bodies not different from those encasing the rest of mankind, were of a different genera. In virtue of their greater intellect and spirit power they were destined to rule the world. Sometimes circumstances conspired to hold them down. There followed in the immediate vicinity of their mundane existence a bending and a straining, an upheaval worthy of a Prometheus Bound, or an Etna in eruption. So out of bondage they writhed to freedom, that freedom which is the assertion of the will to power, the exercise of the intrinsic prerogatives of the superior fraternity. Now Lawrence was not precise or categorical in the elaboration of these ideas. He was loquaciously vague. But I gathered that his afflatus had whispered continually in his ear that he was of the superior caste, that the exigencies of adverse circumstances were but temporary and ephemeral, that the Laurentian spirit was bound to rise and sure to rule.

To me this doctrine explains at once the radicalism and the conservatism of D. H. Lawrence. Against the restrictions and hindrances imposed by vested interests (economic, moral, social, and literary) upon the unknown common man who has ability and aspires, Lawrence kicked and kicked hard. Therefore the iconoclast, the radical. Having booted his way with swift strokes of truth to eminence of notoriety and fame, Lawrence asserted the rights of the esoteric ones who command by cosmic patent. Hence we have Lawrence, the Imperial Englishman, who can say with canker, "Few Englishmen read my books; but I will say that those who do are capable of understanding them." Here the doctrine of the superiority of the cosmic elect becomes in practise somewhat confused with the philosophy of the civis Romanum. That confusion exists, I believe, in Mr. Lawrence. Anyhow he thoroughly enjoys his capacity for scorn.

This is a peeling of Lorenzo, fascinating and repelling. In the alternations of fascination and repulsion there lies energy. And energy—well, good, and sufficient.

FIGURE 72. D. H. Lawrence, drawing of Pueblo Indian Dancers, from
Laughing Horse, no. 13 (1926). In addition to his poetry, essays, and novel
based on his visits to New Mexico, Lawrence frequently sketched and painted
southwestern subjects, though few would argue that his enthusiasm for the
visual arts was matched by his talent for them.

FIGURE 73.
D. H. Lawrence,
cover design for
Laughing Horse,
1920s. It was
never used.

FIGURE 74. Loren Mozley, "Ranchos de Taos," linoleum cut from *Laughing Horse*, no. 13 (1926).

Lawrence's last piece in *Laughing Horse* was published some eight years after the writer's death. "Altitude" is the first scene of an unfinished play Lawrence had written in Taos in the 1920s Illustrated charmingly with drawings by Johnson's painter friend Gina Knee, the play caricatures the attitudes as well as the people inhabiting "Mabeltown." Johnson's editorial note, published along with the play in *Laughing Horse*, no. 20 (1938) explained the circumstances in which it was written and its array of zany characters.

FIGURE 75.
Loren Mozley,
"Mount Lobo,"
linoleum cut from
Laughing Horse,
no. 13 (1926).

Altitude

THE FIRST SCENE OF AN UNFINISHED PLAY
D. H. LAWRENCE

Editorial Note

On the following pages, we present the fragmentary beginnings of a comedy which D. H. Lawrence started to write in Taos more than ten years ago.

He scribbled the opening lines on the back of a candy box one evening in Mabel Luhan's living room, with several friends present offering suggestions as to who the characters should be and what they should do and say. It was an amusing game, and few of those who played it knew until many years later that the next day Lawrence finished this first scene and began a second. Unfortunately, the play was never finished.

Although it is obvious that, contrary to custom, *none of the characters are fictitious*, it should be clearly understood that the "Mary" of the play is by no means the late Mary Austin; that "Mabel" is certainly not the author of *Lorenzo in Taos*; that "Ida" is not, as you might suspect, Ida Ruth Eastman; that "Clarence" is not also named Thompson; and that Lujan is not the patronymic of "Tony." "Mrs. Sprague," although her first name is Alice, should not be confused with Mrs. Carleton Sprague of New York City; Elizabeth is not Mabel Luhan's adopted daughter; and of course you realize that the "Spud" mentioned, is not the editor of this magazine.

We are indebted to Mrs. Frieda Lawrence, and to The Viking Press, for permission to print this fragment; and Mr. Jake Zeitlin for copying the original manuscript while it was on exhibition in the Los Angeles Public Library.

THE CHARACTERS
IN ORDER OF THEIR APPEARANCE
{Graciously described by the Editor}

MARY: A Woman With Ideas, who can also cook.

SPUD: Referred to as a "Young Intellectual,"
but obviously not.

CLARENCE: A "Young Aesthete," addicted to rose-coloured
trousers and jewels.

MILKMAN: Just that.

IDA: A Dramatic Actress, even at breakfast.

MRS. SPRAGUE: A benign wraith.

MABEL: A determined lady who always knows what she
wants—and gets it.

INDIAN: Whose name is Joe.

TONY: An American Indian philosopher, Mabel's husband.

ELIZABETH: Younger and blonder that the others.

The play is illustrated by Gina Knee

{The curtain rises, revealing the kitchen of Mabel's house at Taos.
Mary stands in the sunny doorway, chanting to herself, saying "Om"
resoundingly}

Mary: This country is waiting. It lies spell-bound, waiting.
The great South-West, America of America. It is waiting. . . .
What for? What for?

{Enter Spud, taking in the situation at a glance.}

Spud: Hello! Hasn't the cook come?

Mary: Good morning! No sign of her as yet. ...Isn't morning
wonderful, here at this altitude, in the great South-West? Does
it kindle no heroic response in you, young Intellectual?

Spud: I don't know. Maybe I'd better kindle a fire in the
stove.

Mary: Quite right! Homage to the god of fire. Wait! An
apron! Let me do it. The fire in this house is the woman's fire.
The fire in the camp is the man's fire. You know the Indians say
that?

Spud: No, I didn't know it till you told me.

Mary: Oh, young Intellectual! It is a Woman Mediator you
are pining for. The Woman Redeemer!

Spud: Maybe! Does this look like an apron?

Mary: *{Girding on the apron, and busy at the stove.}*
To do, to know, and to be! Hamlet had hold of only one-third
of the twisted string.

{Enter Clarence in rose-colored trousers and much jewelry.}

Clarence: Oh, good-morning, Mary! Good-morning Spud.—
Why, Mary, won't you let Emilia do that?

Mary: Do you see any Emilia in the neighbourhood?

Clarence: Why, no, I don't. Is it possible she's not coming?
Oh, what a calamity!

Mary: A contretemps, not a calamity, young Idealist. The heroic nature is ready for every emergency. Woman is the great go-between. When the cook does not turn up. *I* am the cook. Mary and Martha should be one person.

Spud: What about Magdalene?

Mary: The men will play *her* role.

Clarence: Oh, but do let me do this.

Mary: Do what?

Clarence: Make a fire and all that.

Mary: The wood-box is empty: bring in some wood. *{He goes out.}*

Spud: Oh, I wish Mabel weren't so temperamental.

Mary: Thank God for Mabel's temperament, young Intellectual. Where would you be without it?

Spud: Why, I might get my coffee.

Mary: You get more than coffee from Mabel.

Spud: Maybe I do. But it's rough on a empty stomach.

{Enter Clarence; lays wood on kitchen table.}

Mary: In the wood-box, young Dreamer!

Clarence: Oh, so sorry!

Mary: Brains and dreams won't start a stove. Hands, muscles, and common-sense must be ready for any emergency, in the new mystic we are bringing into the world.

Clarence: I'll take Mabel her breakfast in bed. That will be much the best.

{The Milkman suddenly appears at the door.}

Milkman: How much? Got the empty bottles? Any cream?

Spud: Oh, yess! Let's have cream!

Clarence: Mabel only lets us have it on Sundays.

Mary: A pint of cream, two quarts of milk. The cook will give you the bottles tomorrow. *{Exit Milkman, slamming the screen door. Clarence follows him out and rings the gong loudly.}*

Spud: Why, what is he ringing for?

Mary: No doubt he thinks the bell will bring the breakfast, as the rooster thinks he brings the sun with his noise. It is all part of the male vanity. Woman brings the breakfast, meanwhile.

Spud: And I suppose she has some hand in making the sun rise, too?

Mary: Certainly. It is the great creative spirit of Woman, the perfected Woman, that keeps the sun in stable equilibrium.

Spud: *{sniggering}* Do you say she keeps the sun in her stable?

{Enter Ida}

Ida: Oh-h! I thought it was breakfast.

Mary: Lay the table, Ida.

Ida: For *everybody?*

{Enter Mrs. Sprague in white muslin. She hovers, then sits at table and looks benignly at the stray bits of wood left there by Clarence, who re-enters at this moment.}

Clarence: Oh—er, Good-morning! Good-morning, Mrs. Sprague; how did you sleep? Good-morning, Ida!

Ida: We're supposed to be laying the table.

Mrs. Sprague: Oh yes! Oh yes! *{Picks up a tumbler and wanders around with it.}*

{Mabel pops in through the dining-room door.}

Mabel: Where's breakfast? Where's Emilia? Who rang that bell?

Clarence: *I* rang the bell, Mabel. I thought we might as well all know that cook isn't coming. —*Won't* you go back to bed? *Please* do! You'll be *so* much more comfortable.

Mabel: *{rushing at stove}* Where's the coffee? Where's the cof-fee-pot? Is that water boiling?

Mary: Mabel, *I* am making the coffee.

Mabel: It's got to boil. It's got to boil several minutes. I want it strong, so it's got to boil.

Mary: Mabel, You may trust many things to me, the least of them being the coffee. Won't you all sit down and discuss the situation, while I solve it?

Mabel: The bacon! *{Rushes into pantry and emerges with a side of bacon}* Who can cut bacon *thin*? It's got to be cut thin. I want it dry. Cut it, somebody, and *I'll* cook it.

Clarence: *{with dignity}* I'll cut it, Mabel. Where is a knife?

{Mabel rushes across and produces a huge knife. Clarence proceeds to saw bacon, on the table-cloth}

Ida: Not on the table-cloth, Clarence.

Mabel *{snatching knife}* Not so *thick*! Somebody cut the bacon who can cut it *thin*. *{silence}* Spud, come and cut the bacon.

Spud: *{reluctantly}* I'll try. My god, be careful with that knife; you look like a Chicago aesthetic. *{crouches on floor to cut bacon.}*

Indian: *{in doorway}* Hello!

Mabel: Hello, Joe! No cook this morning. You know how to cook?

Indian: No.

Mary: Will one of our young Intellectuals go to the well for water?

Mabel: *{to Indian}* Fetch a pail of water, Joe. *{Joe goes out with pail.}*

Mary: Don't you notice, the moment an Indian comes into the landscape, how all you white people seem so *meaningless*, so ephemeral?

Ida: Why, yes! I was just thinking how ephemeral you all looked when Joe picked up the pail.

Mabel: *{snorts}* It *is* extraordinary! It's because the Indians have *life*. They have *life*, where we have *nerves*. Haven't you noticed, Mary, at an Indian dance, when the Indians all sit banked up on one side, and the white people on the other, how

FIGURE 76. "That's enough bacon, Spud!" by Gina Knee (1898–1982), painter and close friend of Spud Johnson, who persuaded her to try illustrating Lawrence's "Altitude" in *Laughing Horse*, no. 20 (1938). Spud slices bacon in the foreground, while Mary Austin pontificates from the stove and Mabel rushes in from the right.

all the life is on the Indian side, and the white people seem so dead? The Indians are like glowing coals, and the white people are like ashes.

Ida: Well, Mabel, and which side are you on?

Mabel: *{snorts again}* The Indian!

Mary: There is something which *combines* the red and the white, the Indian and the American, and is greater than either.

Mabel: *{rushing at Spud}* That's enough bacon, Spud.

Spud: *{rising}* I don't know that I feel so *ashy* at an Indian dance.

Ida: No, neither do I, Spud. *{Spud examines his finger, critically.}*

Clarence: And I *certainly* don't get any glow from the Indians.

Mabel: Well, you all know what I mean. And you do *all feel* it. Anyway, you *look* it.

Ida: Perhaps we're the ashes of your stormy past, Mabel, and you see in the Indians the red glow of your future. —But, my dear, it's all red paint.

Clarence: Exactly: The paint they've daubed on their faces.

Spud: The danger signal.

Mrs. Sprague: Have you cut your finger?

Spud: A little.

Ida: Suck it, Spud.

Spud: I am sucking it. *{Joe re-enters with the pail.}*

Indian: Here's the water.

Mabel: All right, Joe. You can go and chop some wood if you like. *{Joe grunts, doesn't like, but goes out. Mabel rushes at the stove}* I'll fry the bacon, Mary.

Mary: Mabel, *I am* officiating at this altar.

Mabel: But I want my bacon dry, *dry!* You others can have it as you want, but I want mine dry.

Mary: You shall have it as dry as the Arizona desert, Mabel.

Ida: Oh, what about Professor Mack? Is he still desiccating the Arizona desert, studying the habits and misbehaviours of the Cactus?

Mabel: He's coming here.

Ida: Why, how thrilling! Don't you feel awfully bucked, Mary?

Mary: Professor Mack and I have had a perfect correspondence all our lives. This is the first time we shall have slept under the same roof.

Ida: How extraordinary! I wonder what the *roof* will feel about it.

Mabel: Let's sit down now. *(they all sit at table.)* Well, *(ominously)* here we all are.

Spud: Minus a few of us.

Mabel: How are you, Alice? You've not said anything yet.

Mrs. Sprague: Why, I'm fine, Mabel. How are you?

Mabel: Fine! *(snorts)* How is everybody? How are you, Spud? Ida?

Spud: Fine!

Ida: Fine!

Mabel: Mary, how d'you feel this morning?

Mary: Why, fine!

Clarence: If you were going to ask me how I feel, Mabel, I feel fine, perfectly fine. It's *wonderful* to be here.

Mabel: Ye-es! You're *looking* marvelous. But you're not going down to the Plaza in those trousers?

Clarence: Why, yes. I wasn't going to take them off to go down town.

Mabel: What's the idea?

Clarence: As you said, we all *feel* so fine, I thought I'd try to look as fine as I felt.

Mabel: But why in trousers? Why look it in trousers?

Clarence: But why not? You wouldn't have me try to look it *without* trousers. No, Mabel? If we *feel* wonderful, and we *are* perhaps rather wonderful, I think it's up to us to come out in our own feathers.

Mabel: Yes, but why feather your legs?

Clarence: But why not?

Mabel: It's an exhibitionist complex.

Ida: Mabel, I don't think you can quite say that. I *admire* rose-coloured trousers.

Mabel: Yes, all right, indoors, But not to go down to the Plaza. They're all wrong in the Plaza. Think how the people will *jeer*—and then talk. Another sign of vice from over there.

Clarence: But what does it matter whether they jeer and talk—I shall go perfectly unconscious of them, in my rose-coloured trousers.

Mabel: You won't! You can't! You'll be conscious all the time. You'll be conscious all the time that they're jeering at you, and then you'll get all tied up over it afterwards.

Clarence: I assure you, Mabel, I *should* have gone to the Plaza in my rose-coloured trousers *perfectly* unconscious of everybody, if you hadn't started this difficulty.

Mabel: I bet you wouldn't. You *couldn't*. Anyhow, what do you want to go to the Plaza for in rose-coloured trousers? *What* are you conscious of, when you wear them?

Clarence: {*with hauteur*} Of *feeling* wonderful, and I hope, of looking it.

Mabel: Clarence! You know everybody will just say you look a fool. Not wonderful at all.

Clarence: I thought it didn't matter what the crowd in the Plaza says. Anyhow, you've squashed my efforts. I shall go and take off my trousers and never put them on again.

Ida: But you'll put on others, won't you?

Clarence: Yes, *grey* ones.

Ida: But Clarence! Wait. Why don't you walk up and down this room a few times before *us*, and see how you feel: and we'll say whether you're wonderful, or exhibitionist, or whatever it is.

Clarence: No. I shall go and take them right off.

Mary: Stick to your guns, young Aesthete.

Ida: Stick to your trousers, anyhow. No, I mean it quite fairly. Walk up and down a few times past the sink. Yes:—there!

{Clarence walks. Enter Joe.}

Mabel: *{irritably}* Hello, Joe! How're you feeling, hm?

Indian: Fine!

Mabel: Can you stay help wash dishes? Put some water in the kettle.

{Joe crosses in front of Clarence, who is walking up and down.}

Clarence: Excuse me, Joe, will you keep still a minute.

Mabel: I *told* him to fill the kettle.

Clarence: Mabel, I am acting at the request of the majority.

Mabel: You're a pure exhibitionist. I don't care about majorities, anyhow. Leave off exhibiting yourself.

Ida: Oh, but you're *fine*, Clarence! I'm all for rose-coloured trousers.

Clarence: I shall go and take them right off.

Ida: No! No! They're wonderful.

Mary: Let us appeal to true, unspoiled taste, and hear what the vital American has got to say. Joe, what do you think of his trousers?

Indian: Fine! *{Enter Tony.}*

Mabel: Here's Tony! Let's ask Tony. He sees both sides. Tony, Clarence is going to the Plaza in those trousers. What you think of it?

Tony: *{seating himself at table}* Make a guy of himself, sure.

Mary: You wouldn't go down to the Plaza in them, Tony?

FIGURE 77. "Well, I guess I eat a can of sardines," by Gina Knee. Tony Luhan, at left, opens a can of sardines while "Clarence" parades up and down the room in his rose-colored trousers. Illustration from D. H. Lawrence, "Altitude," *Laughing Horse*, no. 20 (1938).

Tony: Me? No. I wouldn't.

Mary: And you, Joe; would you go to the Plaza in those trousers?

Indian: No Mam! They're fine for a dance, for an Indian.

Mabel: That's it! You give them to Joe, Clarence.

Clarence: I shall not, Mabel. But I shall go and take them *right* off, and never put them on again.

Ida: Don't, Clarence! Oh, don't!

Mary: The Indian has spoken.

Ida: Then let the Jew speak. I'm a Jew, and my people are good at speaking. Clarence, I implore you, don't haul down your flag. Keep your trousers. *I'll* walk down to the Plaza with you.

Mabel: *Ida*! Prepare for the consequences.

Ida: What consequences, Mabel?

Mabel: All the *talk*. What'll Andrew say?

Ida: Why I'll have him paint a portrait of Clarence *in* the trousers.

Spud: Keep them, Clarence.

Mrs. Sprague: They're a lovely colour; they make a bright note.

Mary: I wash my hands of them.

Mabel: But it's so *babyish*!

Clarence: I shall take them *right* off! [*Flounces out. A silence.*]

Mrs. Sprague: You know, voices have told me that Clarence is a great Initiator.

Mabel: Initiator of *what*, Alice?

Ida: The fashion in rose-coloured trousers. I agree with him entirely.

Mrs. Sprague: No. If we take care of him, and protect him, and *love* him, he may be a Great Teacher.

Mabel: Well, I protect him, preventing him making a guy of himself.

Mary: I think the Indians are *always* right. I doubt if any young man is capable of having a revelation. I doubt *really* if any man is capable of having a revelation. Next time I *really* believe it will be a *Woman*. The next Redeemer will probably, almost certainly, be a Woman.

Mabel: Meaning yourself, Mary? Why shouldn't *I* have the revelation?

Mary: You're not perfect, Mabel. I'm glad you're not, for I have hardly any place in my life for a woman who is both rich and perfect.

Mabel: Tony!

Tony: What?

Mabel: Like a fried egg?

Tony: Yes, I think so.

Mabel: Well, get up and fry it then. There's no cook today.

Mary: How are you this morning, Tony? It's so good to sit next you.

Tony: I'm fine.

Mabel: The Indians *do* feel fine. They always feel fine. That's because they live right. They've got something that white people haven't got. We've got to get it. That's what we're here for. That's what I married Tony for: to try and get the wonderful something that they've got and that white people haven't.

Tony: *{Getting up at last and looking around vaguely}* Where the eggs?

Mabel: Can't you find any? Well, maybe there aren't any. Have some marmalade.

Tony: Well, I guess I eat a can of sardines.

Mabel: Tony, you don't want a can of sardines for breakfast!

Tony: Guess I do!

Mabel: Oh, dee-ar! *{Tony unwinds sardines.}*

Mary: Mabel, when you say the Indians have that wonderful thing that white people haven't got, I think *I* have it.—Joe, more wood on the fire. —The Indians have the rhythm of the earth. The earth in America has a *special* rhythm, the marvelous American rhythm. And here in Taos that rhythm is at its height.

Ida: You mean altitude?

Mary: I mean the *perfect* rhythm. The white people still haven't got the rhythm of America, the perfect rhythm, of American earth. The Indians have had it so long, maybe they're in danger of losing it. The new revelation will come when the white people, when some white *Woman* gets the perfect rhythm of the American earth. And I think if I stay here all summer, *{looks meaningly at Mabel}* I shall get it.

Mabel: Well, *stay* all the summer, and let's see you get it. We want something to happen. Here we all are, a group of more or less remarkable people, in a remarkable place, at a remarkable altitude. If something doesn't happen of itself, let's *make* it happen. Let's make a Thing! *{Enter Elizabeth, eating an apple and shedding large tears.}* What's the matter, Elizabeth?

Elizabeth: Why I'm so mad at Contentos.

Mabel: What's he done, then?

Elizabeth: Why he's broken his bridle *again*, and got away.

Mabel: Where is he?

Tony: I tell you to take a rope—

Mabel: Go get a rope and catch him. *{Enter Clarence in grey flannels.}*

Ida: Oh, dear the glory has departed.

Clarence: Yes, it intended to depart.

Ida: Too bad.

Mabel: Spud, you finished? Go get the poppies before the sun spoils them. Hurry, now.

Spud: Well, let me drink my coffee first. *{Drinks hurriedly and departs.}*

Ida: Spud's queer this morning.

Clarence: Spud always seems queer, to *me*.

Mabel: Spud *is* queer. —I wonder what it is; whether we can't fix it.

Mrs. Sprague: He has such a swell disposition. I wonder what it can be?

Clarence: I don't know. Of course it mayn't *mean* anything, but I heard his door banging *all* night last night. It really seemed mysterious.

Mrs. Sprague: It was my door. There's no catch on it. It makes me nervous in the night.

Ida: Oh! Why doesn't Mabel have a catch *put* on the door? Of course it makes you nervous, banging in the wind.

Mabel: I forget about it, every day.

Clarence: *I'll* put a catch on the door. *{Exit.}*

Ida: Will he do it, do you think?

Mabel: Who, Clarence? Maybe. But he's more likely to try a safety pin.

Ida: Mabel, you can say the Indians feel fine *all the time*, and that we ought to feel the same; but what I want to know is, what do you mean by feeling fine? Feeling up to the mark, and so on?

Mabel: Oh no, none of those dreary things. I mean feeling good. You have that good feeling, don't you know, when you expand—and you make everybody around you feel wonderful. I know I do it myself. You can't help it—they've *got* to feel good, just because of the thing that's in you. You radiate life, and the people around you feel good. Haven't you seen me do it? Don't you feel it come from me?

Ida: Ye-es, maybe I do. But what does this feeling good mean? Is it just good spirits?

Mabel: No! Not any of that. Tony, you explain how the Indians feel when they feel good.

Tony: *{chewing a sardine}* Well, the Indians, they feel the sun. They feel the sun inside them, and they feel good. Like what the sun inside them, and they love everybody.

Ida: Sunshine, Tony, or moonshine inside them?

Mary: *{heavily}* Let *me* explain what it is. The sun is overhead, and the earth is underfoot. We live between the two—

{At that moment, the telephone rings; Spud enters with poppies, Elizabeth behind him. Mabel jumps to the telephone; Spud poses with poppies; Elizabeth gets a cup and pours herself coffee. All speak at once.}

Mabel: Hello!

Elizabeth: Guess I'll have a cup of coffee.

Spud: Aren't the poppies beautiful!

{Curtain}

FIGURE. 78. "The sun is overhead, and the earth is underfoot." Gina Knee, in witty illustrations of D. H. Lawrence's play fragment "Altitude," captures the agreeable nonsense of utopia-seekers in Mabel's kitchen in Taos. From *Laughing Horse*, no. 20 (1938).

A special word of thanks is due Jane Abrams, whose curiosity and skill contributed mightily to the decision to undertake this book and exhibition. While teaching at the University of New Mexico in the 1970s, Abrams, a printmaker and painter, had come to know the work of many longtime New Mexico artists and had seen their work in galleries and museums around the state. She had also come across their block prints on the pages of old copies of *Laughing Horse*.

In the late 1970s Abrams learned that the blocks from *Laughing Horse* had been given to Zimmerman Library at the University of New Mexico. Though scratched and cracked, the blocks engaged her curiosity. With the cooperation of the Center for Southwest Research, she undertook to print the whole collection—nearly 200 blocks in all. On her own press, on fine paper, the blocks rendered fresh images, often of better quality than Spud Johnson had ever obtained on his little Kelsey press.

This collection of impressions printed by Jane Abrams, preserved at Zimmerman Library, has revived a nearly forgotten body of work by New Mexico artists of the 1920s and 1930s.

405

Brought together in this volume and exhibited for the first time, these prints expand our understanding of their skills, their interests, and their relationships.

Notes

CHAPTER I

1. Claire Morrill, "Spud's Years Touched Many," *Taos News*, 7 November 1968, 3.

2. Spud Johnson, undated application for Guggenheim Fellowship, Spud Johnson Papers, Harry Ransom Humanities Research Center, University of Texas at Austin, hereafter cited as Johnson Papers.

3. Spud Johnson, handwritten autobiographical fragment, Johnson Papers.

4. Frederick Lewis Allen, *Only Yesterday: An Informal History of the Nineteen Twenties* (New York: Blue Ribbon Books, 1931), 229.

5. Ibid.

6. James Kraft, "Biographical Introduction," in *The Works of Witter Bynner: Selected Poems* (New York: Farrar, Straus, Giroux, 1977), LVI.

7. Spud Johnson, quoted in Tricia Hurst, "Spud Johnson Defined an Era," *Taos*, May 1990, 8–9.

8. Spud Johnson, "The Laughing Horse," *New Mexico Quarterly* 21:2 (Summer 1951): 162.

9. Max Eastman, quoted in James Burkhart Gilbert, *Writers and Partisans: A History of Literary Radicalism in America* (New York: John Wiley and Sons, 1968), 21.

10. Lewis Mumford, "The Theory and Practice of Regionalism," *Sociological Review* 20 (1928): 139.

11. Mary Cabot Wheelwright, wealthy Bostonian who founded Santa Fe's House of Navajo Religion (now the Wheelwright Museum of the American Indian) was similarly interested in connections between Asian and Native American religion.

12. "The Rydal Press of Santa Fe New Mexico: A Brief Account of Its History and Its Purpose," *The Colophon: The Annual of Bookmaking* (New York: The Colophon, 1938), reprinted in Marta Weigle and Kyle Fiore, *Santa Fe & Taos: The Writer's Era 1916–1941* (Santa Fe: Ancient City Press, 1982), 175–82.

13. Kraft, *The Works of Witter Bynner*, LVI.

14. Johnson, Autobiographical Statement for Guggenheim Foundation Grant Application, p. 3 [undated, contextually, late 1930s], Johnson Papers.

15. *Adobe Notes, or How to Keep the Weather Out with Just Plain Mud* was reprinted in 1966 in its original style and format by the Spanish Colonial Arts Society and reissued again in 1977 by the New Mexico Publishing Company, Santa Fe. Kate Mueller Chapman was married to Kenneth M. Chapman, artist and authority on Pueblo pottery. She undertook the restoration of a number of old adobe structures, winning prizes for her efforts. Dorothy N. Stewart was a painter, writer, and printer who graduated from the Pennsylvania Academy of Fine Arts. She also wrote *Hornacinas: Niches and Corners of Mexico City* (1933).

16. Johnson, quoted in Hurst, "Spud Johnson Defined an Era," 8.

17. This piece was published in the *New Yorker*, February 26, 1927, 47–48.

18. Walter Mallon [Spud Johnson], "A Poet in a Raccoon Coat! A Sketch of an Interesting Westerner Who is a Demi-God to Young Poets and a Democrat to His Indian Neighbors," *Sunset*, March 1929, 38.

19. Published as *The Autobiography of Lincoln Steffens* (New York: Harcourt, Brace, 1931).

20. Spud's collections of art and memorabilia are now housed at the Art Collection, Harry Ransom Humanities Research Center, the University of Texas at Austin.

21. In 1923 Mabel had married Tony Luhan of Taos Pueblo, after which she added his name to hers.

22. See Lois Palken Rudnick, *Mabel Dodge Luhan: New Woman, New Worlds* (Albuquerque: University of New Mexico Press, 1984), 268–69.

23. Ibid., 271.

24. Georgia O'Keeffe, letter to Rebecca Strand [James] 24 August 1929, reprinted in *Georgia O'Keeffe: Art and Letters*, ed. Sarah Greenough (Washington: National Gallery of Art, 1987), no. 48, 193. Garland was a painter and poet who owned the H & M (for Henwar, her husband, and Marie) Ranch at Alcalde, New Mexico, where O'Keeffe stayed during the summers of 1931 and 1934.

25. O'Keeffe suffered an emotional or physical collapse late in 1932 and was hospitalized early in 1933. She convalesced in Bermuda that spring and repeated the visit the following year.

26. Johnson, journal entry, October 14, 1934, Johnson Papers.

27. Spud Johnson, letter to Gina Knee dated 14 January 1951, copy in Diary 7, Johnson Papers.

28. Frieda Lawrence, quoted in Morrill, "Spud's Years Touched Many," 3.

29. Georgia O'Keeffe, letter to Spud Johnson, [undated], Johnson Papers. Albidia was Mabel Dodge Luhan's longtime housekeeper.

30. Spud Johnson, "The Perambulator," *Santa Fe New Mexican*, 9 February 1930, 4.

31. Johnson Papers.

32. *The Horse Fly*, 1 June 1941.

33. H. L. Mencken, letter to Spud Johnson, April 16, 1935, Johnson Papers.

34. Author's conversation with Earl Stroh, April 18, 1992.

35. Morrill, "Spud's Years Touched Many," 3.

CHAPTER 2

1. Spud Johnson, "The Santa Fe Gadfly: The Real Story," *Santa Fe New Mexican*, 12 May 1968, D-7.

2. Willard Johnson, letter to Mr. Spohn, 28 June 1924, papers of "Laughing Horse Press," Archive 316, Center for Southwest Research, Zimmerman Library, University of New Mexico.

3. Theodore Roosevelt, quoted in Merle Curti, *American Paradox: The Conflict of Thought and Action* (New Brunswick, N.J.: Rutgers University Press, 1956), 74.

4. Walter Lippmann, *A Preface to Politics* (New York: Macmillan, 1913), 85.

5. Haniel Long (1888–1956) was a poet, critic, editor, and some-time professor of English at Carnegie Institute of Technology. Born in Burma and educated a Harvard, he was a visitor to Santa Fe in the 1920s, settling there in 1929. He is best known for his prose poem "Interlinear to Cabeza de Baca" (1936), "Malinche" (1939), and *Piñon Country* (1941).

6. Johnson, "The Laughing Horse," *New Mexico Quarterly* 21 (Summer 1951): 163.

7. Editorial note prefacing D. H. Lawrence, "Chere Jeunesse," *Laughing Horse* no. 4 (December 1922).

8. Upton Sinclair (1878–1968) was a muckraking journalist and novelist. The author of some eighty books, he is best remembered for *The Jungle* (1906). He was an active force in Socialist politics in the 1920s and 1930s, particularly in California.

9. Johnson, "The Laughing Horse," 164.

10. Ibid.

11. Letter from Upton Sinclair to David P. Barrows, 14 December 1922, reprinted in *Laughing Horse*, no. 5 (1923).

12. Idella Purnell Stone had attended Berkeley and had returned to Guadalajara, where her father was a dentist. She was working at the United States Embassy while she began *Palms*. Both Bynner and Johnson contributed advice and poetry to the new periodical.

13. Johnson, "The Laughing Horse," 165.

14. Spud Johnson, "Laughing Horse Feeling Its Oats; Will Ha-Ha Book Censorship Idea," *Santa Fe New Mexican,* 4 February 1930, 4.

15. Johnson, "The Laughing Horse," 166.

16. Wanda M. Corn, *In the American Grain: The Billboard Poetics of Charles Demuth* (Poughkeepsie: Vassar College, 1991), 22.

17. Ibid., 25.

CHAPTER 3, WITTER BYNNER

1. James Kraft, "Biographical Introduction," XLV.

2. Spud Johnson, "The Rabble," *New Mexico Quarterly Review* 19 (1949): 74.

CHAPTER 3, MABEL DODGE LUHAN

3. Lois Palken Rudnick, *Mabel Dodge Luhan: New Woman, New World* (Albuquerque: University of New Mexico Press, 1984), 252.

4. Ibid., 213.

5. Ibid., 152.

6. Plutarco Elias Calles (1877–1945), military and political leader in the Mexican Revolution, served as president from 1924 to 1928; between that year and 1934 he was the power behind puppet presidents chosen by Calles's PNR party.

7. Georges-Louis Leclerc, comte de Buffon (1707–88) was a French naturalist, best known for this thirty-six volumes on natural history.

CHAPTER 3, D. H. LAWRENCE

8. Frederick J. Hoffman, Charles Allen, and Carolyn F. Ulrich, *The Little Magazine: A History and a Bibliography* (Princeton: Princeton University Press, 1946), 266.

9. Spud Johnson, "The Real Story," *New Mexican,* 12 May 1968, D-7.

10. Lawrence, in a letter to S. S. Koteliansky, quoted in Keith Sagar, ed., *D. H. Lawrence and New Mexico* (Salt Lake City: Gibbs M. Smith, 1982), 1.

11. Lawrence, quoted in Bynner, foreword to *D. H. Lawrence: A Composite Biography*, ed. Edward Nehls, vol. 2, 1919–25 (Madison: University of Wisconsin Press, 1958).

12. Mabel Luhan, *Lorenzo in Taos* (New York: Knopf, 1932), 52.

13. Lawrence's second article, "The Hopi Snake Dance," was published in *Theatre Arts Monthly* in December 1924.

Index

SPUD JOHNSON AND
Laughing Horse

This book was designed by Kristina Kachele.
The text was set in Garamond #3, with Bickley Script
and Juniper display, and was composed on a Macintosh II
system using Quark Express, version 3.2.
It was printed and bound by Thomson-Shore, Inc.
The jacket was printed by Thomson-Shore, Inc.